The Gothic Cathedral

The Gothic Cathedral

Wim Swaan

With an historical introduction
The Cathedral in Medieval Society
by Christopher Brooke

Park Lane
New York

Author's Note

Such is the richness of the legacy of great churches that has come down to us from the Gothic era that, to avoid a mere catalogue of facts and figures, a rigorous process of elimination was essential. To this end, it was decided to concentrate on the cathedrals proper – i.e. churches housing the *cathedra* or throne of a bishop – reluctantly omitting such great monastic pilgrimage churches as St Denis and Westminster Abbey, San Francisco at Assisi and Santa Croce at Florence, St Elizabeth at Marburg, and the austere but eloquent brick churches of northern Germany and the Baltic; and the unique beauties of Portuguese Gothic.

Even thus restricted, we were confronted by a considerable *embarras de richesse,* particularly in the case of France and England, and many personal favourites have had to be omitted. The final choice of thirty-three cathedrals would seem to strike a happy mean, permitting a treatment in depth both in text and illustrations, yet providing a sufficiently representative selection to enable the reader to follow the structural and aesthetic evolution of Gothic cathedral architecture.

A special effort has been made to emphasize the modifications which the *opus francigenum* underwent in different climates and areas – from the extreme cold and snowfalls of Vienna to the heat of Seville – and in response to national characteristics and preferences then already apparent.

One of the greatest triumphs of Gothic architecture lay in its integration of architecture and the arts, notably sculpture and stained glass. The cathedrals selected are particularly rich in these and other works of art, and they are amply illustrated so as to permit constructive comparisons, for example, between the smiling angels of Rheims, Regensburg and León.

W.S.

Professor Brooke and the author are aware that readers may find certain differences of interpretation in their various discussions of the social background of the building of the medieval cathedrals; they have read each other's texts and respect each other's views, but hope that readers will realize that such differences are not fundamental but result from the personal emphases that each of them has given to the historical evidence.

Published 1984 by Park Lane,
distributed by Crown Publishers, Inc.,
One Park Avenue, New York, New York 10016.

Copyright © MCMLXIX by Paul Elek Productions Limited
All rights reserved.

ISBN 0-517-343835

Printed and bound in Hong Kong by South China Printing Co.

Contents

1 *Frontispiece* St Matthew writing and receiving inspiration from the Angel, from the *jubé* of Chartres Cathedral, mid 13th century. *Paris, Musée du Louvre*

2 *Left* Detail of rare and very fine *Madonna and Child* in wood by Andrea Pisano, mid 13th century. *Orvieto, Museo dell' Opera del Duomo*

Acknowledgements

I should like to express my sincerest appreciation to the *Direction des Monuments Historiques de France,* to the ecclesiastical authorities in France, Germany, Spain, and Italy, and to the Deans and Chapters of the English cathedrals and York Minster, for their kind permission, courtesy and assistance in taking photographs in the interiors and on the roofs of the cathedrals, often from positions involving a great deal of inconvenience and, occasionally, even hazard; and also in the treasuries at Rheims, Cologne, Pamplona, and Toledo. A particular debt of gratitude is due to the cathedral authorities in Orvieto for opening the marble tabernacle enclosing the Reliquary of the Sacred Corporal to enable me to photograph details of the enamelled plaques by Ugolino di Vieri. Thanks to the co-operation of all concerned and to the generosity of the publishers, it was possible for the author personally to take all the photographs for the volume—with the exception only of certain manuscripts and engravings and the *grisaille* painting of *St Barbara* by Jan van Eyck, where a subjective approach was of less moment and excellent photographs were available from the museums concerned. For better or worse, text and photographs, therefore, present a single viewpoint of the architecture, sculpture, stained glass, paintings and *objets d'art* of the Gothic cathedral.

My thanks are due to the following museums for permitting me to take photographs of works in their collections: *Musée du Louvre,* Paris, *Musée de l'Œuvre Notre-Dame* and the *Musée Rohan* at Strasbourg, the *Stadtmuseum* at Cologne, the *Augustiner Museum,* at Freiburg-im-Breisgau, the *Historisches Museum,* Vienna, the *Museo de Navarra,* Pamplona, the museums of the *Opera del Duomo* at Orvieto, Siena and Florence, the *Uffizi,* Florence, and the archives of the *Veneranda Fabbrica* at Milan. The Commune of the City of Florence graciously gave permission to photograph the fresco by Andrea da Firenze in the Spanish Chapel of the *Chiostro Verde* of Santa Maria Novella. Photographs of manuscripts in their collections were supplied, and are reproduced, by kind permission of the Trustees of the British Museum (Plates 61, 65, 66, 74, 194, 195), the Victoria and Albert Museum, London (Plate 285), the *Bibliothèque Nationale,* Paris (Plates 39, 59, 69, 84, 87, 88, 89, 90, 93, 94, 105, 132, back endpapers), the *Bibliothèque Royale,* Brussels (Plates 63, 79), the Pierpont Morgan Library, New York (Plate 67), and the Walters Art Gallery, Baltimore (Plate 70). *St Barbara* is reproduced by kind permission of the *Museum van Schone Kunsten,* at Antwerp.

Any work on a subject that has fascinated one since childhood, especially when so amply documented as the Gothic Cathedral, cannot but—albeit subconsciously—reflect the opinions, hypotheses and conclusions of the scores of scholars who have devoted a lifetime of study to the subject. All the works listed in the select bibliography have been consulted with profit. I should, in addition, like to acknowledge my profound debt to the definitive works on the Gothic style by Marcel Aubert, Henri Focillon, Paul Frankl, Louis Grodecki, Erwin Panofsky and Otto von Simson; to Emile Mâle's classics on medieval iconography; and, in the specialized field of building organization, methods and techniques, to the researches of Douglas Knoop and G. P. Jones, John Harvey, Pierre du Colombier and Jean Gimpel. Professor Christopher Brooke has also contributed a most valuable introduction. Most of the research was done in the Library of the Victoria and Albert Museum, where the staff were their customary models of courtesy and efficiency.

London, December 1968   W.S.

3 St Martin and the Beggar, late 13th century. *Regensburg*

List of Plates

List of Diagrams

Front endpapers
Two original architectural drawings for the west front of Strasbourg: left, detail drawing dating from about 1300, an elaborated version of the earliest drawing dating from about 1275; right, the gable over the central portal, ornamented with sculptured *Lions of Judah,* attributed to Master Michael Parler, about 1385. *Strasbourg Musée de l'Œuvre Notre-Dame*
Back endpapers
Two drawings from the sketchbook of Villard de Honnecourt, one with a plan of the apse of a church and a lying figure and the other indicating figures 'constructed according to the Art of Geometry'. *Paris, Bibliothèque Nationale*
Jacket front
Part of the great northern rose window of Notre-Dame; *Paris*
Jacket back
Detail from 14th-century gilded and enamelled silver *retablo* of the main altar, carried out by Masters Bartomeu, Andreu and Pedro Barness, between 1320 and 1357. *Cathedral of Gerona, Spain*

The Cathedral in Medieval Society

The Cathedral in Medieval Society

by Christopher Brooke
Professor of History, Westfield College, University of London

Every walk of life in medieval society can be seen portrayed in the art and decoration of a medieval cathedral. At Notre-Dame in Paris a peasant gathers winter fuel (Plate 4); another, with boots laid aside, toasts his feet before a fire to represent February in the calendar at Amiens (Plate 28); others again are seen with plough and horse and cart at the entry to 'Giotto's Tower' at Florence. At Bourges the coopers ply their task (Plate 12); and in the windows of Chartres Cathedral no less than forty-three of the trades of the city can be seen at work; at Florence two of the crafts most closely linked with the cathedral itself, metalwork and sculpture, have been portrayed by Andrea Pisano (Plate 377). Three German potentates look down from Strasbourg Cathedral; in former times Duke Rudolf and his wife – now in comfortable retirement in a museum – stood on the west front of the Stephansdom at Vienna. The west front of Wells Cathedral (Plate 230) offers a show of kings more numerous than the witches gave Macbeth.

Every order of society had made its contribution to the building, and it was fitting that this should be recorded. A cathedral was partly built from its endowments – so the kings at Wells, the founders and patrons of the cathedral, had earned their place – but mainly, then as now, from gifts and offerings, and the craftsmen at Bourges and Chartres appear in windows which they themselves had given. The way in which such contributions were collected is most vividly revealed in the accounts of the building of Milan Cathedral. The proud device of the Visconti dukes reflects the important part they played; but the Duomo was essentially the product (as will be more fully described below) of a communal effort in which every corner of the city, every walk of life was involved. On September 23, 1387 the drapers came to offer their work and over 42 lire in cash – in the lire of the day, worth many times the lire, or even the pound sterling, of 1969; on September 20 the twelve servants of the commune came to offer their labour, but were foiled by the weather, and so had to be content with offering 14 lire. So the tale goes on, over many years, involving thousands of folk, drawing the whole community of a great city and duchy into a single enterprise.

No doubt there were many in that as in all ages who were indifferent: there were puritans who disapproved of the lavish adornment of churches, there were heretics who disapproved of churches altogether. But in a special way many great churches and cathedrals represented the common effort of the cities they adorned, the communities whose centres they were, and the hierarchical society whose homes they were intended to be: an astonishing concentration of effort for a

4 *Winter*. bas-relief from the West Front. *Paris*

world in which all countries were underdeveloped.

Medieval society was a pyramid in which dead and living mingled, presided over by God himself. In the popular view, the saints performed a function akin to that of the Gods in Homer: alive, active, intensely interested in mortal affairs, each enjoying his or her own local cult centres and intervening for the protection of their subjects – a kind of superior aristocracy. Like the Greek Gods, the saints had exceptional, miraculous power, and were commonly expected to use violent methods on occasion to protect their own; but unlike the Gods, they had (for the most part) a genuine human past of heroic virtue, and valued in their subjects the qualities they had striven so

earnestly to foster in themselves. Under God and the saints two ladders led down to the rank and file of humanity: a spiritual, ecclesiastical ladder, with pope and bishops at the top, abbots and monks, archdeacons, cathedral canons and the like in between, and the parish clergy at its foot; and on the secular side kings and emperors, princes and barons, knights and gentry, merchants and artisans, peasants and slaves.

Kings and barons lived in palaces and castles; peasants lived in huts and hovels; churches and cathedrals were built as homes for all the elements in society.

God's presence was universal; but a cathedral was his home in two special senses. First, he was the architect of the universe, the supreme master-mason, as he is shown in the Bible of St Louis at Toledo: earthly architectural skills were a reflection of his and an offering to him, as is more naively expressed by the manner in which he presides over the making of the Ark in the Bedford Book of Hours. Secondly, one of the centres of its design was the High Altar where the central act of worship of the cathedral was enacted, and where day by day his Body and Blood were present in the Mass.

At the outset of the history of Gothic design, before it was normal to break up a cathedral into compartments with lofty screens and reredoses, and before it became the normal practice to reserve the Sacrament, there was a sense in which the most permanent and conspicuous inhabitant of many great churches was the saint whose shrine dominated the vista. The importance of the saint, whose physical presence was guaranteed by his relics, is revealed in the lavish craftsmanship of reliquaries, in portrayals, as in the glass at Bourges, of the discovery of relics; but never more dramatically than in Canterbury Cathedral, where the whole design was recast as a monument and a home for St Thomas Becket, and a chapel of unusual shape, the crown or *corona,* devised to symbolize and house the crown of his head, severed in the brutal attack of his assassins.

Canterbury Cathedral was dedicated to Christ Himself, and no mortal folk could claim it as their home in quite the way in which it was Christ's and Thomas's. Yet in a measure, and in various proportions, it was the home of every order of society, from peasant to king.

For the peasants, for the most part, the cathedral was a distant vision. But when it was being built, they might find work helping to carry the enormous quantities of wood and stone needed for its building–or they might find themselves compelled to lend their carts and their labour for the purpose; they might feel themselves involved in the work by contributing, according to their resources, to the building fund; and when it was finished, they might join their parish priests on Whit Sunday for the great processions to the cathedral, or go as pilgrims on the feasts of the saints who were buried there. The enormous naves of medieval cathedrals were in part intended to provide shelter for large throngs of ordinary folk on such special occasions.

The cathedral of the late Middle Ages was a house with many rooms. Many of the smaller rooms were chantry chapels, where priests specially hired for the purpose said mass for the souls of the founder of the chapel and his family, or for a society, community or 'guild'. By the end of the Middle Ages there were over fifty chantry priests at Laon alone. But the record, so far as I know, was held by St Paul's Cathedral in London, where in the fourteenth century there were seventy-four chantries; not all separate chapels, for several chantry

5 *Left* The interior with rose windows. *Palma*

6 *Above* Reliefs of Sleeping Guards on the 14th-century Easter Sepulchre, where the ceremonial entombment of an image of Christ took place on Good Friday. *Lincoln*

priests might celebrate at one altar, but all representing a special interest within the common world of the cathedral. Some were founded by bishops and canons; some by leading city merchants; some by great lords. It is here in particular that one meets the higher strata of lay society.

The great layman, like the peasant, was only an occasional visitor to a cathedral; but when he came, he might find, as at Autun, a stirring reminder of the Last Judgement to greet him over the west portal; or as in the Pardon Cloister at Old St Paul's, painted in imitation of models widely disseminated in France and later copied in Germany and Spain, a dramatic representation of the Dance of Death; or at the end of the Middle Ages a stone cadaver under a tomb to remind him of the physical destiny of his earthly pomp. Great men commonly endowed chantries to help their souls in the doubtful and dangerous encounter with Death; more often in churches or

7 *Above* A Groom holds the bridle of the horses of the Magi. Note the realistic carving of the hinges and escutcheon of the stable door. Fragment from the *jubé*, Chartres.

8 *Right* Detail of the Angel Gabriel from *The Annunciation* by Simone Martini, painted for the chapel of Sant' Ansano in 1333, Siena. *Florence, Uffizi*

abbeys intimately connected with their own family, but sometimes in cathedrals.

Cathedrals lay in cities; most drew their canons from far and wide; some (as Cologne) from the great nobles of the area. But often the cathedrals were more intimately connected with local burgess communities than with the greater landlords. Medieval Europe was an agrarian society; but the rôle of merchants and artisans was not a secondary one. The peasant might live near to subsistence level, but in the mid and late Middle Ages neither he nor his lord was wholly dependent for survival on a single year's harvest. And the structure of society – the lord's warhorse and weapons, his house, his large household, and his chantry – depended on the surplus that could be sold for cash; in a society in which transport (by our standards) was incredibly slow and cumbersome, carrying trades played a part out of all proportion to what we should

expect. In the twelfth and thirteenth centuries new towns were built by kings and nobles in northern Europe; in the weekly markets within and the annual fairs without their walls their produce was sold for money and the money exchanged for the necessities of life and the luxuries which provided the incentive for economic growth. Among the rich city men who organized the markets and ran the towns could be found immigrants bringing the skills of other mercantile communities to the town, sons of poor men who had prospered by their enterprise, and the younger sons of local gentry who could not expect to inherit land, but could be set up in business by their families – men like the Dick Whittington of history who started with 'no more capital than a cat' and rose to be Lord Mayor of London.

In the Mediterranean lands, especially in Italy, the towns were not a new revival of the central Middle Ages; nor were they in the long run subject to external control by kings and princes to the same extent as, for example, in England or France. The break with the social organization of late Roman times had been less complete, less rapid, and towns always remained the social as well as the economic centres of the land. Peasants, knights, merchants and artisans jostled together within the walls of the Italian cities, and also slaves, for in southern Europe (partly because of the greater survival of old ways of life) domestic slaves remained throughout the Middle Ages a normal part of the scene, although they had disappeared from northern Europe.

The distinction between North and South can be exaggerated. The baptistry attached to the Cathedral of Florence – late Roman in design, though many different centuries have contributed to the present building – is a striking witness to the continuity of life and the sense of civic community in a great Italian city: to it all the children of the city were brought to be baptized. But cities like Florence and Milan passed through many vicissitudes, and grew again like a northern city from small foundations; and the intense sense of civic community which played so vital a rôle in inspiring the citizens of Florence to adorn the city in the heyday of the Italian Renaissance, or the citizens of Milan to encrust their cathedral with Gothic pinnacles past counting, can be paralleled in many northern cities. The stained glass of Bourges and Chartres reveals the zealous patronage of the crafts and guilds of the city: the groups of men engaged in the various trades of medieval industry, especially in the various processes of cloth-making, and the stone-masons, to whose gargantuan activities the whole cathedrals bear witness.

In the making of Chartres Cathedral every element in the society of the town and the diocese, and of the country round, played its part, including the king himself. The summit of the lay hierarchy was the king – or in Germany and (more remotely) in Italy the Holy Roman Emperor. In many people's eyes he was more than a secular figure; he was anointed with oil of a special sanctity before his coronation, and he expected to hold sway over bishops as well as over barons and burgesses. With this view not all agreed, for there were two systems of authority set in the world, that of the church, with the pope at its head, forming a monarchy of its own, even if a spiritual monarchy, to which all owed allegiance as well as to the king; and the popes took pains to emphasize that monarchs were secular men, not priests, still less bishops; and that bishops were not subject to their authority. In practice, the two systems of authority lived in the world, and within men's minds, in

uneasy harmony; the largest example of the complex structure of divided loyalty to which all men were subject in the Middle Ages.

In many cathedrals the king had a special place as patron and 'founder': his ancestors had really founded the cathedral, and he continued to exercise patronage – to give protection, to be received with respect and honour,. to have a share in appointing to canonries and sometimes to exercise a measure of influence in other ways. There was an unusual custom at St Paul's that a large allowance of bread and beer was issued every week to all the canons, whether they were resident or not. In the fourteenth century only a small proportion of the thirty canons were in residence, and they tried to corner as much of the resources of the cathedral estates as they could; and so they shut down the brewery and the bakehouse. They were met by an eloquent denunciation from the king, not because Edward III was personally much interested in the brewery of St Paul's, but because many of the non-resident canons were civil servants, and so found it an easy matter to issue royal letters patent in their own interest. This story illustrates the nature of a cathedral chapter in the late Middle Ages. In principle it was often a large body, and the rights of the whole chapter of canons were never quite forgotten; in principle too all were under the bishop's direction and were appointed, or 'collated', to their canonries by him. In practice, in many parts of Europe, a small nucleus of canons came to enjoy a large measure of independence, and the non-resident canons and even the bishops were wise if they made their visits to their stalls in the cathedral and their seats in the chapter house, where the chapter's business was conducted, very infrequent. At St Paul's the majority of canons were men whose first call of duty lay elsewhere – in the service of king, or pope, or of some other great man. They were all members of the upper clergy, the privileged, educated clergy; and by the fifteenth century a large majority had university degrees. The rank and file of the clergy were quite distinct in status, and only had entry to cathedral offices at a much humbler level, as vicars choral and chantry priests. These were indeed very numerous, but the magnificent stalls which are often such fine examples of late medieval craftsmanship in cathedrals as far apart as Lincoln and Seville were primarily intended to offer a convenient, commodious, tolerably comfortable and appropriately splendid setting for the resident canons.

In different parts of western Europe there was much variety. The chapters varied in size and organization: some lived in common, some were comparatively humble and poor; more often the canons lived in fine houses in the close and were comparatively well off. In the fourteenth century the resident canons in London kept their numbers small by demanding from a new recruit a lavish round of hospitality beyond the pocket of any but a man of means comparable to the city merchants among whom they lived. This was quite exceptional in the cost it involved a new canon; even more exceptional in Christendom at large was the very different arrangement under which a number of English cathedrals, and a small number in Normandy and Sicily and elsewhere, were served by monks or (as at Sées and Carlisle) by canons regular, canons living under a rule and in community. The monastic chapters were set up in the tenth, eleventh and twelfth centuries – the idea was originally developed by St Dunstan and his associates as part of the monastic revival of the tenth century; and the monastic chroniclers of Canterbury Cathedral provide us with the most vivid impression of how a great cathedral appeared to those who spent a substantial part of each day attending mass and singing the offices within its walls.

The best of these is Eadmer, an English monk whose life spanned the Norman Conquest and the early twelfth century. Monks and archbishops were his human companions; but the saints of the cathedral, Dunstan and Ælfheah (Alphege), and Christ himself, to whom it is dedicated, were equally alive and present to him. Most real of all was the master who inspired him to write, and who to Eadmer was a living archbishop and a saint rolled into one: Anselm of Aosta, Italian philosopher, monk and spiritual leader, who represented in Eadmer's otherwise local, parochial world, the universal nature of the medieval Church and of its culture. Of the royal court and of secular society Eadmer wrote in a quite detached way. When he compiled a *History of Recent Events,* it mainly consisted of the public life of St Anselm. It starts a century back, in the days of St Dunstan, the first of the saintly archbishops whose relics actually lay in the cathedral: earlier archbishops were buried in St Augustine's Abbey or elsewhere. It contains a lively account of the Norman Conquest, but characteristically traces the first beginnings of the fall of the house of Godwin (King Harold's father) to the day he stole a manor belonging to Christ and the saints of Canterbury Cathedral. The arrival of the first archbishop of the new régime, Lanfranc of Pavia and Bec, in 1070, was clearly an event of greater impact even than the arrival of the Conqueror himself – though both were dimmed by the advent of St Anselm (1093-1107). Eadmer felt himself a part of a small world, of the cathedral's community, its relics, its local traditions, its English past; part too of a larger world, for his own archbishop was a man of European reputation who lived much in exile and took Eadmer to the papal court – and in any event, even before St Anselm's coming, the monks were ruled by Christ and St Dunstan, whose home was in Heaven.

On December 29, 1170 Canterbury Cathedral won its greatest relic when Thomas Becket was brutally murdered within its walls. A well-timed fire four years later gave the monks the excuse for a major rebuilding; and the new choir, designed by the French master-mason William of Sens, the hero of Dorothy Sayers' *The Zeal of Thy House,* is the first major expression of 'Gothic' fashions in England. The last act in this great enterprise was delayed until 1220, when Archbishop Stephen Langton presided, in the throne which still exists, over the translation of the relics of Thomas Becket, St Thomas of Canterbury, the blissful martyr whom Chaucer's pilgrims went to seek, to the magnificent new shrine in the centre of the sanctuary. Langton's throne was set in the middle of the apse, facing west; on either hand sat his fellow archbishops and bishops; behind him rose the new shrine, dominating a great vista, visible to the throng in the nave, still the Norman nave built by Lanfranc. On either side of him lay the chapels, and the shrines, of Dunstan and Ælfheah; before him the High Altar, Christ's altar, on which Christ himself reappeared in visible form when the celebrant elevated host and chalice in the mass for the faithful to see and to worship.

Langton thus sat surrounded by the visible evidence of the superiors and comrades in whose name he acted as archbishop: all the permanent inhabitants of the cathedral, the chapter of monks, the relics of the saints, Christ himself. Langton was probably visible to the throng in the nave, though not so visible as Lanfranc would have been when he presided in the choir of his cathedral 140 years earlier, and this for two reasons: first, because the choir had twice been extended, once in Anselm's time to make more space for monks and shrines; and again in the recent rebuilding to provide an ample and fitting context for Becket's shrine. Thus the archbishop was considerably further away than he had been. In the meantime too, it is probable that the open vista of the Romanesque cathedral had been broken by screens between nave and choir of greater height. The building of great screens was a characteristic event of the late Middle Ages in most parts of Europe; and it reflects in a vivid way the relation between the cathedrals and their world. In the fourteenth and fifteenth centuries large screens rose to separate nave and choir; and in cathedrals

again, in human view, in the new and more stately throne of wood in what was now the normal situation, to the South of the sanctuary. This absurd rigmarole emphasizes the remarkable change by which the cathedral ceased altogether to be a single room and became a house of many mansions.

The idea of privacy, of separating great men from their households, of any kind of domestic comfort, as we should understand the term, had been alien to the early Middle Ages. An eleventh-century castle was essentially a building with two rooms: in the hall the lord feasted with his household, and many of his followers slept; in the chamber, which was almost equally large, he could retire to be with his family. Private rooms were virtually unknown. In the late Middle Ages private rooms multiplied; standards of privacy and comfort

with major shrines behind the high altar, the lofty reredoses of this age also separated the altar from the saint. At the end of the Middle Ages Langton's successors were enthroned in his stone chair, still set before Becket's shrine, facing West. But as the reredos made them invisible even to the monks (let alone to the throng in the nave), they had to be enthroned

9 With tender gestures, angels carry the souls of the elect to rest 'in the bosom of Abraham'. *Judgement Portal, Rheims*

grew – anyway for the well-to-do. The nave of a large church was a social centre as well as a religious; decrees had to be passed forbidding ball games in cathedral naves, and checking the use of missiles for attacking birds within the walls. Canons and monks in the late Middle Ages expected to be able to keep the wind and the noise, and the busy throng, at a certain distance; they expected to have furniture of a certain magnificence; they expected to find such things in God's house even more than in their own. The busy throng could not, however, be entirely confined to the nave: it expected to come closer to the shrine behind or beside the high altar. So privacy dictated that the saint and the side aisles, by which he was approached, should be screened off as well as the nave, and a house made within the cathedral, in which the central worship of the cathedral could be conducted in decent seclusion.

Domestic comfort was not, however, the only, nor perhaps the main motive for this seclusion. In the more open vista of a Romanesque or early Gothic cathedral the saint's shrine was liable to make him the most conspicuous of the church's main inhabitants. The design of a late medieval cathedral was reckoned to emphasize the place of God himself at the head of the social hierarchy in which the saints still played a large rôle and the canons were certainly not neglected. To most visitors mass at high altar and the local presence of God at high mass – local, for he was, of course, always present everywhere and to all – were invisible, remote, mysterious; to the canons his presence in the mass was as visible as ever, uniquely so, in that it was without the distraction of a shrine or of the presence of layfolk; and God's presence was not confined to mass, since the practice was growing in the late Middle Ages of reserving the Sacrament, and sometimes already, in some parts of Europe, of providing a costly tabernacle for the purpose. In this way both the permanent character, and the subtle but substantial changes, in medieval Gothic cathedrals show that they were homes for all the many folk who made up the Christian world, but especially for their permanent inhabitants, the higher strata of the spiritual hierarchy, canons, bishops, saints, God himself. In every age there were men who repudiated these conceptions; and the motives of the cathedral builders were doubtless mixed: love of magnificence, social ostentation, fashion, played their part; many master-masons doubtless worked, like the fourteenth-century merchant of Prato, 'in the name of God and of profit'; but the rich profusion and variety of craftsmanship revealed in the splendid photographs in this book bear witness to a powerful concentration of effort, witness in turn to a view of society widely and deeply held, as a ladder and a hierarchy, with its summit, throne and justification in the same God in whose eyes there is neither Jew nor Greek, bond nor free.

10 Figure of St Peter from the north porch, about 1240. *Rheims*

The World of the Cathedral Builders

1 The World of the Cathedral Builders

It had been widely predicted that the end of the first millenium of the Christian era would also bring the end of the world, and when the critical date passed without the expected cataclysm, a wave of relief and thankfulness swept over Europe. 'It was as if the whole earth, having cast off its age by shaking itself, were clothing itself everywhere in a white robe of churches,' wrote the Cluniac monk, Raoul Glaber, three years after the event, and for the next century and a half there arose the splendid and monumental churches that are the great glory of Romanesque art (1).

A large number of these were abbey churches, for the very real spirituality resulting from the Cluniac and other reform movements (2) had captured the imagination of the times, confirming the monastic way of life as the ideal of sanctity and inspiring great endowments over which the temporal lords retained a considerable degree of control. Everywhere, new monasteries were founded and existing ones rebuilt. It was perhaps the golden age of monasticism. The decline of the Carolingian dynasty had seen a process of political fragmentation and the triumph of an almost anarchical feudal system. The population of the towns had declined or even dispersed to the countryside. Still less were there any capitals, since the nominal rulers usually had several residences and set up court now in a castle, now in an abbey. In a virtually moneyless society, landed property was the only source of wealth and income. The basis of social and economic life in France had shrunk to the *mansus* or feudal manor, semi-independent and with an almost self-sufficient economy, in which there was no inducement to over-produce since the poor state of communications, and the absence of a merchant class, made it impossible to supply more than local needs. But, it was out of this feudal society that the modern world was gradually to grow.

In the eastern Mediterranean Venice, Pisa and other Italian towns were beginning to play a leading rôle in a great revival of trade with Byzantium and the Muslim world, and these centres were also engaged in vigorous trade with the far North via the great waterways of the Dnieper, linking the Black Sea and the Baltic. Beyond the confines of Western Europe proper, these developments acted as a powerful stimulus to the revival of commerce in the West, where the marked decrease in feudal warfare that followed the 'Truce of God' suggested by the church, gave rise to a new spirit of confidence and initiative (3). Land was drained and forests cleared; the horizon broadened, and a new figure, the merchant, appeared on the scene. The extraordinary rise of a merchant class within the feudal system

11 Carved boss showing the Lamb of God from the vestibule of the undercroft. *Wells*

and the concomitant revival of urban life is something of an enigma. Who were these merchants and where did they come from? Henri Pirenne, one of the leading authorities on the period, came to the conclusion that they were recruited not from the ranks of the landowners, far less the clergy, nor yet again from the settled peasantry living on the manorial estates, but from the landless poor, 'the nomadic folk who wandered about the country, working for hire at harvest time, living from hand to mouth . . . a floating scum . . . that had nothing to lose but everything to gain' (4). These merchant-adventurers were dominated from the start by a capitalist spirit. Originally, in one and the same person 'broker, carrier, sharper, and chevalier of industry' (5), they became merchants when commerce had already become a distinctive way of life, settling down at some convenient place such as a landing stage for river-craft protected by a castle, or an episcopal see, equally well fortified (6). The settlers attracted other merchants, for only in association could security be found, and in their wake came artisans and craftsmen, lured by the promise of steady employment. The process of urbanization had begun.

Spreading around the nucleus of the feudal fortress or *bourg*, the new settlements would in turn be surrounded by fortified walls forming a *faubourg* or outer fortress, whose inhabitants were known as *bourgeois* or burghers. It was this new urban class of burghers, vaunting its new-found strength and freedom, imbued with an acute civic consciousness, and engaged in ruthless competition with neighbouring towns, that was instrumental in building the great Gothic cathedrals, each designed to outdo its rivals; to proclaim not only the primacy of Faith, but the commercial pre-eminence of the town.

With the Crusades (the First was proclaimed in 1095) considerable numbers of people came into direct contact for the first time with the refined and much more highly-developed civilization of Byzantium and the Muslim world. Trade followed war, and in Europe there was a considerable rise in the standard of living, particularly in articles of furnishing and clothing, with the introduction of brocades, taffetas, damasks and watered silks. Many new plants, for both pharmaceutical and culinary use also made their appearance. Sugar was first used for sweetening (to a limited extent) and European gardens were scented with the fragrance of a new flower: the rose.

By the first half of the twelfth century, the 'medieval renaissance' was in full flower. Despite vigorous opposition, the new towns had won an ever-increasing measure of autonomy, culminating in the proclamation of 'Free Towns' and 'Communes' recognized by royal charter. Money came to replace landed property as the most desirable form of wealth, undermining the whole basis of the feudal system. Existing urban complexes were thriving and everywhere new towns were being laid out. Thanks to a veritable population explosion, the countryside, too, was booming, despite the constant defection of serfs to the cities, where they had only to spend a year and a day without being reclaimed, in order to earn their freedom (7). Deforestation and land reclamation continued now at a faster pace, so that the scene in town and countryside alike must have been not unlike the expansive pioneering days of America.

Communications also improved; Italian merchants began to visit Flanders from the tenth and eleventh centuries, and by the thirteenth century traffic in cloth in particular was considerable. The conveniently located fairs of Champagne drew crowds from all over Europe. Formerly most of the travellers had been pilgrims: now crusaders, merchants, scholars, masons and other building craftsmen were constantly on the move.

Of particular significance were the cultural contacts with Islam through the cosmopolitan Courts of Spain, Southern Italy and Sicily. Much of the wisdom of the classical world, Persia and India had been assimilated by the Arab conquerors and, together with original Arab contributions, was available to students in their universities. Arabic numerals and the decimal system, Euclid's geometry (translated from the Arabic by Adelard of Bath), the *Optics* of Ptolemy and the eleventh-century Arab astronomer Al-hazan, treatises on algebra and

trigonometry (both Arab sciences *par excellence*) and a vast body of literature in Latin, Greek and Hebrew, found their way to Europe from Islam (8). Particularly far-reaching in its consequences was the re-introduction to Europe of the works of Aristotle (chief classical authority for the philosophers of Islam), first in translations from the Arabic and later direct from the Greek, and also of the celebrated commentaries on Aristotle by the Moorish philosopher, Ibn Rushd (Averroës).

Within the new towns of Europe there was an insatiable thirst for knowledge: education, centred in the cathedral schools, many of which dated back to Charlemagne, took on a new importance. For half a century the prestige of the great teacher, Anselm (died 1117) ensured the importance of the school of Laon; later Chartres became another important centre of humanist studies, under a succession of brilliant scholars, Bernard and Thierry of Chartres and William of Conches. The great John of Salisbury (died 1180) ended his days there.

The 'schools' gave their name to the religious philosophy of the day, 'Scholasticism'. Until the middle of the twelfth century the influence of St Augustine who, as early as the fourth century, had tried to effect a reconciliation between Neo-Platonism and Christianity, remained dominant. To St Augustine the experience of God was the exclusive purpose of life. The world of the senses was a snare and a delusion and Reality was to be sought behind mere physical appearances, in the spiritual truth – that reflection of the Divine within all things – discernible only by the inner eye of contemplation. Nature, in fact, ceased to exist, except as a symbol of that supra-natural world revealed by Faith.

The curriculum in the schools was restricted to the traditional Seven Liberal Arts, the *trivium* (grammar, rhetoric and dialectic), the more advanced *quadrivium* (arithmetic, geometry, astronomy and music) and the 'mother of the arts', philosophy, together with Christian revelation, theology. To the modern mind, the natural sciences are conspicuous by their absence. In a comparatively bookless age, where the master alone had a book, a Socratic form of instruction was favoured, and traces of this method were retained even in written works in the Scholastic tradition (9). The dialectical method underlined the debt to classical philosophy, but there was a basic difference. True, free inquiry was welcomed, but few teachers, knowing the danger, would dare flatly to contradict the Church Fathers, let alone the letter of the Scriptures. Working within these circumscribed limits, the early Scholastics effected a synthesis of Neo-Platonic and Christian ideas. Their elaborate cosmological speculations, and especially their interpretation of the metaphysical nature of light and the importance of mystical numerical relationships in ensuring Divine order and harmony, were to play a decisive rôle in the evolution of Gothic architecture.

Growing familiarity with the works of Aristotle, transmitted through Islam, particularly his *Metaphysics* with its emphasis on knowledge obtained by empirical methods, opened up new vistas of thought, including the possibility of applying reason to dogma. Perception, by means of the senses, began to play a leading rôle in philosophical speculation, and the world of appearances and the beauties of nature, hitherto disdained, were invested with a new significance.

The need to reconcile faith and reason was increasingly felt

12 *Right* Vignette depicting the work of the Wheelwrights' and Coopers' Guilds which had donated the window; 13th century. *Bourges*

EZECHIEL

and brought into sharp focus in the dramatic confrontation of two of the most celebrated personalities of the day: the scholar, Peter Abelard (1079-1142) and the mystic, St Bernard of Clairvaux (1091-1153). Abelard – best remembered by some for his love-affair with Héloïse – was the outstanding intellect of his day, an undaunted searcher after the truth, remarkably independent of Patristic tradition. In his greatest work, *Sic et Non* (Yes and No), he examined a large number of crucial theological questions and exposed apparently conflicting answers from the Scriptures, the Church Fathers and the Church councils. This subjection of faith to the scrutiny of reason was intolerable to St Bernard, who was outspoken in his denunciation of Abelard, 'this man who is content to see nothing in a glass darkly, but must behold all face to face'. At Bernard's insistence the Council of Sens (1140) passed judgement on Abelard, condemned certain of his conclusions and forced him to retire to the monastery of Cluny. St Bernard had won the day, but his triumph was short-lived. Within a decade, Gratian's *Concordance of Discordant Canons,* based directly on Abelard's principles, had imposed order on the mass of often contradictory source-material, been enthusiastically received and henceforth formed the foundation of Church Law. Albertus Magnus (1193-1280) the great German scholar, too, had vigorously espoused Aristotelian principles and an emphasis on reason, but it was left to his Italian pupil, Thomas Aquinas (1225-1274) to effect the long-needed synthesis of St Bernard's faith and Abelard's reason in his monumental *Summa Theologica.*

Drawing heavily on Aristotelian reasoning, and particularly on the master's *Metaphysics,* he evolved a vast, coherent system of thought within which faith and reason, man and nature, Church and state, pagan and Christian knowledge, all found an integral place. Constructed with masterful logic, the *Summa* represents the apogee of 'High Scholastic' thought and justifies St Thomas's reputation as the greatest of medieval philosophers and Catholic theologians. With St Thomas Aristotelian thought had triumphed completely. Perception through the evidence of the senses was vindicated. Henceforth, in Erwin Panofsky's words, 'a plant would be thought to exist as a plant, and not as the copy of an idea of a plant' (10).

During the twelfth century there was thus a dramatic change in outlook accompanied also by the gradual eclipse of the cathedral schools by a new, semi-secular institution, the university. By the beginning of the thirteenth century there were five: Paris, Montpellier, Oxford, Salerno and Bologna. Three universities were supreme in their specialist fields: medicine at Montpellier and Salerno; Canon and Roman law (based on Justinian's Corpus) at Bologna. In every other sphere Paris reigned alone and unchallenged. From the time of Abelard to the end of the fourteenth century there was hardly a theologian or philosopher of distinction who did not either study or teach at Paris. If the body of the Church was in Rome, its mind was in the university of Paris, a fact tacitly acknowledged in the Papal decree of 1292, exempting its graduates from having to take any further examinations wherever they might teach. Johann of Osnabrück in the North and Brunetto

14 *Above St Anne holding the infant Virgin and Christ,* about 1320 (the Head of the Virgin is a copy of the original in the Landes Museum, Linz); from the high tower of the *Stephansdom,* Vienna. *Vienna, Historisches Museum*

Latini in Italy alike acknowledged the supremacy of French culture (11). The proud boast of Eudes de Châteauroux in the mid-thirteenth century was merely a statement of the truth: '*La France est le four, où cuit le pain intellectuel de l'humanité*' ('France is the oven where the intellectual bread of mankind is baked'). All Europe looked to France for leadership, a factor that goes far to explain the rapid diffusion and acceptance of the *opus Francigenum* or 'French Style', as the Gothic style was called abroad.

With the secularization of learning came a great increase in the production of books. In the twelfth century Bernard of Chartres, one of the greatest teachers of his day, bequeathed the whole of his library to the cathedral: a total of twenty-four volumes; a century later, books – though still written by hand – were being 'mass-produced' by professional scribes and a whole street in Paris was occupied by the illuminators and book-sellers.

According to the English chronicler, Matthew Paris (died 1259) there were no fewer than 3,000 students at Paris, with six colleges reserved for English students of theology alone, and at Bologna the students organized themselves in guilds, also according to 'nations', symptoms of one of the most significant developments of the period: the emergence of a form of national consciousness and the increasing importance of national languages.

The practical education of the merchant gave a great

13 *Left* Three examples of Gothic stained glass composition within a lancet shape; from left to right, *Virgin and Child,* 14th-century window donated by the Guild of Tailors – note the symbolic pair of scissors. *Freiburg. The Prophet Ezekiel,* 13th century. *Bourges. St Lô,* 13th century. *Coutances*

impetus to the study of the spoken language; at the feudal courts the humble minstrel was supplanted by the aristocratic troubadour of Aquitaine with his refined lyric poetry in the vernacular of the South, the melodious *langue d'oc*. The heroic *chanson de geste* which so strengthened the sense of a common European heritage was joined in the thirteenth century by the courtly novel of chivalric romance, and later on by its bourgeois counterpart, down-to-earth tales full of lively observation and humour, such as those of Chaucer.

The synthesizing spirit of the age, epitomized by the religious philosophy of the Scholastics, found its consummate artistic expression in Dante's *Divine Comedy*. Like the Gothic cathedral and the *Summa* of St Thomas Aquinas, it has an encyclopaedic richness, attempts to embrace all life within its compass and to reflect cosmic order in its formal structure (12). With Dante we reach not only one of the supreme artists of all time, but the paragon of a new type, the lay intellectual, writing in a newly-formed tongue. In fact, had Dante lived a century earlier, there would have been no Italian tongue for him in which to write.

One of the most intriguing aspects of Gothic culture is the important rôle played by women. After the largely male-dominated world of the early Middle Ages, the female voice is heard again: women like Eleanor of Aquitaine and Blanche of Castile changed the course of history; woman is not only the subject of court poetry, her feminine sentiments are voiced through the mouth of the poet; with the 'Courts of Love' and the institution of chivalry, the noble-born knight sues humbly for the favour of his liege-lady, elevated to the status of a goddess. This same chivalric love finds expression in a growing devotion to the Virgin, whose cult had been given great impetus by the teaching of St Bernard, and maintained its momentum until, in France at least, she had almost everywhere displaced the saints to whom the cathedrals had earlier been dedicated, and ruled supreme as *Notre-Dame* (Our Lady).

The society that developed the Gothic style was still largely feudal in organization – but no longer anarchic as in the early Middle Ages. It was strictly hierarchical. John of Salisbury compared the state to a human body in which the priesthood was the soul, the king the intelligence, and so on, down to the farmers: the feet. In practice such organic unity could not be maintained and there was at best a precarious balance of opposing forces, recalling in a sense the dynamic equilibrium of Gothic architecture. These were the centuries when the pretensions of the papacy to universal rule came nearest to realization. The problem of unity was very much on men's minds and the scholastic philosophers devoted a great deal of thought to the theoretical basis of an harmoniously organized society in which the conflicting interests of Church (*sacerdotium*) and State (*imperium*) would be reconciled. The ideal of the Christian ruler found its embodiment in St Louis of France, who brought a new – almost unheard of – sense of honour and integrity to politics. With such reforms as that of the judiciary, he made it possible for even the humblest of his subjects to obtain redress. The aim of the state, at least, was to protect rather than to extort, the monarchy was strengthened and endowed with an incomparable lustre, and the moral and cultural supremacy of France was confirmed.

15 *Left* The Gothic Age was above all the age of 'Our Lady', *Notre-Dame;* detail of the French 14th-century coloured marble sculpture known as the *Virgén Blanca,* 'White Virgin', in the Cathedral. *Toledo*

16 Detail of the Reliquary of St Galgano. *Siena, Museo dell' Opera Metropolitana*

Perhaps the finest flower of the medieval church was not a pope but rather St Francis of Assisi (1182-1226). St Bernard in his quarrel with the Scholastics had, in place of reason, reasserted the pre-eminent rôle of faith and charity (love) in understanding Divine Mysteries, and by emphasis on the innate dignity of man as a child of God and brother of Christ made man, strengthened the concept of the brotherhood of man. With St Francis even the birds became 'brothers'. Significantly, the new mendicant orders (both Franciscan and Dominican) no longer turned their back on the world but recruited support and worked among the burghers.

Many of the great abbeys had, by preference, been isolated from the world in aristocratic seclusion, and the Cistercians were known deliberately to have chosen unhealthy surroundings, on the grounds that an ailing brotherhood might well be a more spiritual force – an astounding theory endorsed by even so liberal a mind as Abelard, although rarely practised. No such life-denying impulse characterized the cathedral. The heart of the town, it was jostled by buildings crowding like chicks around a hen. Even the cathedral square, the *parvis* (from the French for 'paradise') was small; and with the centuries came accretions to the structure, not only oratories, chapels, sacristies, etc., but shops, booths, even dwellings, clinging to the flanks of the cathedral like barnacles, as can be seen in so many old and nostalgically charming engravings. The intimate, informal *parvis* surrounded by picturesque, half-timbered structures and filled with flower-sellers' and other stalls, have all too often been replaced by a sea of gleaming motorcars and charabancs, jam-packed on the vast, characterless squares which the nineteenth-century town-planners considered a suitable setting for the cathedral. Occasionally, it is true, the 'improvements' were prompted by other than purely aesthetic considerations. The resemblance of the Place Notre-Dame in

Paris to a parade-ground is no coincidence; it was specifically made large enough to station artillery in the case of a civil uprising.

In the medieval town the cathedral was the focal point of civic aspirations. Here the citizens would gather for the great festivals of the Church, celebrated with solemn splendour; here they would come to pray alone at the shrine of a saint or, on the contrary, to seek company. The medieval cathedral was far from being a place of worship alone. Within its walls people strolled and chatted openly, not hesitating to bring their pet dogs, parakeets and falcons. It was a favourite rendezvous for lovers – a fact casually noted without a hint of criticism by so high-principled a person as Christine de Pisan (about 1364–about 1433). At goals of pilgrimage, people even slept

and ate in the cathedral. Civic meetings were regularly held in cathedrals, so satisfactorily that some towns found it unnecessary to build a town-hall. The cathedral was sometimes the scene of lawsuits, disputations and university graduation ceremonies, even of everyday business. The mayor of Strasbourg habitually used his pew in the cathedral as his office, conducting his affairs from there. At Chartres, the cathedral housing the most sacred relic of the Virgin and inspiring greater religious fervour than perhaps any other, the wine merchants had their stalls in the nave and were only induced to move when the chapter set aside a portion of the crypt for their exclusive use.

The guilds that donated precious stained glass windows took care to choose locations where they could best be seen and did not hesitate to advertise their craft in vignettes that provide us with one of our best sources of everyday life in the Middle Ages (Plates 12 and 18). The great pair of scissors emblazoned on the window donated by the tailors at Freiburg-im-Breisgau (Plate 13) is as effective a piece of advertising as the *mon* or crest of a great Japanese commercial house. The multifarious activities that took place in the cathedral did not result in quite the bedlam one might have imagined. The prodigious scale of the interiors – many, like Amiens, able to house the entire population of the day – made it possible to isolate conflicting activities quite effectively. A hubbub at the west door might be quite inaudible in a chapel opening off the choir. Then, too, the fact that the interiors were unencumbered with chairs, people either standing (as they customarily did for sermons) or kneeling, ensured the maximum flexibility in the use of space. Above all, clearly defined areas or zones were set aside for specific purposes: the laity were only admitted to the nave and aisles and, occasionally, for a pilgrimage, to tombs accessible only from the choir ambulatory. The choir itself was reserved exclusively for the clergy who performed the regular services of the Church, conducted with appropriate splendour and dignity, that, theologically speaking, constituted the very *raison d'être* of the cathedral. Whether the laity participated in these services or not was irrelevant. The choir was customarily closed off from the choir aisles and later, in many cases, even from the nave, by a solid screen wall known as a rood-screen (from the fact that it was usually surmounted by the great 'rood' or cross), so that the choir became a kind of interior within an interior. Most of the French rood-screens or *jubés* were swept away in the eighteenth century when the taste of the times demanded an all-embracing view, to be replaced by the gilded iron grilles in the Louis XIV and Louis XV styles that consort so strangely with their Gothic setting (Plate 104). A rare survival of a stone *jubé* is the magnificent example at Albi (Plate 179).

The cathedral was the theatre of the Middle Ages. The liturgy had a strong dramatic element and the building's consecration would begin with pure 'theatre'. The bishop would lead a splendid procession towards the new cathedral, attended by all his clergy – except one, playing the rôle of an evil spirit, who lurked inside the locked doors, in ambush (*quasi latens*). Arriving before the closed door, the bishop rapped upon it three times with his staff and the procession raised the anthem: 'Lift up your heads, O ye gates, and be ye lifted up, ye everlasting doors, and the King of Glory shall come in.' First silence, and then a voice from within, 'Who is the King of Glory?' and the roared response, 'The Lord of Hosts, he is the King of Glory.' At this signal the bolts would slide open, the

vanquished 'spirit of evil' slipped out into the crowds and the bishop and procession entered the cathedral for the consecration ceremony.

On Maundy Thursday the great cross of the cathedral was taken down and, together with the Host in its pyx, laid within the shrouded 'Easter Sepulchre', a portable shrine which occasionally developed into a permanent stone structure, the size of a small chantry chapel (Plate 6). In its early form the Easter Sunday ceremony consisted of an anthem in dialogue between the angel at the tomb and the Three Marys. Later the dramatic element was elaborated to include watchers in armour (Pilate's guard) keeping vigil night and day beside the candle-lit tomb, and a simulated burst of thunder and smoke would mark the climactic moment when Christ rose from the tomb.

17 *Left* Two masons carry material in a hand-barrow while a third drinks from a jug; above masons build a crenellated tower. Details from a 13th-century window donated by the Masons' Guild. *Bourges*

18 *Above* Mixing mortar. Detail from a 13th-century window donated by the Masons' Guild. *Bourges*

19 *Overleaf* Flying vaulting ribs in the chapel of St Catherine. *Vienna*

20 *Overleaf* The tympanum of the St Anne Portal, made between 1160 and 1170 for an earlier, less steeply pointed archway and then adapted to its present location. On either side of the Virgin are (left) Bishop Maurice de Sully with the Dean of the Chapter reading and (right) the kneeling King Louis VII. *Paris*

Some cathedrals provided a particularly original spectacle at Pentecost, when a dove trailing blazing tow was let down from the roof and flew hither and thither representing the tongues of fire descending upon the Apostles.

A dramatic enactment of the 'Flight into Egypt' is recorded at Beauvais, when a procession headed by a beautiful young girl with a baby in her arms and seated upon an ass entered the cathedral and advanced to the altar. Then came a solemn mass, conventional in every detail except that the terminations of the *Introit, Kyrie, Gloria* and *Credo* ended not with the customary words but with mock braying, echoed by the celebrant himself, using 'the prose of the ass'. The rubrics for the 'Feast of Asses', as celebrated in the cathedral of Rouen, went one step further still, indicating the points in the service when the animal's tail was to be pulled sharply three times so as to achieve perfect synchronization with the priest's thrice-repeated benediction: *Dominus vobiscum* (13).

In its early struggle for converts the Church had absorbed many pagan customs, among them the great fertility festival falling in mid-winter. One of the characteristic features of the Roman Saturnalia was that for one day the established social order was reversed and the underling took control. This custom survived in the liturgical farces of which the most famous or notorious was the 'Feast of Fools', celebrated chiefly in France. Successively banned and revived through the centuries, the feast took the form of wild revels revealed only too clearly by numerous directives laying down what was *not* to be permitted. During the ceremony of 'Deposuit', at that point of the *Magnificat* when the words were uttered, '*deposuit potentes . . .*' ('He hath put down the mighty from their seat'), the precentor of the cathedral handed over his staff of office to the 'Lord of the Feast', one of the subdeacons, who, together with the choir-boys, assumed control and ran riot. 'Priests and clerks may be seen wearing masks and monstrous visages at the hours of office, dancing in the choir dressed as women, pimps, and minstrels, singing wanton songs and eating black-puddings at the altar itself, while the celebrant is saying Mass. They play at dice on the altar, cense with stinking smoke from the soles of old shoes, and run and leap throughout the church . . .' (14) – which became for this one day at least, a setting for music-hall burlesque.

St Francis had enacted the Adoration of the Magi in a real stable with living animals, and the great popularity of the crib or *presepio* dates from this act. Gradually the elaborated dramas that accompanied such feasts as that of the Epiphany could no longer be contained within the choir and spread first to the nave where half a dozen *tableaux vivants* might be set up against the piers, the public watching from the aisles, as the three Magi followed a star of lighted candles, suspended from the roof and often moved mechanically from scene to scene.

From here a further step took the liturgical drama outdoors – the first step also towards secular theatre. The later liturgical and miracle plays with their elaborate stage scenery and simultaneous action in Heaven, Earth and Hell, took place against the backdrop of the cathedral. Lasting for hours and sometimes for days, the dramatic cycles of the new 'outdoor theatre' had necessarily to take cognisance of the weather, and in northern Europe, at least, summer performances began to take precedence over those in the cold winter months. Initially the stage representations were, no doubt, strongly influenced by their counterparts in sculptured stone but towards the end of the Gothic period we have an interesting counter-current of influence from the theatre to the visual arts manifested in extravagant 'theatrical' costumes and histrionic attitudes. Hitherto sacrosanct iconography was modified when, for example, the classic depiction of the dead pushing open the lids of their sarcophagi at the Last Judgement gave way to the macabre concept of the dead pushing their way up out of the earth – inspired by the theatre where the actors popped up through trapdoors in the floor of the stage.

The cathedral was also a concert-hall. The period saw a great development in polyphonic vocal music, achieving a triumphant first-flowering during the latter half of the twelfth century in the compositions of Léonin and Pérotin of the *Ecole de Notre-Dame* in Paris – the Ile-de-France dominating the musical field as effectively as those of philosophy and the plastic arts. Pérotin also composed music to accompany the actions of the early liturgical drama, and the fascination with the simultaneous development of several melodic lines found a perfect form in the liturgical *motet* for several voices, a highly complex form which, as contemporary musicians emphasized, was not for simple folk. They, no doubt, voiced their praises in the semi-impromptu *laude* advocated by the mendicant orders.

Although Aelred the Abbot of Rievaulx in the mid-twelfth century could complain, 'Why, I pray you, this dreadful blowing which recalls the noise of thunder rather than the sweetness of the human voice?', the organ did not play as great a rôle in the music of the Gothic era as one might have imagined. There is not a single reference to an organ at Notre-Dame in Paris until the fourteenth century, and even then it was, apparently, a small instrument, primarily for study purposes. In the field of organ music, at least, we have a clear advantage over the medieval music lover, who could never have heard the triumphant sonorities of the *Te Deum* made possible by the perfection of the instrument in subsequent eras. On the debit side, the great eighteenth and nineteenth century organs are disastrous visually in many Gothic interiors, for example at Notre-Dame in Paris (Plate 23) (15).

The religion of the Middle Ages was the very antithesis of our 'Sunday Worship'. From birth to grave, religion and life were integrated in one indissoluble unity. The Liturgical Calendar set down not only the Saints' Days and the Feasts of the Church, but with them dictated the cycle of daily life. When the Feast of St Barnabas approached in June, the peasant knew it was time to mow the tall grass, and the vignette of a peasant carrying home his bundle of logs depicted on the portal of the cathedral provided a gentle reminder (Plate 4). For all its ceremony, religion retained a spontaneous and unself-conscious quality. Life drew its whole meaning from faith; the Church did not hesitate to draw inspiration from life. Fra Salimbene of Parma relates how the celebrated humanist, Henry of Pisa, delighted by the love-song of a maid-servant, appropriated the tune for his *Christe Deus, Christe meus, Christe Rex et Domine* (16).

To the unlettered masses of the Middle Ages the cathedral

21 *Opposite* Windows provided the *Biblia Pauperum* of the masses. Here, read from the bottom up and from left to right, are: the *Flight into Egypt,* in two scenes; the *Three Magi* warned in a dream to return by another route, and their journey home; and a 'concordant' episode from the Old Testament: Daniel prophesying the *Fall of the Idols*. Detail of medallion window from the early 13th century. *Laon*

was the *Biblia pauperum.* 'I am an old woman who knows nothing and never read a word. I see at the church . . . a painted paradise with harps and lutes, and a hell where the damned are boiled. The one makes me afraid, the other happy . . .' (17). Such are the words François Villon puts in the mouth of his illiterate mother. The church was well aware of the power of the visual image. St Gregory himself had written: 'For what writing supplies to him that can read, that does a picture to him that is unlearned and can only look' (18). With so consciously didactic a purpose in mind, it was unthinkable that the subject matter should be determined by the artist's fancy although it is unlikely that the iconographic scheme could always be understood by the uneducated or uninstructed layman. Emile Mâle (19) has shown that the iconography of the cathedrals was as carefully organized as the treatises of the Scholastics. Like the contemporary *Summa Speculum* (Mirror) or *Imago Mundi* it provided an encyclopaedic picture of this world and the next.

On the sculptured walls and in the glowing glass of the cathedral the four 'Mirrors' of Vincent of Beauvais' *Speculum Majus* unfold before our eyes. In the *Speculum naturale* we see the Acts of Creation and the world of nature – viewed as both fact and symbol. On the central tympanum of the *Portail Royal* at Chartres, inspired by the vision of St John the Divine, we can see Christ in Glory within a *mandorla*, surrounded by a man, an eagle, a lion and an ox (Plate 26) (20). These 'Emblems of the Evangelists' have not only inspired some of the greatest masterpieces of Christian art, but in their triple-tiered symbolism, as expounded in contemporary lectionaries, afford a good insight into the ideas of medieval man. The emblem of St Matthew is a man since his gospel commences with a genealogical table of the ancestors of Christ; St John is the eagle (that was believed to be able to gaze straight at the sun just as St John had transported man straight to the very heart of divinity); St Mark is the lion in reference to the voice crying in the wilderness of his opening verse; St Luke is the ox, the sacrificial victim of the Old Law, for his gospel commences with an account of the sacrifice by Zacharias. Secondly, the four creatures could be considered as symbolizing the Four Mysteries of the life of Christ: The Incarnation (God made man); the redemptive Offering (the ox); the Resurrection (the lion which, according to the Bestiaries, slept with its eyes open and was likened to the Redeemer, 'who in virtue of His divinity was living and watching even when by virtue of His humanity he appeared to sink into the sleep of death'); and the Ascension (the eagle soaring heavenward). Thirdly, to complete the triple tier of this symbolism, the emblems expressed the virtues necessary for salvation: the intelligence of man; the renunciation of the sacrificial ox; the courage of the lion, and the vision of the eagle 'who with direct gaze contemplates the things of eternity' (21).

The belief that the lion slept with open eyes and that the eagle gazed straight into the sun derives from the Bestiaries. These collections of animal fable and pseudo-science dating from Classical times, overlaid with symbolism by the early Christians and endowed with authority through quotation by the Church Fathers who found an image of the Saviour's life

23 The interior of Notre-Dame; note how the 18th-century organ obscures the western rose. *Paris*

and death in the habits of the animal kingdom, enjoyed enormous popularity throughout the Middle Ages, especially in the rhyming verses of a collection of sermons by the celebrated preacher, Honorius of Autun (22). Beneath the magnificent figure of Christ Blessing at Amiens (the so-called *Beau Dieu*) there is a rather endearing creature with one ear pressed to the ground and the other stopped with the tip of its tail (Plate 24). This is the adder of the Bestiaries, not, as we might expect, a viper, but 'a kind of dragon which can be charmed by song', and which assumes this protective attitude when it senses danger. 'The adder', adds Honorius, 'is the image of the sinner who closes his ears to the words of life.' Another reason why the lion was regarded as a symbol of the Resurrection was related to the belief that the lioness gave birth to lifeless cubs which were roused to life by the roaring of the father on the third day. So, too, the owl that sleeps by day is likened to the Jews who shut their eyes to the light of truth, and the legend of swan-song makes that bird the symbol of the soul crying in joy or anguish at the approach of death and the prospect of eternal bliss or woe.

Parallel with the medieval preoccupation with symbolism, it is precisely here in the 'Mirror of Nature' that we also find that spontaneous delight in the beauties of this world – the flowers of field and hedgerow, the birds and beasts, so lovingly observed and delineated, and quite devoid of any symbolic intent – that reflects the revival of interest of the Gothic period in natural appearances. The art of the Gothic era is, in fact, notable for its sensuous and even sensual element. As Arnold

24 *Above* The Medieval 'Adder', with one ear pressed to the ground and the other stopped with the point of its tail, was the symbol of the sinner 'who closes his ears to the words of life'. Bas-relief on the pedestal of the *Beau Dieu. Amiens*

25 *Right* A personification of one of the Liberal Arts, *Geometry. Freiburg*

Hauser observes: 'There is hardly an epoch of Western history whose literature so revels in descriptions of the beauty of the naked body, of dressing and undressing . . .' (23). This, of course, is in the field of a secular art form, but a parallel undercurrent can be detected even in the cathedral. If the theologians responsible for the iconographic scheme saw to it that the nude appeared only where explicitly demanded by the Scriptures – for example, in the rise of the dead at the Last Judgement – the sensual spirit of the times found an outlet in lewd devils and demons and, where the rein was removed, erupted in fantastic and even obscene grotesques and drolleries.

The Fall has condemned man to labour by the sweat of his brow and in the *Speculum doctrinale* (24) we see the occupations of the months of the year, presided over by the signs of the zodiac: the farmer sows and reaps, threshes the corn and presses the vintage, slaughters a hog for the revels of Christmas and in the cold month of February warms himself before a fire (Plates 27 and 28). Few ages have accorded honest labour greater honour. Work, whether in the cornfield or the sheepfold, the bakery, the smithy, the tailor's shop or the mine is depicted with sympathy and respect; often with humour, never with a hint of condescension or caricature.

The Liberal Arts that formed the basis of instruction are personified by stately women with distinguishing attributes. Thus, Grammar, birch rod in hand, supervises two diligent young pupils (Plate 274); Geometry holds her straight edge and compasses (Plate 25); Astronomy an astrolabe, or occasionally, a bushel (supposedly a reference to the fact that the movement of the stars dictated the time for sowing and reaping); while the concept of the scholar with head in the clouds finds expression in a figure of Philosophy at Laon, head literally disappearing in a cloud, and shown with a ladder, indicating the rungs of knowledge that must be climbed to master this 'Mother of the Arts'.

Sometimes celebrated personages associated with the Arts appear in conjunction with the Muses. At Chartres beneath the figure of Music, a woman striking a carillon of bells with a hammer, there is a small figure writing industriously, probably Pythagoras, credited with formulating musical theory. The *Speculum morale* depicts the virtues and vices. The age-old concept of a struggle between good and evil

26 *Left* Central tympanum of the *Portail Royal. Chartres*

27 *Top* A peasant, stripped to the waist, threshes corn with a flail; *The Month of August,* from the Calendar series. *Strasbourg*

28 *Bottom* A bearded figure in winter garb warms his bare feet before a fire; *The Month of February,* from the Calendar series. *Amiens*

found concrete expression in the *Psychomachia* or inner 'Battle of the Soul'. Personified as beautiful maidens, the Virtues transfix with their lances the monsters (Vices) beneath their feet (Plate 30). Dominant in the Romanesque and early Gothic periods, this interpretation gradually lost favour to a second in which the Virtues and Vices were juxtaposed in paired medallions or bas-reliefs. The Virtues, now stately women accoutred in knightly armour – an echo of the Psychomachia – bear a shield emblazoned with their distinguishing device: a dove for Humility, a serpent for Prudence, a lion (or a bull) for Courage. Though effectively expressing the imperturbability of virtue, these formidable Wagnerian Brunhildes can be, it must be admitted, singularly unprepossessing. The scenes depicting the vices, on the contrary, are most enjoyable – all movement, life and interest. A crowned rider falls headlong from his horse (Pride); a man beats his wife (Discord), and a young knight startled by a hare, drops his sword and runs (Cowardice) (Plate 29).

In the fourth and final 'Mirror', the *Speculum historiale,* the whole vast panorama from Eden to the Saints is surveyed and interpreted. The sources are the Old Testament and the Gospels, the Apocryphal Books and the lives of the saints

as assembled by Jacobus de Voragine in his *Legenda Aurea*, for history for the Middle Ages was the history of the Church. Secular history – even such momentous events as the Crusades – finds hardly an echo in the art of the cathedral. The exploits of the greatest kings are denied the space allotted to the daily round of peasant and craftsman.

'The Old Testament is nothing but the New covered with a veil, and the New is nothing but the Old unveiled', St Augustine had written in his *De Civitate Dei,* and the theologians vied with each other in finding Christ's advent foreshadowed in the Old Testament. Abraham's sacrifice of Isaac was patently a symbol of God the Father's sacrifice of his Son (25); Noah, 'the only just man' was likened to Christ, the perfect man, and the ark floating on the waters of the flood to the Church and the water of baptism. Never was the concordance of mystic numbers taken to more incredible lengths. St Augustine, himself, went so far as to dispute the generally accepted age of Christ at his Crucifixion (thirty-three) in favour of thirty – on the grounds that the ark was thirty cubits high. The Apocrypha, against whose 'deliramenta' St Jerome had fulminated, provided precisely the plethora of marvels in which the men of the Middle Ages took such delight. Supplemented by the equally numerous and fantastic exploits of the Saints, they provided an inexhaustible mine of inspiration to the artist.

The cathedral was a compendium, didactic and admonitory, of the worlds of nature, of the mind and of the spirit, past, present and future, culminating in the awesome prophesies of the End of the World, the Last Judgement and the establishment of the Heavenly Jerusalem of which the cathedral was the earthly embodiment.

29 *Above Fortitude* and *Cowardice* – a young knight drops his sword at the sight of a hare – two details from the paired bas-reliefs of Virtues and Vices. *Amiens*

30 *Left* Represented as a beautiful maiden, a Virtue transfixes a monster with her lance. *Strasbourg*

31 *Right* Detail of the head of a Virtue with a rather seductive smile. *Strasbourg, Musée de l'Œuvre Notre-Dame*

32 *Overleaf* A vigorously carved head from the arcading beneath the 'Five Sisters' window could almost be the work of the German expressionist, Barlach. *York*

33 *Overleaf* Detail of the original 13th-century decorative wrought iron hinges on the doors of the St Anne Portal. *Paris*

The Gothic Style

2 The Gothic Style

At times the crowd of pilgrims who strove to flock in to worship the holy relics became so dense that no one among the thousands of people could move or do anything but stand benumbed, like marble statues, or, as a last resort, scream . . . Squeezed in by the mass of strong men as in a winepress, the distress of the women was frightful: pale as death, they cried out as if in labour. Several, miserably trodden underfoot, were lifted by the men above the heads of the crowd and were marched forward . . . Moreover, the brethren who were showing the tokens of the Passion of Our Lord to the visitors, had often to give way to the riotous crowd, and having no place to turn, had to escape with the relics through the windows (1).

This evocative picture of the crowds at a great Church festival – deliberately heightened for reasons of policy as we shall see – is typical of the style of the great Abbot Suger of St Denis, one of the first great enthusiasts of the Gothic style.

Suger (1081-1151) had a dazzling career. Of peasant stock, he was placed in the Church as a child and must have shown precocious talent, for as an oblate aged ten he was admitted to the exclusive abbey school of St Denis, attended by the sons of the nobility and, since the abbey was used as the royal residence, even by princes of the royal house. Suger's unique administrative and diplomatic gifts brought the young monk rapid promotion and he represented his monastery at church councils and at the papal court while still in his twenties. The Capetian monarchy had allied itself with the Church in its effort to curtail the power of the feudal barons. In this struggle the Royal Abbey played an important military rôle and, as deputy for his abbot, Suger came into direct contact with a former school-fellow – now King Louis VI. Their youthful acquaintance was cemented in a warm friendship. For the rest of the king's life Suger was his chief minister, most trusted adviser and confidant, credited by historians with much of the success of his reign.

Two years after Suger's election as Abbot of St Denis in 1122, the kingdom found itself in great danger from a threatened invasion by the German Emperor Henry V, son-in-law of Henry I of England. Louis VI hastened to St Denis and made a vow of rich donations to the abbey if the patron saint of France, and of the royal house, should avert the danger. Then, at a dramatic ceremony, semi-religious, semi-political, brilliantly stage-managed by the astute Suger, the king appealed to the assembled nobles for support and received an overwhelmingly favourable response – even from those lords traditionally hostile to the Crown. Faced with this unexpectedly united front, the enemy reconsidered his plan and the threat

34 *On page 44* The *cimborio* over the crossing; as at Rheims angels keep guard on the parapets. *Burgos*

35 *Above* The nave buttresses. *Chartres*

passed. The result was a strengthening of the monarchy, still greater wealth for the abbey and a further increase in the prestige of Suger whose career reached its climax when, during the next reign, of Louis VII, the king departed for the Crusade of 1147, leaving the abbot as regent of the realm and primate, in fact if not in name, of France.

Suger's amazing success underlines the truly liberal and progressive attitude of the twelfth-century Church which, alone in the hierarchical society of the times, could offer such an opportunity of advancement. Small wonder that Suger should have regarded the Church as his mother, to whom he owed everything and for whose honour he would spare no pains. Ever since his boyhood Suger had dreamed of rebuilding his beloved abbey and remedying the congestion he described so graphically. After the political events of 1124 and the heightened importance of St Denis, the need became even more pressing and he set aside a large sum annually towards the fabric fund. It was only in his sixtieth year (1140), however, that the first stage of the rebuilding was ready for consecration.

He commenced by building a new west front. While stressing the flanking towers – as the Normans had done at the Abbaye aux Hommes at Caen – Suger laid a new emphasis on the three great doorways which not only helped solve the problem of the circulation of large crowds, but were to be regarded as the veritable 'Gateway of Heaven'. For the first time, the central doorway was surmounted by a rose window. Internally, the western block formed three aisles at ground level, corresponding to the entrance doors, with chapels above, the central one serving as the *camera* or treasure-house, illuminated by the rose window (2). Both aisles and upper spaces were roofed with pointed arches and cross-ribbed vaults. Leaving the Carolingian nave intact, Suger then turned his attention to the choir, which he rebuilt within the short space of 39 months, again using a structural system of pointed arches and cross-ribbed vaults. The new choir terminated in a semi-circular, double ambulatory from which radiated nine shallow chapels with tall windows, 'an elegant and praise-worthy extension', in Suger's own words, 'by virtue of which the entire sanctuary was pervaded by a wonderful and con-tinuous light entering the most sacred windows' (3). Here, in the choir of St Denis, we have the manifesto of Gothic architecture. Light is to be the theme and generating element – 'light of Divine essence' (4), filtering through radiant stained-glass windows and bathing the interior with a glow not quite of this world. Determined to allow more and yet more of this magic light to enter, the Gothic architects were to pare their structures to the bone, to defy the laws of gravity in ever higher and more delicate buildings, to risk all to create the first and greatest architecture of glass.

The new style of architecture was inaugurated with con-siderable publicity. The dedication of the choir on June 11, 1144, was attended by King Louis VII, his queen, Eleanor of Aquitaine, the great nobility and a host of distinguished prelates. Characteristically, Suger made of the ceremony not only a great religious and social occasion, but also one of profound political importance, the service deliberately exalting the king's prestige, emphasizing his alliance with the Church and the homage due by the nobility to God's anointed. The five archbishops and fourteen bishops present no doubt returned to their sees determined to emulate the brilliantly-lit choir of St Denis, admired not only for its intrinsic merits but also for its associations with the Crown.

Thanks to Suger's statecraft the monarchy, the Church of France, the Abbey of St Denis and its new style of architecture were linked indissolubly, and the triumphant progress of the House of Capet was accompanied by the equally triumphant progress of the Gothic style. It is no coincidence that the greatest French cathedrals all arose within the Royal Domain. 'The French Cathedral', as Viollet-le-Duc so rightly observed, 'was born with the monarchical power' (5).

The Gothic passion for light had a profound theological significance. Plato's metaphorical association of sunlight with

goodness and knowledge was greatly elaborated by the pagan Neo-Platonists who identified light with Ultimate Reality and the generating principle of the universe. Light, they argued, was also the means by which the intellect perceived truth. This concept found confirmation in the magnificent passage in the Gospel of St John where the Word is compared 'to a light that shineth in darkness, by which all things were made, and that enlighteneth every man . . .' On this dual basis of pagan and Christian thought, a fifth-century Syrian mystic, Dionysius the Areopagite, built a highly complex philosophy which constituted no less than a theology of light. For Suger there was a personal reason for a particular interest in this philosophy, for this Dionysius (Denis), already mistakenly confused in the Middle Ages with another Dionysius, the Athenian disciple of St Paul, had also long been identified with the third-century martyr and Apostle of Gaul to whom the Abbey was dedicated. Mistakenly or deliberately created, this triply-compounded personality certainly provided just the combination of qualities befitting a patron saint of the realm. We have seen how with the help of the great abbot, the Saint's prestige became second to none. Small wonder that the author of a new translation of the writings of Dionysius the Areo-pagite, dedicated to Suger's successor at St Denis, should have claimed that he held first rank after the Apostles; small wonder also that his philosophy of light and Suger's interpreta-tion of that philosophy should have been taken very seriously, or that when the sharp-witted Abelard expressed his doubts as to the identification of the writer with the Apostle of Gaul, he should barely have escaped trial – not for heresy, but for treason.

Suger's infatuation with light which had so decisive an influence in formulating the Gothic style was but an extreme manifestation of a view widely supported by the Scholastics which received expression from men as different as Hugh of St Victor, Gilbert de la Porrée, St Thomas Aquinas and Robert Grosseteste, who hailed light as the most direct corporeal manifestation of the Divine, 'the mediator between bodiless and bodily substance, at the same time spiritual body and embodied spirit'. Light, which could pass through glass with-out breaking it, was likened to 'the Word of God, Light of the Father, that had passed through the body of the Virgin' and became a symbol of the Immaculate Conception. Some of the enthusiasm accorded light itself was also bestowed on sub-stances that transmitted light. This concept, too, derived from Dionysius the Areopagite, who had propounded the thesis that the contemplation of the light emanating from material objects could aid in a comprehension of Divine Light. And what closer physical approximation to spiritual light than the glittering surfaces of precious metals and, above all, the matchless beauty of gems? Suger, contemplating the cabochon gems adorning the great golden altar-cross, felt himself trans-ported to 'some strange region of the universe between the slime of earth and the purity of heaven' – an opinion frequently echoed by medieval theologians, tireless in their praise of the anagogical power of gems, with their property of giving off light 'and glowing from within'.

The same virtues are ascribed to stained glass which, not surprisingly, attempted to simulate the glow of gems, so successfully that even today the two colours most widely used

36 *Right* Detail of exterior showing pillars and statues. *Chartres*

by the cathedral builders are still most accurately described as ruby-red and sapphire-blue.

To medieval man the cathedral was truly the House of God, in a very real and awesome sense difficult for us to understand today. It was conceived as no less than the earthly embodiment of the Heavenly Jerusalem; as a microcosm of a Divinely-ordered universe, clearly manifesting the *splendor veritatis* or radiance of Truth.

The arts achieved significance in so far as they reflected this *splendor veritatis,* by conforming to the system of perfect proportions and numbers which ensured the cohesion of the universe; the ultimate speculative source for this belief was Pythagorean number theory and Platonic cosmology. Just how this came to have any bearing on the activities of church builders in the twelfth century is not certain; but for medieval scholars generally the *locus classicus* of these ideas was probably Plato's account of the five regular solids in the *Timaeus.* In the *Timaeus,* Plato put forward the view that the five regular solids constituted the geometrical elements out of which the Universe was compounded. They were also identified with the physical elements: earth with the cube; water with the icosahedron (i.e. a solid made up of twenty equal hexagons); air with the octahedron (i.e. eight equilateral triangles); fire with the tetrahedron (i.e. four equilateral triangles); while the dodecahedron (made up of twelve pentagons) was associated with the Universe as a whole.

The three basic plane figures which underlie the construction of the five regular solids are the equilateral triangle; the right-angled isosceles triangle of which two make a square; and the pentagon. If these figures formed the geometrical starting point for the Divine architect of the Universe itself, there was every reason to use them in the construction of churches, which were veritable symbols of the Universe. There is in fact a good deal of evidence that the number systems associated with the square and the equilateral triangle were widely used in church designs. The pentagon was also used on occasion. It is interesting that the construction of the pentagon involves the use of the ratio known as the Golden Section ($\cdot618:1\cdot0$), in which the lesser dimension is to the greater as the greater is to the sum of the two together (i.e. A is to B as B is to A plus B). This ratio seems to have been known to the Middle Ages in the form of the Fibonacci Series (named after the eminent mathematician Leonardo Fibonacci of Pisa, who lived at the end of the twelfth century), in which any given number is the sum of the two preceding numbers, and any pair of numbers gives an approximation to the Golden Section. One such pair of numbers is 5:8, and this relationship also appears frequently in buildings of the twelfth and thirteenth centuries, for instance Chartres.

The ratio 5:8 also happens to be the mathematical form for the minor sixth in music, and it has often been suggested that the musical ratios played a part in architectural design. St Augustine himself had placed music and architecture together above the other arts, as being 'sisters of number', and on occasion made much use of Pythagorean and Neo-Platonic number theory for his own purposes. The series 1:1, 1:2, 2:3, and 3:4 which correspond to the intervals of the perfect musical consonances: unison, octave, fifth and fourth, were heavily overlaid with Christian symbolism (6). The two

38 The church flooded with 'light of divine essence'–the ideal achieved; detail of the north transept. *Amiens*

geometrical progressions which Plato used to great effect in the *Republic*: 1:2:4:8 . . . and 1:3:9:27 . . . were also invoked, and likewise the sequence of Perfect Numbers.

A simple and striking example of the application of the ratios of musical consonances to medieval architectural design is afforded by the plan, from the sketchbook of a thirteenth-century architect-master-builder, of a Cistercian church with a square end and double-square vaulting bays (Plate 39). The ratio of the fifth (2:3) determines the relationship of the width across the transept to the total length; that of the octave (1:2) the relationship between the side aisle and the nave and also between the length and width of the transept; the musical fourth (3:4) is echoed by the proportion of the choir, while 'the crossing, liturgically and aesthetically the centre of the church, is based on the 1:1 ratio of unison, most perfect of consonances' (7).

What is perhaps more surprising to us is that the stability of buildings could also be conceived in terms of perfect numbers. The medieval architect certainly seems to have attributed mechanical virtues to the square and equilateral

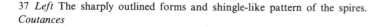

37 *Left* The sharply outlined forms and shingle-like pattern of the spires. *Coutances*

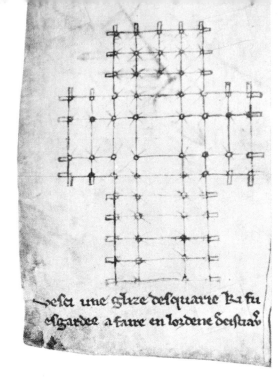

39 The design for a square-ended Cistercian Church illustrates the application of the ratios of musical consonances to architectural design; detail from the Sketchbook of Villard de Honnecourt. *Paris, Bibliothèque Nationale*

triangle. This is made abundantly clear by the difficulties which faced the builders of Milan Cathedral. Uncertain how best to proceed, they called a conference of master-builders to determine the section through the church; they asked not so much how high the vaults should be, but, rather, which geometric figure should govern the section. After maintaining that the design under construction was structurally unsound because of inadequate foundations, piers and buttressing, and because the geometrical basis had been compromised, one of the German consultants, Heinrich Parler, who was steeped in Gothic structural theory, actually proposed that the height be *increased* yet further to make the section conform to a square. The inference was that the increased stress on structural members, already allegedly defective, would in some way be offset by the structural soundness ensured by a design 'ad quadratum', in harmony with the laws that assured the indissoluble stability of the cosmos.

Viewed in this light, it is easy to see why geometry, which ensured 'true measure' should have been accorded so predominant a rôle in construction; why Dominicus Gundissalinus of Segovia, the celebrated twelfth-century scholar, could repeat the late antique formula that defined architecture as applied geometry.

Abbot Suger was not alone in promoting acceptance of the Gothic style; a second 'godparent', strange as it may seem, was the redoubtable St Bernard. This ascetic aristocrat abhorred the ostentatious display of riches and found it difficult to approve of 'a Church resplendent in her walls, beggarly in her poor; clothing her stones with gold and leaving her sons naked'. Reluctantly he conceded the possible necessity of valuable materials and elaborate decoration in raising the minds of a worldly laity to things spiritual. For the clergy themselves there should be no need for such a stimulus to devotion.

The fantastic beasts that had proliferated in the lavish decoration of the late Romanesque Abbeys of the Cluniac Order – now in spiritual decline – particularly incurred his wrath. 'What purpose is there in these ridiculous monsters, in this deformed comeliness, and comely deformity . . . in these unclean apes . . . monstrous centaurs . . . this creature with many heads united to a single body . . . this four-footed beast with a serpent's tail . . . ?' In a place like a cloister, did they not merely tempt the monks 'to spend the whole day in wondering at these things rather than in meditating on the law of God? For God's sake, if men are not ashamed of these follies, why at least do they not shrink from the expense?' (8)

What connection could there be between the austere spirituality advocated by St Bernard and the elaborate style of architecture, decoration and furnishing inaugurated by Suger at St Denis? The answer was that if Suger wished to give expression to his natural taste for the costly and magnificent, so closely associated with the style of Cluny, which St Bernard so disliked, he had to produce a convincing argument to justify his choice, for St Bernard was not a figure whose views Suger could ignore. Suger's approach was outlined in two treatises that provide us with a most valuable insight – albeit indirectly –

40 *Left* A gargoyle aims his backside in the direction of the Prelate's Palace – the sculptor's protest, so local folklore asserts, against some grievance. *Freiburg*

41 *Right* Head of the Magdalene; detail from a polyptych by Simone Martini, 1320. *Orvieto, Museo dell' Opera del Duomo*

into the concepts which the design of the medieval church was intended to convey. Throughout, he emphasizes the necessity to 'clarify' and 'enlighten'. In describing his special pride, 'the luminous and most sacred windows' he relates at length the edifying subjects portrayed on each, 'urging us onward from the material to the immaterial', while the use of precious materials for the liturgical vessels and ornaments was justified not only on metaphysical grounds but by reference to the Old Testament.

'If golden pouring vessels, golden vials, little golden mortars are used to serve, by the word of God or the command of the Prophet, to collect the blood of goats or calves or the red heifer: how much more must golden vessels, precious stones, and whatever is most valued among all created things, be laid out, with continual reverence and full devotion, for the reception of the blood of Christ.' With obvious reference to the attitude of St Bernard he continues: 'The detractors object that a saintly mind, a pure heart, a faithful intention ought to suffice for the sacred function; and we, too, explicitly and especially affirm that it is these that principally matter. [But] we profess that we must do homage also through the outward ornaments of sacred vessels, and to nothing in the world in an equal degree as to the service of the Holy Sacrifice, with all inner purity and with all outward splendour.' (9)

The symbolism of the entrance portal as the Gateway to Heaven and the Church as a vision of the Heavenly Jerusalem was reinforced by verses inscribed on the splendid, gilded-bronze doors. The beholder was urged to avail himself of the elevating power of their beauty to 'illuminate the mind so that it might travel through the true lights to the True Light, where Christ is the true door' (10). Above, on the lintel, a touching verse revealed another side of the character of the great statesman-prelate:

Receive, O stern Judge, the prayers of
Thy Suger;
Grant that I be mercifully numbered
among Thy own sheep. (11)

This was in reference to the sculptured tympanum depicting Christ in Glory, presiding at the Last Judgement. This was one of the favourite Romanesque subjects for the west front of a church, where the last rays of the setting sun illuminate the last moments of a dying world; but how differently it is treated here. In the tympanum at the Cluniac Abbey of Beaulieu, completed but a few years previously, the scene was one of turmoil and confusion. At St Denis the various elements have been subjected to a thorough-going reconsideration and reorganized in an arrangement calculated best to elucidate the significance of the event. Order rules supreme. A majestic Christ, serene and omnipotent, surveys the other participants in the drama – angels, apostles and the risen dead – whose scale and location conform to their importance in the hierarchy. The 'comely monsters', the griffins and fish-tailed beasts that loomed larger than the apostles themselves at Beaulieu, have been banished to limbo. Not a detail remains that could be criticized as irrelevant to the theme; the orthodoxy of the statement would defy the scrutiny of the Grand Inquisitor.

At St Denis a systematic and didactic order has been imposed on the arrangement of the sculpture. Here, too,

43 Decorative sculpture from the south transept, early 15th century. *Milan*

'column statues' representing ancient Kings of Israel adorn the splayed jambs of the portals for the first time, further reinforcing the 'Gateway' symbolism: the New Testament (Christ and His Church) being entered by way of the Old, with Christ's royal ancestors providing a guard of honour as it were. With the sculpture of the tympana and these 'column statues' the elements of the Gothic portal have been assembled. (Unfortunately, the sculpture was mutilated by revolutionaries and restorers to such an extent that its original beauty can, today, only be guessed at from the engravings published by Montfaucon in the eighteenth century.) At Chartres can be seen a triumphant first-flowering in the sculpture of the *Portail Royal* – 'l'avant-printemps de la sculpture gothique' (12).

The success with which Suger vindicated his aesthetic philosophy may be gauged by the fact that the new St Denis evoked not a word of hostile criticism from St Bernard, whose relations with Suger remained extremely cordial until the latter's death. At the same time, the extremely effective exposition of the *splendor veritatis* in the light-flooded choir of St Denis, and the integrity of its naked structural system, so

44 Interior of the choir looking towards the great east window. *York*

effective a vehicle for the expression of the musical consonances that reflected Divine Order, had an irresistible appeal for the Cistercians later on. In the thirteenth century an austerity version of Gothic with neutral-coloured *grisaille* glass in non-figurative designs replacing the scenes resplendent with ruby and sapphire at St Denis, and sculptural decoration restricted to a few foliate motifs, was carried over the length and breadth of Christendom in the monasteries of the Cistercian order.

To the architectural historians of the nineteenth century, with their strong rationalist-technical bias, the history of Gothic architecture was closely identified with the history of its characteristic structural elements: the pointed arch and ribbed-vault. The introduction of these elements was seen as setting in motion a seeming inexorable chain of reaction, a structural evolution that proceeded, in a series of logical steps, to call into being the Gothic style. Today scholars take a very different view. The structural elements are generally recognized as playing a fundamental part in the evolution of the style, but only as a means to an end. They made it possible to give perfect

expression to the spirit of the times: to religious fervour given expression in a soaring verticality, to the longing for 'light of spiritual essence', clarity, order and synthesis. It was the spiritual climate of the day, that potent compound of Mysticism and Scholasticism, that provided the essential motivation; the interaction of idealistic and technical factors that produced the Gothic style.

The insecurity of the early Middle Ages was reflected in churches with thick walls and small openings, a 'Fortress' of God in a dangerous, and often hostile world. Before the eleventh century no one thought of covering the wide span of a nave with anything but a light timber roof. In the eleventh century, with its spirit of increased confidence and initiative, attempts were made to replace the timber covering, so susceptible to frequent and disastrous fires, with stone, first using a continuous waggon or barrel vault (Fig. 1). The result was one of the characteristic forms of the Romanesque church. Small windows, at best, could be inserted along the length of these crude, tremendously heavy barrel vaults without threatening their stability, so that the nave had generally to rely on the light admitted at the two ends and on indirect light from windows in the external walls of the side aisles. These were vaulted either with the same barrel vaults (involving a much smaller span and, therefore, presenting far less acute problems) or with groin vaults. The groin vault results when two barrel vaults are made to intersect at right angles, the line of intersection of the vaulting surfaces being known as a groin (Fig. 2). The weight of such a vault is directed towards the supports at the corners of the bay. Provided these supports are suitably braced to resist the thrust, they can be of small cross-section, while the space between can be pierced with ample openings for light.

The obvious solution was to use the groined vault over the nave as well, but this presented great problems occasioned by the height of the springing of the arches and the large spans involved. Before the end of the eleventh century, some naves of moderate scale were successfully covered with groin vaults, examples surviving in Lombardy, the Pyrenees and the Rhineland, and in the early twelfth century even some naves of larger churches, notably Vézelay in Burgundy. Simultaneously, in Périgord, a series of domes was used to cover the nave – structurally satisfactory, but very expensive. The future development of vaulting lay elsewhere.

There is much to be said for Paul Frankl's assertion that 'the Gothic style begins with the *combination* of diagonal ribs with a groin vault . . . that only their combination produced Gothic ribs and Gothic vaults'(13). The earliest surviving combination of these elements occurs in the vaults of the choir-aisles of the Cathedral of Durham, commenced in 1093. The nave of Durham cathedral also includes some of the earliest pointed arches in Western Europe. Originating in Mesopotamia in ancient times, the pointed arch was widely used in Muslim architecture(14). The earliest pointed arches in Christian buildings almost certainly occurred in the Mediterranean area and the form was probably transmitted to the West via Italy. The Normans may have become familiar with its use either in Sicily, which they wrested from the Muslims during the last third of the eleventh century or as a result of the First Crusade. The architect of Durham was undoubtedly a Norman.

It will be noticed that the early experiments in the evolution of Gothic structural elements all took place outside the Île-de-

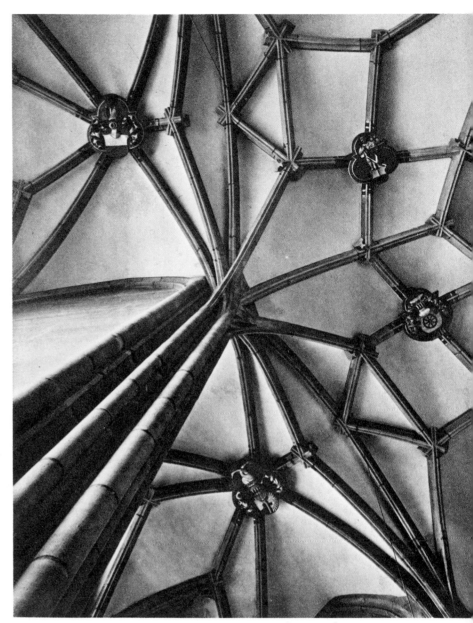

45 The combination of ribbed vault and pointed arch also facilitated the vaulting of bays of irregular shape; detail of the vaulting in the ambulatory. *Rheims*

46 Late Gothic vaulting of the 'Parler School'. *Freiburg*

47 *Overleaf* The palisade-like south façade, towering above the sea-wall. *Palma*

France which can, however, still claim to be the cradle of the style; for it was there that the possibilities inherent in the technical advances were first realized, and that 'architects first drew the inevitable conclusions from the vault rib . . . making it the progenitor of an entire style' (15). The very fact that the Île-de-France, unlike Burgundy, Normandy or Languedoc, had produced no great regional school of Romanesque art tended to be an advantage, for the new style filled a hiatus and was not presented with the problem of displacing a well-established style.

In the ribbed groin vault two diagonal ribs under the groins divide the surface of the vault into four triangular compartments. The French word used since the thirteenth century for these diagonal vaulting ribs is *ogives* (generally supposed to be from the Latin *augere*: to strengthen). The English, German and Italian words ribs, *Rippen* and *costoloni*, are particularly significant and apt since they draw attention to the linear character of the strengthening element, true, indeed, of every feature of Gothic structure which is skeletal rather than monolithic, articulated rather than homogeneous.

Do the diagonal ribs help support the vault? Fifty years ago such a question would have been greeted with incredulity and utter scorn. It was obvious that they did. This belief, the cornerstone of the whole rationalist theory of Gothic structure championed by Viollet-le-Duc and Choisy has, however, been seriously questioned of recent years and one critic, Pol Abraham, created a furore by denying the rib any statical significance whatever (16). Its value, he maintained, was purely formal or aesthetic. The rib merely created the illusion that it supported the vault. His supporters pointed for confirmation to Gothic buildings damaged in the World Wars where the ribs had fallen, leaving ribless vaults standing. On the other hand, one could quote a far larger number of cases where the vaulting webs have gone leaving only the ribs standing, particularly where buildings have only been subjected to the ravages of time and weather and not to unnatural shocks which they could hardly have been designed to sustain. (The crossing at Lindisfarne provides an example.) The skeleton of

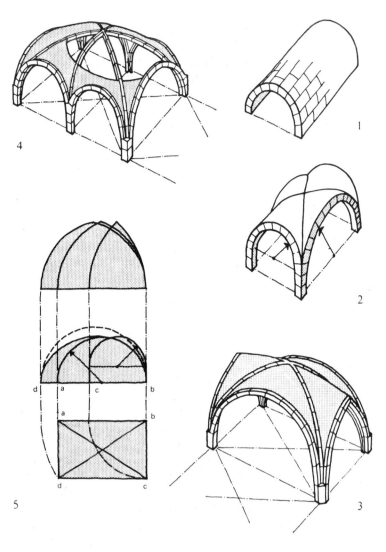

Figs. 1–5 *The Evolution of Gothic Vaulting*

Fig. 1 A waggon or barrel vault.

Fig. 2 Romanesque vaulting of a rectangular bay with a stilted arch over the shorter span.

Fig. 3 Early Gothic vaulting with a pointed arch over the shorter span only.

Fig. 4 Domical sexpartite vault (see Glossary) using a unit of two nave bays.

Fig. 5 *a,b,c,d* represents the plan of a rectangular vaulting bay. Since the height of a semicircular arch is half the span, such an arch over distance ab would be higher than that spanning the smaller side bc, and the smaller arch would have to be stilted (i.e. have its springing point raised) if the apices were to be kept level. Similarly, a semicircular arch over the diagonal db would rise higher still (indicated by broken line), and was often depressed to an elliptical form to reduce its height. Using pointed arches, the problem of keeping the apices of three arches of different spans level could be conveniently and elegantly solved simply by using more or less acute pointed arches.

ribs alone left standing, defining space without enclosing it, provides one of the greatest aesthetic delights of ruined castles and abbeys.

Even accepting Pol Abraham's thesis that the *final* strengthening function of the rib was not significant, this does not mean that the ribs did not play a very important part in ensuring stability during the *initial* settlement of the vault. The early Gothic builders were themselves quite certain that the rib fulfilled a real structural function and was far from being a purely aesthetic device. The very word *ogive* implies

this, and direct confirmation is afforded by the report of the committee of master-builders who in 1316 gave a report on necessary repairs to the fabric of Chartres Cathedral occasioned by the wear and tear of a century. They definitely saw the ribs as structural members. The major practical significance of the rib was technical: it simplified the construction of the vault. To begin with, the daunting size of a large groined vault was broken down into more manageable units. The diagonal ribs and the arches enclosing the bay could be erected first, and the vaults, now reduced to thin stone webs or 'severies' (10 to 14 inches thick in the very largest buildings) could be tackled section by section.

Scaffolding and centering to support the arches and vaults under construction could also now be erected section by section, instead of necessarily under the entire groin vault, while the smaller size of the vaulting compartments and the lighter weight of the vaulting panels permitted the extensive use of a simple form of movable centering known as a *cerce*. The enormous saving in centering was of the greatest importance, not because there was a scarcity of timber (large areas of Europe still being covered with forest) but because the sawing of wood was not yet practised, and timber for planking had to be reduced to size with an adze – a laborious, time-consuming operation. The diagonal ribs also concealed the groins, particularly unsightly and difficult to construct when the layout of the medieval church made it necessary to vault bays which were not square but rectangular. Even the Romans had often constructed their great groin vaults over square bays, rather than face the additional problems presented by rectangular bays. How the medieval cathedral builders solved these problems using the ribbed vault, is illustrated in Figures 1 to 5, where the evolution leading to the perfect high-Gothic solution is traced, step by step.

Figure 3 shows the plan of a rectangular vaulting bay over a nave, enclosed by the transverse arches spanning the nave, and wall ribs or formerets over the clerestory walls, and with diagonal transverse ribs under the groins, intersecting at the keystone. Using the semi-circular arch throughout, the transverse arch rises far higher than the wall rib over its shorter span, while the diagonal rib rises higher still (5 *db*). The result is a vault of domical form of the type used in Anjou and Poitou (4). An early solution to the problem of keeping the apices of all three arches more or less level was to stilt the small wall arch (i.e. place the springing of the arch at a higher level) bringing it up to the height of the transverse arch, while the diagonal rib was lowered by using a segmental rather than a semi-circular profile (5 *c*). An alternative, avoiding the problems associated with the segmental arch – notably its excessive thrust – was to make the diagonal rib semi-circular and stilt the other two arches even further; but the result left much to be desired, especially visually. The decisive advance was to retain the semi-circular diagonal rib and bring the wall and transverse ribs up to the same height using pointed arches of different radii (5 *d*). This solved virtually all the problems, not only for a rectangular bay, but also for bays of irregular shape, such as were encountered in the rounded choir end. In addition, the lateral thrust of the vault was much reduced. The final stage in the evolution of Gothic vaulting, characteristic of the high-Gothic phase, was to point even the diagonal arch, the motive for this last development being chiefly aesthetic, in the interest of consistency of form.

None of the subsequent elaborations of the Gothic vault,

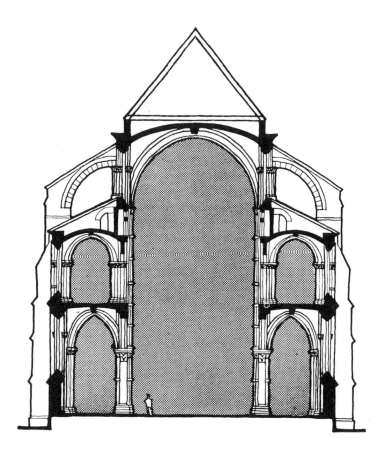

Fig. 6 Transverse section. *Laon*

48 The fantastic but compellingly real creatures that peer down as gargoyles. *Amiens*

the additions of tierceron and lierne ribs, or the creation of net, fan or pendant vaults, fulfils any real structural function. There is much to be said for the French viewpoint that all these later developments merely compromise the purity of the perfect, classic solution and are but symptoms of decadence. Patriotic scholars of other nationalities naturally disagree. This is particularly understandable in the case of the English, for English medieval vaulting, as we shall see, is a perfect expression of the national temperament; and it must be admitted that it is difficult to resist the attraction of these highly decorative webs of stone.

The lateral thrust transmitted by the nave vaults had to be resisted. The earlier Gothic churches followed Romanesque precedent and placed a gallery or tribune over the side aisle, as at Laon (Fig. 6). The vaulting of the tribune acted as a stiffener, rather like a restraining chain round the nave. So long as the main vaults were not of excessive height above the 'chain', this generally sufficed, but additional strength at the vulnerable points above the tribune vaulting could be provided by building cross-walls on the vaults, enclosed within the timber roof. Initially built in horizontal courses of masonry like any other wall and resting on the tribune vaults, the stroke of genius came when an arch form was adopted, for with it was born the principle of the flying buttress (17).

This flying arch transmitted the thrust across the aisle to a narrow but deep buttress-pier and thence down to the ground, the whole system acting rather like a person with arms outstretched, propping up a toppling cupboard. The early 'four-stage' interior elevation consisted of the main arcade between nave and side aisle, the tribune gallery, the triforium (an arcaded wall passage in the thickness of the wall at the level of the aisle roof) and the clerestory windows above. Thanks to the invention of the flying buttress, the tribune gallery, which so obstructed the passage of light, could be omitted and the four stages reduced to three (Fig. 7). Once brought out from hiding under the tribune roof, the flying buttress could be raised to any height, and the arches doubled or even trebled, if need be, enabling the cathedral builders to raise the nave vaults, and the height of the clerestory windows, to a hitherto undreamed of extent.

With the aid of the ribbed vault, pointed arch and flying buttress it was possible to direct and concentrate weight and thrust, and to resolve these forces within an articulated skeleton of structural elements whose form was determined to a large extent by their function. Neither the result of aesthetic caprice, nor yet of engineering pure and simple, Gothic structure provides a graphic diagram, as it were, of the mechanical forces at work. On the exterior, a forest of taut, free-standing forms – reminiscent of a modern 'space-frame' – provides a permanent stone scaffolding, holding the opposing forces in a delicate equilibrium. Within, all is soaring insubstantiality as befits a 'Celestial City' and the glowing colours of the stained glass stretched between the vaults and piers give little indication of the complex machinery of support without.

Compared with the self-contained and passive forms of the Romanesque church, the Gothic church 'seems to be in a process of development, as if it were rising up before our eyes; it expresses a process, not a result. The resolution of the whole mass into a number of forces, the dissolution of all that is rigid and at rest . . . gives us the impression of a dramatic conflict . . . And this dynamic effect is so overwhelming that beside it all else seems a mere means to this end' (18).

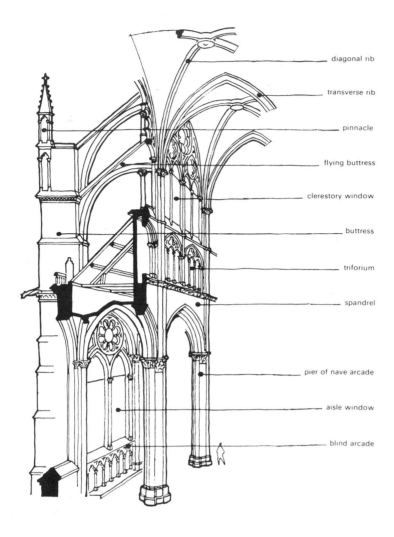

diagonal rib

transverse rib

pinnacle

flying buttress

clerestory window

buttress

triforium

spandrel

pier of nave arcade

aisle window

blind arcade

Fig. 7 Diagrammatic section through the nave of *Amiens* showing the names of the various parts of a Gothic cathedral (after Viollet-le-Duc).

49 Bronze funeral effigy of the founder bishop Evrard de Fouilloy, died 1222. *Amiens*

Hand in hand with the evolution of Gothic architecture, and its dissolution of the wall-surface, went that of stained glass, the 'painted' art form *par excellence* of the period. Stained glass has a long history. Small pieces of translucent glass dating from the fifth century survive in window openings at Hagia Sofia in Constantinople. A decisive advance came with the introduction of lead framing during the tenth century (19). Not only was the weight substantially reduced, but the thinness of the leading strips and the ease with which they could be bent to any shape, made an enormous extension of subject matter feasible. Hitherto, geometric patterns had been used almost exclusively; now the whole field of figurative design was open to the glass designer, who quickly responded to the new possibilities. The monk, Theophilus, in his celebrated treatise on art techniques, *De Diversis Artibus,* written in the early twelfth century, specifically refers to the painting of faces, hands and draperies. In the field of stained glass, as in architecture, Suger's new choir at St Denis was a milestone, opening the way to the glories of Chartres and the Sainte-Chapelle.

The very malleability which made lead such an eminently suitable material, had an inherent disadvantage: a lack of strength, particularly in resisting wind-pressure. This was solved by subdividing large windows into smaller areas by means of stout iron reinforcing-bars, firmly bedded into the stonework (20). This iron armature not only accomplished its practical purpose, but in its uncompromising rigidity contrasted most effectively with the irregular-shaped glass fragments, bestowing on the window an appropriately architectonic stamp.

By the Gothic era, dense cast glass had long been superseded by blown glass, obtained by forming a cylinder, cutting it along the length and flattening it to produce a sheet, which could then be cut or broken to the desired shape with a nipper-like tool called a grozing iron. This glass was still relatively thick and had many bubbles and flaws, but it was precisely these irregularities, cunningly exploited by the artist, which gave to early Gothic glass its inimitable subtlety and variety, its murky depths shot through with fitful flashes of light. A severely restricted palette was characteristic of the finest medieval glass, that of the late twelfth and thirteenth centuries. A brilliant sapphire blue and a glowing ruby red generally predominated, while greens, yellows and purples and small areas of colourless glass provided subsidiary accents. The blue was integrally coloured with a special cobalt-oxide-bearing sand obtained from Bohemia, which, with its ready access to raw materials, early achieved great fame as a glass-producing area. It was found, however, that the copper-oxide used to produce the red glass was so powerful that a sheet of glass coloured integrally was almost opaque. To overcome this difficulty the technique known as 'flashing' was devised, in which a sheet of colourless glass was coated with a layer of the red glass. Even the pigmented portion was sometimes composed of alternate laminations of colourless and red glass and it is to these laminations – produced by a process whose secret has been lost – that is attributed the uncanny and inimitable effect of old ruby glass, 'as if glowing from within' (21).

Details such as features, hands and drapery folds were painted on the glass with 'enamel-brown', a black pigment composed of metallic oxides, resin and glass. This was then

50 *Right* Old Testament king; detail from northern rose. *Paris*

fired at a low temperature, but even when vitrified, remained relatively 'soft' and vulnerable and has in many cases deteriorated seriously. In this respect the bold draftsmanship of the earlier period has survived far better than the more delicate later work, especially when this was allied with thin enamel glazes. This deterioration of the painted portions of the design is in direct contrast to the patina acquired by the dyed or stained glass. In this case the corrosion and pitting of the outer surface of the glass by the elements over the course of centuries has, in fact, enhanced the aesthetic effect by the further dispersion of light rays penetrating the glass through the roughened surface. With the fourteenth century, improved techniques of glass production made available thinner sheets in larger sizes. Colours became lighter and the drawing more precise and elegant, if at times a trifle precious and finicky. The medallion-type window with its numerous small scenes gave way to large figures often isolated within an aedicule (miniature building) adorned with the complete decorative vocabulary of cusped arch, crocketed gable and finial, etc. This elaborate architectural 'tiara' permitted the human figure, while still retaining its natural proportions, to be accommodated within the tall, narrow window openings characteristic of the period. Large areas of colourless glass appear, enlivened with designs drawn in a luminous yellow, produced by the 'silver stain' technique of fusing a wash containing silver-oxide or nitrate.

In the late-Gothic period it became possible to dispense with a conspicuous metal armature over a considerable area. Large and complex compositions, many reflecting the influence of the Miracle Plays, often spread over several windows, while

53 Interior of the choir looking east. *Gloucester*

51 *Left* The St Etienne window. *Bourges*

52 (*a* & *b*) Two fine examples of alabaster relief produced in Nottingham and exported all over Europe in the Middle Ages; (*a*) The Trinity, (*b*) The Annunciation, from the Dean Hussey monument of about 1440. *Wells*

the technique of stained glass, using transparent enamels on colourless glass, approached closer and closer to that of easel painting. With the introduction of elaborate effects of shading and perspective the mural character suitable to such an architectonic art was seriously impaired and the great period of stained glass was over.

Only with the twentieth century have we witnessed a renaissance of the art of stained glass, inspired largely by the early glass of the cathedrals. With a return to first principles has come a recognition that the glory of medieval glass depends primarily on the skill with which jewel-like fragments of thick glass have been arranged in an effective abstract pattern, and that the black accents of leading and armature, far from being undesirable, enhance the brilliance of the coloured glass considerably by contrast. And so we have the strange anomaly that completely abstract modern glass often evokes an emotional and aesthetic response far closer to that of genuine Gothic glass than the most painstakingly 'correct' essay in the medieval style painted by the nineteenth-century revivalists.

54 View of the cathedral from the gardens of the Archbishop's palace. *Bourges*

55 *Right* The figures of the jambs (seen here under snow) seem to be frozen into rigid attitudes and contrast forcibly with the suave grace of the *Vierge Dorée* on the adjoining *trumeau* (see plate 150). *Amiens*

56 *Overleaf* Angle of the west façade. *Siena*

How the Cathedrals Were Built

3 How the Cathedrals Were Built

The magnitude of the cathedral-building achievement which, within a couple of hundred years, covered Europe with a mantle of great churches – in France alone, eighty cathedrals and some 500 churches of monumental scale – presupposes not only a singleness of purpose but a highly efficient organization and building industry. The motivating force was provided by the religious fervour of the times, fostered and channelled by an exceedingly wealthy and virtually all-powerful Church, which also had the personnel and experience to administer such vast projects.

The usual method was to create a fabric fund, the nucleus of which was provided by setting aside a proportion of the regular revenues of the church. The fund was supplemented in various ways. Bishops and canons taxed themselves voluntarily, and so, occasionally, did citizens. Legacies also provided important contributions. Numerous documents have survived urging notaries to remind testators of their duty towards the fabric fund, while from about 1200 onwards episcopal and papal indulgences were granted at one time or another in the building of nearly every great cathedral.

Our Lady of Chartres had long inspired extraordinary devotion and the most fascinating eye-witness account of the fervour of the laity is contained in an account written by the Abbot Haimon of Saint-Pierre-sur-Dives in Normandy, dated 1145. 'Who has ever seen or ever heard tell, in times past, that powerful princes of the world, that men brought up in honour and in wealth, that nobles, men and women, have bent their proud and haughty necks to the harness of carts, and that, like beasts of burden, they have dragged to the abode of Christ these waggons, loaded with wines, grain, oil, stone, wood and all that is necessary for the wants of life or for the construction of the Church?' The picture conjured up is one of noise and joyful bustle, but Abbot Haimon stresses an almost ritualistic decorum: '. . . they march in such silence that not a murmur is heard, and truly, if one did not see the thing with one's eyes, one might believe that among such a multitude there was hardly a person present. When they halt on the road, nothing is heard but the confession of sins, and pure and suppliant prayer to God to obtain pardon. At the voice of the priests who exhort their hearts to peace, they forget all hatred, discord is thrown far aside, debts are remitted, the unity of hearts is established. But if anyone is so far advanced in evil as to be unwilling to pardon an offender, or if he rejects the counsel of the priest who has piously advised him, his offering is instantly thrown from the waggons as impure, and he himself ignominiously excluded from the

57 The west front with its 500 ft twin towers. *Cologne*

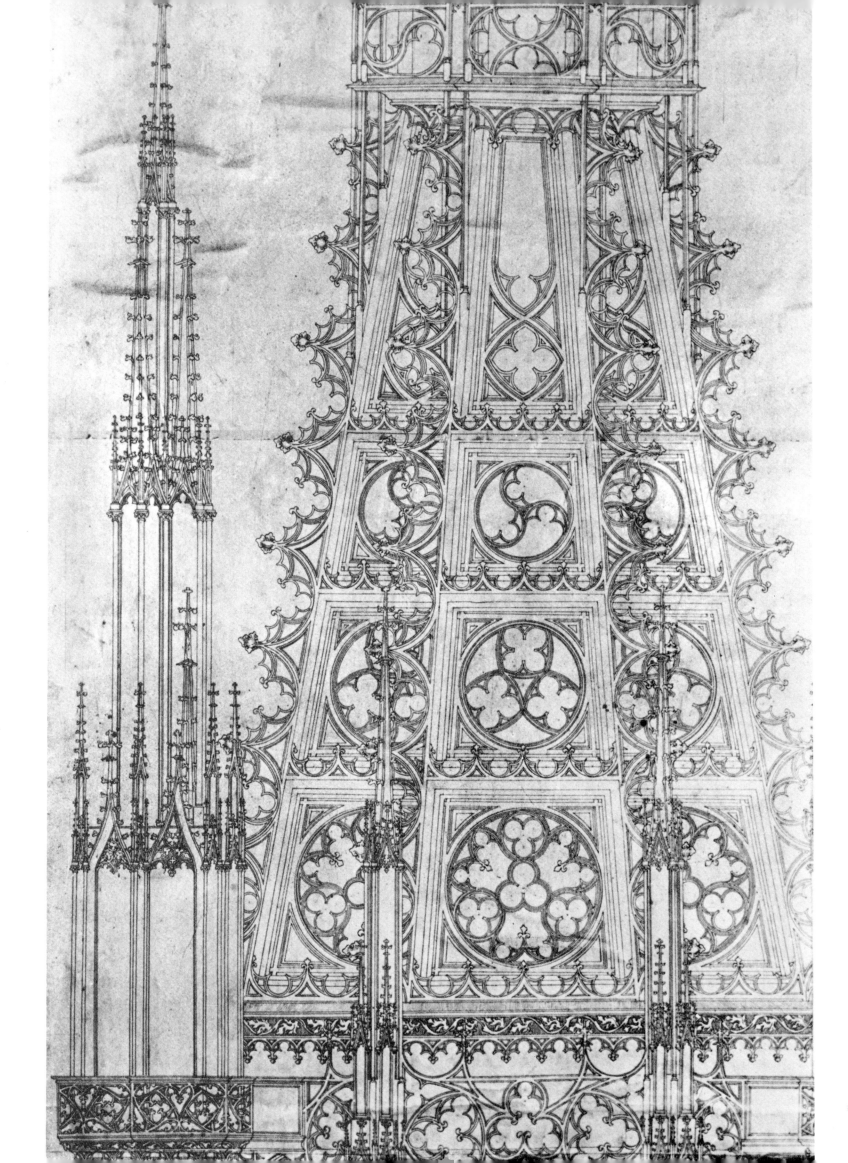

society of the holy . . . After the people, warned by the sound of trumpets and the sight of banners, have resumed their road, the march is made with such ease that no obstacle can retard it . . . When they have reached the church they arrange the waggons about it like a spiritual camp, and during the whole night they celebrate the watch by hymns and canticles. On each waggon they light tapers and lamps; they place there the infirm and sick, and bring them the precious relics of the Saints for their relief. Afterwards the priests and clerics close the ceremony by processions which the people follow with devout heart, imploring the clemency of the Lord and of His Blessed Mother for the recovery of the sick . . .' (1)

Such enthusiasm was obviously most exceptional, though apparently not unique (2), and the significance of gesture remains, even if as some authorities maintain, 'The Cult of the Carts' should be regarded as symbolic. Detailed accounts of the financing and construction of Milan Cathedral have survived. In an entry of the Register of the Building Works dated September 17, 1387, we find mention of free services rendered by advocates and notaries and the mayor himself. Gian Galeazzo Visconti, Duke of Milan, and his family themselves launched the campaign for funds for the building with gifts of jewels and stuffs of gold laid on a provisional altar, which, together with the cheeses, grain, poultry and pelts donated by the various corporations, were afterwards sold by auction. An ass given by the parish of San Marcellino is recorded as fetching one *lira*, seven *soldi*; a fat calf from the Porta Orientale, eight *lire*, eleven *soldi*. Publicity stunts helped to maintain the public interest. Thus, the ladies of the Porta Vercellina staged a presentation of the story of Jason and Medea and with the example of the Golden Fleece implored the donation of a real fleece, while groups of young girls dressed in white and accompanied by trumpets and pipes toured the city and surrounding districts begging for alms. A generous donation by the prostitutes of Milan is also noted.

Where a church was fortunate enough to possess particularly celebrated relics, these could provide an important source of revenue. Within three months of the fire which damaged the old cathedral of Laon in the civic disturbances of 1112, a group of canons took their most sacred relics, salvaged from the fire, and travelled from town to town over a wide area of France soliciting contributions. Everywhere, the relics excited enthusiasm and, according to the chronicles, wrought numerous miracles (Plate 59). The funds assembled, however, were not very great and the following spring they went to England, then enjoying particular prosperity, where several disciples of Anselm, the famous teacher of Laon, held important ecclesiastical office. Journeying via Arras and St Omer, fleeced by Flemish merchants and attacked by pirates during the crossing, the canons nevertheless managed to reach Dover. During a seven month tour they visited most of southern England including Canterbury, Winchester, Salisbury, Exeter, Bristol and Taunton, and returned to Laon with sufficient funds for the repairs.

The enormous veneration accorded the 'Chemise of the Virgin' preserved at Chartres contributed signally to the great success of the fund-raising appeal that enabled the structure of that cathedral to be erected within the short space of

27 years. The theory that the Gothic cathedrals necessarily took hundreds of years to complete, is untrue. When building funds were available, progress could be very rapid. When they fell off, a period of respite would follow while another appeal was organized. It is important to note that even in Abbot Haimon's account there is no mention of the pious volunteers at Chartres taking part in the *actual construction*. The picture of chanting volunteers piling stone upon stone, and the cathedral rising as an unselfconscious paean of praise, an expression of 'folk art' as it were, is a fabrication of the Romantics. Patently ridiculous to anyone acquainted with the technical side of building – particularly such a complex building as a Gothic cathedral, where the disposition of elements at plinth level already reflects the layout of the

59 The exhibition of relics, a detail from the Belleville Breviary illuminated by Jean Pucelle and his workshop. *Paris, Bibliothèque Nationale*

vaulting – it has proved very difficult to dispel from the popular imagination. Even the rôle played by the 'monk-builders', naturally greatest in the building of their own abbeys, and most significant among the Cluniac and Cistercian Orders, has been grossly overrated. The monumental buildings of the Gothic era, like those of any other age, were largely the work of professional artisans, attested to by numerous documents that have survived in the archives of Church and State.

Exceptional prelates, like Abbot Suger, exerted a profound influence on the development of religious architecture, establishing new criteria of taste, and determining the iconographic scheme. Only rarely, however, did they take such a direct interest as Suger. Many bishops acted as the patron or sponsor of the new cathedral, little more. The practical charge of these great building projects was entrusted to the canons of the chapter, a body of priests under a dean, whose duty it was to assist the bishop in the administration of his diocese. When evidence becomes plentiful in the fourteenth century it appears that each individual canon, not bound by the rule of poverty, had a generous income from a prebend, enjoyed the life-tenure of a comfortable house and could dispose of his personal possessions by bequest. Originally under the direct authority of the bishop, the chapter gradually became an almost autonomous body, often in conflict with the bishop, whose power it attempted to curtail, and ever ready to resort to litigation to protect and extend its rights. It was the chapter which, generation after generation, concerned itself with the

58 *Left* Early project for the spire of Strasbourg Cathedral by Johan Hültz of Cologne, inspired by the openwork octagon of Freiburg. Ink on parchment, after 1419. *Strasbourg, Musée de l'Œuvre Notre-Dame*

60 The decorative *baldaquin* porch provides a perfect contrast to the cliff-like wall of brick, unbroken to a height of 45 feet above the floor. *Albi*

financing, construction and maintenance of the cathedral fabric, ensuring the collection of the revenues set aside for the fabric fund, entering into contracts, arranging the payments for material and labour and appointing a master-mason in charge of the technical side of building operations. They themselves administered the business side through one of their members to whom was given the title *custos fabricae* (keeper of the fabric) (3).

Concurrent with the production of a design, the first concern would be to arrange for adequate supplies of material and labour. Most important was the supply of stone. Care was needed to select stone that both worked and weathered well. The Westminster Fabric Roll cites the expenses paid to a mason sent to select stone: '6d per day for 8 days for riding to the quarries . . . to choose and examine good stones.' On large projects it was customary for the chapter to work a quarry itself or even open a new one. The location was of great importance in view of the high cost of transport. Professors Knoop and Jones (4) cite several cases where transport cost

three to four times as much as the quarrying. The actual distance from the quarry to the building site was secondary to convenience in transportation. Water carriage was far easier and far cheaper, so that stone could even be obtained from abroad at competitive prices; for example, the fine creamish-white sandstone of Caen in Normandy, soft when quarried but hardening on exposure, and therefore ideal for delicate carving, was imported into Britain in great quantities.

Land transport was by ox and, increasingly, by horse-drawn cart and waggon, and by pack-horse, belonging to the organizers, or exacted as service from tenants on church lands, or requisitioned (in the case of the Crown), or hired. As Professors Knoop and Jones have shown, the building accounts for the Abbey of Vale Royal (5) for the years 1278-80 detail the expenses incurred in carting stone from the quarry to the abbey, a distance of some five miles. One-horse carts were hired for 2d or 2½d per trip; two-horse carts for 3d or 3½d. Two journeys were generally made per day and an average of twelve per week. For this project alone more than 35,000 cartloads of stone were carried from quarry to building site over a period of a couple of years. The labour involved in cutting such amounts of stone from the rock face without the aid of explosives, and only with simple picks, axes, chisels and wedges, can easily be imagined. Iron tools were quickly blunted and carried by relays of boys back to the smithies, a feature of every mason's yard, whether at the quarry or the building site. Quarries were all the more quickly exhausted since, as in the case of mining, it was impossible to go deep, chiefly because of the difficulty in getting rid of water from excavations.

The high cost of transport encouraged the working and at least the rough-finishing of stone at the quarries. Marble from the Isle of Purbeck, so extensively used in the Early English cathedrals, was often even polished at the quarries, and towards the end of the Middle Ages, sculptured figures and interior furnishings were increasingly carved by schools of sculptors established at famous quarries. Peter of Nottingham carved an elaborate reredos in the famous alabaster of the district for the chapel at Windsor Castle and sent it off, complete for erection, in ten carts. This was a special order. For lesser jobs, routine workshop-production sufficed, and popular images in convenient sizes were 'mass-produced' for stock; clearly the case in a lawsuit of 1491 involving the sale of fifty-eight heads of St John the Baptist – symptomatic of the spirit of the age, when ardour had cooled and Faith degenerated into pietism.

Despite the use of stone vaulting and the economies in centering effected by the ribbed vault, enormous quantities of timber were still required, particularly for the construction of the great roofs of the North, so aptly referred to by the French as 'forêts'. These roofs, it is interesting to note, were often erected as soon as the skeleton of vaulting ribs was completed, so as to provide protection from the elements and permit the consecration of the church. The completion of the severies could then proceed at leisure.

The most important craftsman in the construction of the Gothic cathedrals was the stone-mason and his associated workers. Two Latin words were used in the Middle Ages to describe masons: *cementarius* and *lathomus*. The first, strictly speaking, refers to a 'clayer' or 'setter', sometimes mentioned as a 'rough-mason'; the second, *lathomus*, to a worker in 'freestone', the name given to a fine-grained sandstone or lime-

61 *Above* A medieval forge; note the puffing 'servant of the bellows'. Detail from the Gorleston Psalter. *London, British Museum*

62 *Right* Reliquary of the True Cross dated 1401, of gilded silver set with enamel and precious stones. *Pamplona, Cathedral Treasury*

among the mortar-mixers and the carriers that we find most of the women workers involved in building operations (7). In addition there were, of course, the quarrymen, removing mountains of stone for the cathedrals. Although there is evidence of masons working as quarrymen on occasion, and certain modern authorities are inclined to the view that the quarries served as important 'nurseries' for masons, the quarrymen were, generally speaking, a group apart, engaged in a backbreaking, ill paid and thankless task.

Legislation of 1212 in London set a maximum wage of 4*d* a day for qualified masons, carpenters and tilers, and until the advent of the Black Death (1348) wages remained more or less constant. The Black Death claimed a third of the population and the dire shortage of labour that followed saw a sharp increase in wages and prices, despite legislation to peg them at their former levels, including, in England, the first Statute of Labourers (1349). For the period 1350-1500 the average wage was approximately 6*d* a day (8). A clear indication that medieval building craftsmen were comparatively prosperous members of their society is afforded by their tax rating, and by the property left in their wills, at a time when only a very small proportion of the population even made a will. In addition to their wages, building workers received various other incentives. Thus at Ely in 1324 a carpenter was given a bonus (*ex curialitate*) of 2*s* on his annual pittance of 13*s* 4*d* (i.e. a 15 per cent bonus) for working conscientiously, while another instance records a payment of 4*s* for drinks 'that the carpenters and tilers may sweat more diligently at their work.' Then, as now, the completion of important stages of the work was a cause for celebration. 'Gloves given to the mason and

stone that can be freely worked in any direction and is hence capable of undercutting and particularly suitable for carving. Such a worker was a 'freemason' (6). In practice, however, the terms *cementarius* and *lathomus* were almost interchangeable, also with the Norman-French term, *masoun*. The distinction between artist and craftsman took a long time to emerge: accounts do reveal considerable differences in pay to various masons, but the difference was simply between more- or less-skilled workmen; one of degree not of kind. The labour alone involved in executing the great sculptural programmes of the French cathedrals was prodigious. We have documentary evidence that fifteen master-masons, at least three of them assisted by an apprentice, worked for fifteen years on the main portal of Rouen Cathedral carving the thirty-four large statues, the numerous small figures and the tympanum.

The master stone-mason served a long apprenticeship followed by years as a journeyman before he could submit his 'masterpiece' for consideration by the guild. By the fourteenth or fifteenth centuries fathers would commonly pass on their skill to sons, and many of the higher-paid workers belonged to families long connected with the craft. Associated with the fully qualified master-mason were numerous assistants and 'servants'. The fact that the *cementarius* (or layer) generally had more assistants than the *lathomus* (or freestone carver), is not as surprising as it seems, for it was with the layer or setter that the mortarmen and carriers, who made up quite a high proportion of the total labour force, would be grouped. It is

2d spent on drink on the completion of the arches of the chapel,'
reads an Ely account of 1425.

The sharp difference between wages at different seasons of
the year (5d a day in summer, 4d in spring and autumn, and
only 3d in winter, as set down in an ordinance of 1275) reflects
the number of working hours, dictated by the hours of daylight.
At York Minster workers were supposed to start before 5 am
in summer and continue until between 7 and 8 pm; with half
an hour's break for breakfast, an hour and a half for a combined
midday meal and siesta, and a further half an hour for a late-
afternoon snack and drink. In many cases building operations
were suspended and workmen laid off during the winter
months, the unfinished masonry being covered with reeds or
thatch to protect the vulnerable, exposed jointing from frost
as depicted in Plate 63. Where work did continue, a nine-hour
working day was probably the average for the six winter
months, compared with an average of twelve hours for the
six summer months – a very long working day indeed. Work
stopped at noon on Saturdays, however, and there were
numerous Saints' Days and holidays, generally no less than
thirty weekday holidays, as many as forty in some instances.
A portion of these were paid holidays at least for the most

63 *Construction of the Madeleine at Vézelay;* notice the unfinished masonry
(in the top left hand corner) being covered with straw to protect it from frost.
Detail from 14th-century manuscript, *L'Histoire de Charles Martel et ses
Successeurs. Brussels, Bibliothèque Royale*

skilled workers. An ordinance of 1352, for example, relating
to the building of York Minster, stated that if two feasts fell in
one week, a day's wage was to be deducted; if three feasts, then
half a week's wage. All told, the medieval worker did not fare
badly compared, say, with his counterpart in nineteenth-
century industrial society.

How much did it cost to build a Gothic cathedral? By good
fortune we know the amount spent on the one cathedral in
England for which the information is most relevant: Salisbury,
which alone was built on a virgin site, was completed rapidly
(1220-1266) and has survived virtually unaltered. The cost of
construction over these forty-six years was 42,000 marks,
estimated as roughly equivalent to a million pounds today (9).

Only the great tower and spire added a century later are not
included in this amount. The modern equivalent figure
suggested is, of course, rather misleading. Even assuming that
craftsmen were available, it would obviously cost many
millions to erect such a building today. And how many millions
more a Chartres or an Amiens?

As in the time of the pyramids – and still today – the new
work was set out on the site with pegs and cord, geometrical
principles, such as the use of the pythagorean triangle with
sides in the convenient proportion of 3, 4, and 5, being
employed to ensure true right angles. The sites of abbeys had
generally been ample – the spacious closes of the English
cathedrals usually testify to a monastic origin – but the typical
Gothic cathedral arose in crowded towns constricted by
expensive fortifications, where every square inch was precious.
Apart from the existing church, parts of which it might be
considered desirable to incorporate in the new structure,
it was common, when rebuilding on the greatly increased
scale of the Gothic period, to find part of the site encumbered
with other buildings: dwellings, hospices, almshouses and
other charitable organizations, and often several additional
churches. Such properties would have to be expropriated
and the owners compensated. There was often lengthy
litigation and there are records of religious communities
refusing to budge until other accommodation had been
provided and a large indemnity paid. Such problems as
these not only greatly complicated the process of setting out,
but often dictated the order of procedure. The sequence in
building a new church would normally be to start and complete
the choir first so that the High Altar could be consecrated as
soon as possible. Where this order was modified or reversed,
as at Amiens, this can usually be traced to the desire to retain
existing buildings on the site as long as possible.

Foundations were generally simple, consisting of a deep
trench filled almost to ground-level with rubble, and have often
given trouble where later generations added far weightier
superstructures than had originally been intended. At York
Minster, a 25,000-ton tower over the crossing, added in the
fifteenth century, and carried on four great piers, themselves
carrying stresses three and a half times greater than permitted
in modern building practice, transmits its load to inadequate
Norman foundations. Yet the tower has stood for 500 years.
Only today are the foundations at last giving way, due chiefly
to the effect of the gradual lowering of the water-table, which
has led in turn to the exposure of the wooden piles to air, which
makes them deteriorate – a cause the builders could hardly
have been expected to anticipate.

There are, however, cases where the substructure was built
with unusual care, for example, Notre-Dame in Paris, where the
great retaining-wall running continuously around the entire
perimeter is of carefully-dressed masonry, even where hidden
from sight. Wood piles reinforced with iron heads were
extensively used on wet sites, the tops afterwards sawn off
level – a surviving thirteenth-century treatise illustrates a
method of doing so even when the piles were under water –
and then covered with layers of heavy planking, serving as a
foundation for the stone footings. (At Salisbury, on the other
hand, there are practically no foundations at all.)

Although the construction of the great cathedrals was rarely

64 *Opposite* The finest example of sexpartite vaulting. *Bourges*

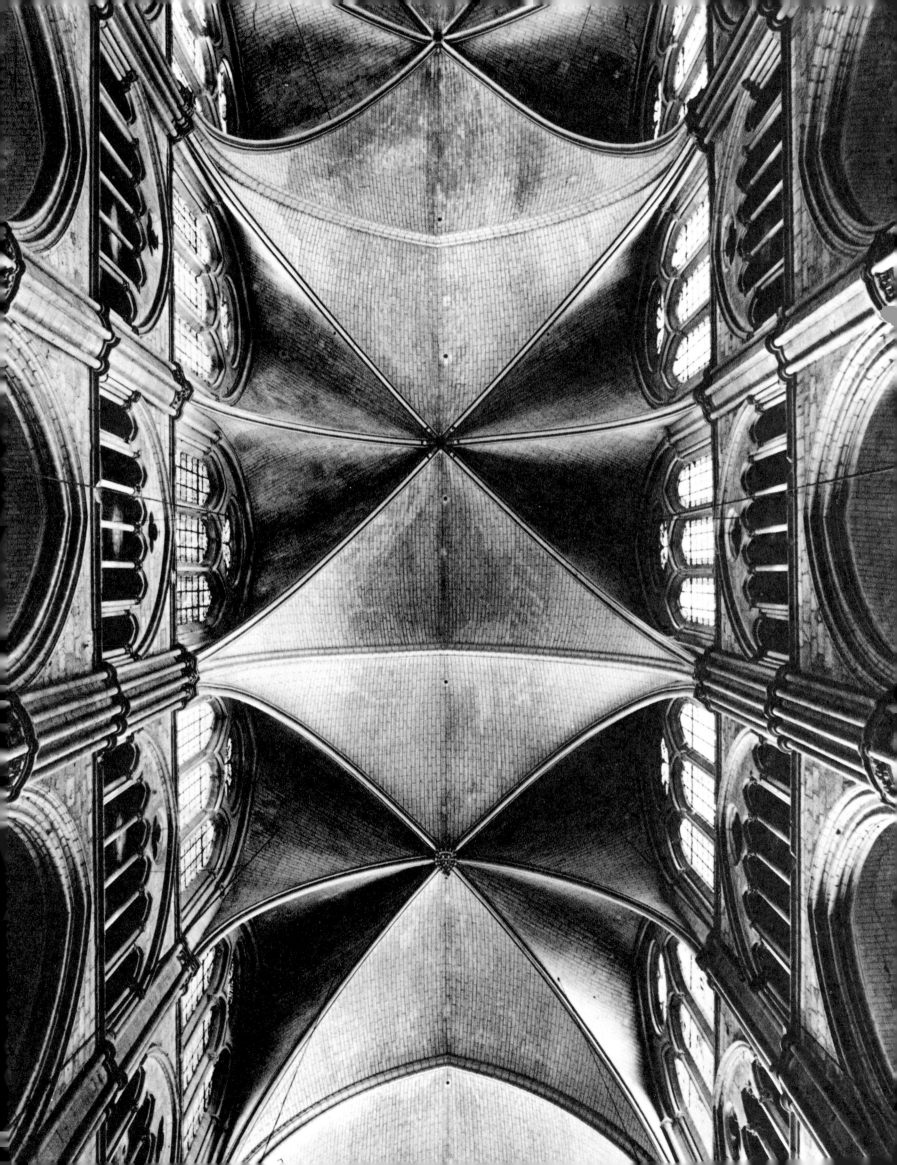

65 *Below The Building of the Ark* from the Book of Hours and Psalter of the Duke of Bedford. *London, British Museum*

regarded as a subject worthy of the artist, usually restricted to events from the lives of the Saints and from the Scriptures, a fairly clear picture of contemporary methods emerges from illustrations purporting to depict such events as 'The Building of the Ark', 'The Tower of Babel' or 'The Construction of the Temple at Jerusalem' (Plates 66 and 69); this is because medieval artists very seldom attempted to capture the atmosphere of a bygone age by a 'period' setting, but simply mirrored the costume and manners of their own day. One of the most informative of the earlier illustrations of Gothic construction is a miniature in a mid-thirteenth-century French Bible, now in the Pierpont Morgan Library in New York (Plate 67). The subject is 'The Tower of Babel', presumably at a stage when all was still proceeding smoothly. In the foreground a mason chisels away while his companion checks a right angle with his square. Two labourers carry stone in a hand-barrow; a third mounts a ladder with a basket containing mortar. On the tower a stone-setter, hands protected from lime burns by gloves, works with a trowel identical to that still used today. His companion steadies a basket of stone, hoisted by means of a crane operated on the treadmill principle. One or two men commonly worked these great wheels, apparently not too

arduous a task. Here the treadmill worker has breath enough to munch a snack, while the Almighty, accompanied by angels, surveys the proceedings from a cloud.

'The Building of the Ark' from the 'Book of Hours of the Duke of Bedford' (10), gives a good idea of contemporary carpentry methods (Plate 65). It will also be noted that, except for the advent of power-machinery, there has been no marked change in tools or methods since that date. One important labour-saving invention was that of the wheel-barrow, increasingly used to replace the hand-barrow. Unique alike in its exquisite delicacy and the air of actuality it conveys, is the superb *grisaille* sketch – or more precisely, under-painting – by Jan van Eyck in the Museum of Fine Arts at Antwerp (Plate 68). The subject, St Barbara, provides the excuse for the detailed representation of the building of the tower in which her father had had her imprisoned, envisaged here as a great Gothic church tower. On the right the masons work in their lodge, a simple, thatched lean-to shed, preparing the stones that are hoisted to the roof by a crane operated by an enormous wheel which can just be glimpsed through the tall, traceried openings. A similar crane on the top of the unfinished tower of the Cathedral of Cologne was a landmark of the city

66 *Left Tower of Babel* from the Book of Hours and Psalter made for the Duke of Bedford in the first half of the 15th century under the direction of Herman Scheere. *London, British Museum*

67 *Below left Construction of the Tower of Babel* from a mid 13th-century French bible, later a gift to Shah Abbas of Persia for whom the Arabic transcription of the text was added. *New York, Pierpont Morgan Library*

68 *Below right St Barbara*, grisaille painting by Jan van Eyck. *Antwerp, Museum van Schone Kunsten*

for three centuries (Plate 261).

A miniature by Jean Fouquet, also at the very end of the Gothic period, provides a most detailed picture of the construction of a Gothic cathedral (Plate 69). The churchgoers entering the doors call to mind a fact that we are inclined to forget: that for hundreds of years the services were accompanied by the clang of hammer and chisel, by the shouts of the workmen and the creaking of pulleys and windlasses. The lighter colour of the new work on the upper stage of the west front would seem to indicate a break in building operations, perhaps while new funds were being raised. Apparently cathedrals did not, even then, remain 'white' for long.

The medieval stone-mason worked almost exclusively for two clients, the Church and the ruler (whether king or great feudal lord), responsible for the castles and fortifications which, together with the religious buildings, constitute the two monumental building types of the period. Almost all other buildings, including dwellings, were of light construction, timber framing with wattle and daub or brick infilling being common. Only towards the end of the Gothic period did a third client, the municipal corporation play a significant rôle (11). While such craftsmen as carpenters, plasterers and tilers could

Auo en amli de quan
tes vertus et de quants
biens il a este aucteur
a ceulx de sa lignuee. et
combien plam de giant aige il est
mott nous lauons declaire ou li

ne deuant dit. Quand salomo
son fil: ancores icune enfant cut
pms le ropaume de son pere. et fa
assis ou siege ropal. tout le peuple
solennelement faueur. comme on
seult fanr a un rop au commence

69 *Above The Construction of the Temple at Jerusalem*, a miniature by Jean
Fouquet in *Antiquités et Guerres des Juifs. Paris, Bibliothèque Nationale*

70 *Above right* Bricklaying, the construction of the temple from a 13th-century
bible. *Baltimore, The Walters Art Gallery*

71 *Right* Detail of clerestory and triforium, north transept. *León*

hope to find steady and continuous employment in the towns, the mason was often obliged to move in search of work. He might also be compelled to do so. The Crown, particularly in England, enjoyed the prerogative of impressment on royal building projects, and this power was, occasionally, also delegated to ecclesiastical authorities (12). County sheriffs were ordered to choose the required number of men and send them off where needed. A standard travelling allowance was paid for every 20 miles; 4*d* in the early thirteenth century, it had risen to 6*d*, 250 years later. In England, workers were quite often sent more than 100 miles; on the Continent rarely so far. The lot of the impressed worker was not pleasant. Although his pay at the 'King's Wage' was not always lower than the normal rate, he was often separated from his home and family for long periods and might even encounter hostility from local workers, as when London masons in 1306 threatened impressed men with a beating if they accepted lower wages than those current in the city. Numerous desertions are also recorded.

The extreme mobility of the medieval mason, in such sharp contrast to the sedentary existence of most workers, resulted in certain unusual features of his corporate existence – some perpetuated to this day in the institution of honorary free-masonry. Often away from home, it was natural that the mason should turn to his colleagues for companionship and for the masons' lodge, originally just a shed to protect him from the weather and store his tools, to become also a place of discussion in the nature of a club. Secret signs and passwords were used to distinguish fellow freemasons. It is interesting to note that the secret handshake apparently originated in a part of Scotland where numerous builders of the traditional 'dry-walling' posed as freemasons, and the quality of the local stone made a quick assessment of a stranger's ability impossible. During the thirteenth and fourteenth centuries, the building lodges were loose associations for the common weal, but as they grew in strength in the later Middle Ages and changed to building guilds, they adopted ever more restrictive practices, aimed at protecting the members' interests and preserving the *status quo*.

Before discussing the rôle of the architect, whose very existence has been challenged, it is as well to define the term: by architect we mean primarily the person responsible for the design of the building and its supervision to ensure that the work is carried out according to that design. That there was such a person, who corresponded quite closely, *mutatis mutandis* to his modern counterpart, is clear. The fact that he was seldom known by the name of 'architect' is of minor importance, but has been responsible for much of the confusion on the subject. The commonest medieval name for the architect was the national equivalent of the Latin *magister*: 'master' in England; *maistre* or *maître* in France, *maestro* in Italy and Spain and, more specifically, *baumeister* in Germany.

The master was generally a stone-mason with a practical knowledge of the craft who had at a certain stage left the mason's bench for the 'tracing house'. There he extended his knowledge, particularly on such subjects as geometry, and learnt to produce plans. Evidence points to his generally being literate. In charge of actual building operations, he supervised the master-carpenter, master-smith, etc. and directed his own

73 Expressive corbel heads terminate the shafts of early English vaulting over a Norman nave. *Gloucester*

masons. On such large projects as cathedrals, the master also required an ability to estimate quantities of material and labour and in certain rare instances even took over the functions of the financial administrator (*custos fabricae*) or, in other words, became a contractor. That the master was not merely a glorified builder's foreman, but had a very different status in every way is also clear. As regards salary, for example, it emerges that the master earned at least twice and very frequently three to four times as much as a fully qualified stone-mason – this from an analysis of numerous examples in different countries and during the early, high and late Gothic periods.

One of the clearest indications of a very different status to that of the other masons is afforded by conditions of employment. Whereas most masons were hired by the week, the master was often employed by the year and occasionally even for life. Thus, at Ely Cathedral in 1359, at the same time that seven other masons were hired by the week, John Stubbard was engaged by the year. At the rate of 2*s* per week, he was paid £5 4*s* for the year and given a robe. In the same year an agreement between the Chapter of Hereford Cathedral and John of Evesham bound him to live in Hereford, work diligently on the fabric, give instruction to those placed under him and not accept other work without the permission of the Chapter. In return he was to be given a house at the nominal rent of 10*s* per annum, receive a white loaf of bread daily and a salary of 3*s* a week for life. A further clause stipulated that in the event of a short illness of up to two weeks he was to be paid

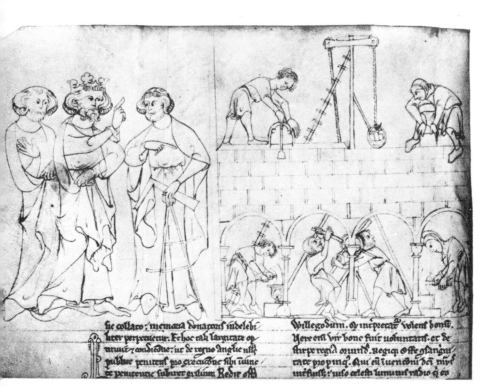

74 King Offa and his architects supervise building operations; drawing by Matthew Paris in the *Lives of the Offas. London, British Museum*

in full; for a longer illness at the rate of 1*s* per week: a similar clause in the contract between the Chapter of York Cathedral and William de Hoton specified that in the event of his becoming blind or incurably ill, half his annual allowance of £10 was to be taken to provide a deputy. In France, Eudes de Montreuil, the royal master-mason, received a daily salary of 4 *sous*, an annual robe allowance of 100 *sous,* his food at court and fodder for two horses.

That capable masters were much in demand, and in a position to bargain, can be gauged by many clauses in contracts. In that between the Chapter of Lugo Cathedral in Spain and a certain Maestro Raymundo, dated 1129, the master, apparently lacking confidence in the stability of the local currency, had a clause inserted whereby he should be paid in kind if the currency fell in value. Instead of his annual salary of 200 *sueldos* he would then receive 'six marks of silver, 36 yards of linen, 17 *cords* (loads?) of wood, and shoes and gaiters as he had need of them; and each month two *sueldos* for meat, a measure of salt and a pound of candles' (13).

The numerous clauses in contracts attempting to restrict masters from accepting other work shows that this must have been fairly common practice. They also sometimes acted as contractors. Then, as now, serious defects occurred through lack of efficient supervision. An entry in the Royal Accounts of England for the year 1256, stipulates that the king's mason, Master John, and the king's carpenter, Master Alexander, shall in future personally supervise new projects and that they shall receive double their normal wage while away from home to cover travelling expenses. In Spain, one of the architects engaged on the reconstruction of the Cathedral of Gerona, and living in Narbonne, was given an annual retainer of 1,000 *sueldos* on condition that he paid six visits a year to the site, while Ulrich von Ensingen, the designer of the great towers of Ulm and Strasbourg, worked in both cities, furthering his monumental schemes by encouraging the authorities in each to outdo the other. He also supplied designs for the

Cathedral of Basle and went to Milan, where several French and German masters had at various stages been called in to give advice. In the later Gothic period at least, consultants' fees provided a valuable supplementary source of income for architects. In Spain there are several instances of the chapter calling upon outside opinion to settle particularly difficult issues. The *junta* or advisory committee assembled at Gerona in 1416, for example, consisted of twelve masters, who were paid a handsome fee in addition to their travelling and living expenses.

A rare, if not unique, instance of what was no less than an architect's 'study-tour' is recorded in a grant made on May 18, 1414 by the authorities of Valencia Cathedral, at the time engaged in building a new bell-tower: 'It is settled that Pedro Balaquer, an "able architect", shall receive 50 florins from the fabric fund of the new campanile . . . in payment of his expenses on the journey which he made to Lerida, Narbonne and other cities, in order to see and examine their towers and campaniles, so as to imitate from them the most elegant and fit form for the Cathedral of Valencia.' (14)

In an age when everyone dressed strictly according to his professional and social status, the gifts of apparel so often included as conditions of the contract are significant. Gifts of gloves were a common indication of an honourable status, while a comparison of prices would seem to indicate that the robes were normally furred and, in England, of Esquire's rank. Clearly the master expected to dress like a gentleman. A drawing from the *Lives of the Offas* by the Benedictine, Matthew Paris (died about 1259) shows King Offa viewing building operations, accompanied by his master-mason holding a large compass and square (Plate 74). Modernize the details of dress and machinery, and the scene could represent a client and architect in conversation on a visit to the site today. The distinction in dress between the professional man and the artisan could not be more explicit.

In a manuscript dating from about 1200 in the archives of Modena Cathedral (15), Lanfranc, the architect of the re-building of the cathedral in 1099, is several times eulogized in the text as *mirabilis artifex* and *mirificus edificator.* Depicted with the caption '*Lanfrancus Architector*' over his head, he appears in several illuminations, directing building operations, but not doing any manual work himself. That this is no coincidence is again supported by the distinction in dress, and by such comments as those of the Dominican friar, Nicholas de Biard, in the mid-thirteenth century. Criticizing certain sections of the clergy of his day he compares them to the master-masons on great projects who, 'rod and gloves in hand, say, *Cut it for me thus!* and do no work themselves, and yet receive a far higher fee than the others . . .' All the evidence therefore points to the medieval architect-master-mason being a very different character, indeed, from the simple, anonymous 'building-foreman' of popular imagination.

The names of the architects of some of the greatest thirteenth-century French cathedrals were recorded for posterity in an

75, 76 *Opposite* Details from the 13th-century windows in the Corona, *Canterbury.* Top left, A King of Israel from the *Stem of Jesse,* and right, *The Return of the Messengers from the Promised Land,* laden with grapes.

77 *Top right* Detail of the *Life of the Virgin* from early 13th-century windows in the choir. *Laon*

78 *Overleaf* General view. *Albi*

extraordinary manner. On the paving of the nave was depicted a labyrinthine maze. Deriving ultimately from classical mythology and the legend of Daedalus, it would appear that in the cathedrals these mazes served as a form of record of the names of the master-masons. The labyrinth at Chartres, 39 feet in diameter and with a maze almost 1,000 feet in length, survives (Plate 80), but not its central plaque which would contain the names. At Amiens again, the labyrinth has gone, but the plaque survived until 1828 and its text is known. This showed incised effigies of the founder bishop, Evrard de Fouilloy, and the first three architects of the cathedral. The inscription reads: 'Work on this church was begun in the year of Grace 1220. The bishop of this diocese at that time was Evrard; the king of France, Louis, son of Philip Augustus. The master of the works was named Robert de Luzarches, followed by Thomas de Cormont, and, after the latter, his son Renard, who had this inscription made in the year of the Incarnation 1288.'

What higher honour could be accorded an architect than this association with the greatest in the land? Some of the inscriptions incorporated as integral parts of the sculptural decoration are equally fascinating:

'MASTER JEHAN DE CHELLES COMMENCED THIS WORK TO THE GLORY OF THE MOTHER OF CHRIST ON THE SECOND DAY BEFORE THE IDES OF FEBRUARY 1258.' So runs the inscription in letters eight inches high, situated at eye level on the plinth of the south transept at Notre-Dame at Paris. Erected by Pierre de Montreuil (or Montereau) who completed the transept, this act of homage to an illustrious predecessor provides a striking testimony to the spirit of *cameraderie* that prevailed among medieval masons and also to the self-effacing modesty of Pierre de Montreuil.

The Musée de l'Œuvre Notre-Dame at Strasbourg preserves an equally monumental inscription from a chapel of the cathedral (Plate 82):

79 *Left Beatus* page from the Peterborough Psalter showing scenes of daily life, sport and birds. *Brussels, Bibliothèque Royale*

80 *Above* The Labyrinth (diameter 12.87 m). *Chartres*

81 *Above right* Tombstone of the architect Hugues Libergier, died 1263, holding a model of a church. *Rheims*

82 *Right* The signature of Master Erwin von Steinbach. *Strasbourg. Musée de l'Œuvre Notre-Dame*

MCCC · XVI · **AEDIFICA**VIT · HOC · OPVS · **MAGISTER** · **ERWIN** · ECCE · ANCILLA · DOMINI · FIAT · MIHI · SECVNDVM · **VERBVM** · TVVM · AMEN (16). Constituting a virtual signature by the still-active Master Erwin, this would today be regarded as flagrant and unpardonable advertising on the part of an architect, and

83 Self-portrait of the master mason, Anton Pilgram, 1513, peers down from an organ console. *Vienna*

84 Page from the Sketchbook of Villard de Honnecourt giving details of the construction of a 'Tantalus' cup and portable hand-warmer. *Paris, Bibliothèque Nationale*

Master Erwin would undoubtedly be charged with unprofessional conduct by his institute.

The tombstone of Hugues Libergier, the architect of the beautiful church of Saint-Nicaise at Rheims, destroyed in the Revolution, shows an extremely dignified figure, elegantly clad in what might well be taken for academic dress (Plate 81). This is probably no coincidence. The word *universitas* commonly designated a corporation or guild and the University of Paris itself was originally but the 'guild of masters of letters' and their pupils. Neither is it perhaps so surprising that the author of the epitaph on the tombstone of the same Pierre de Montreuil (about 1266), royal mason, wishing to emphasize the ultimate professional distinction attained by Pierre, should have drawn an analogy with the academic world and styled him *doctor latomorum* (doctor of masonry).

Fortunately, a single work has survived that throws considerable light on the cathedral-designer's working methods and interests: the sketchbook of a master active in France in the thirteenth century, the most creative period of the entire Gothic era. The album or sketchbook of Villard de Honnecourt is a fairly large book, its vellum pages of unequal size stitched into a heavy, well-worn leather cover. It now consists of thirty-three pages with drawings on both sides, but was originally far larger, for many pages have been rather untidily snipped out. Originally preserved in the library of the Abbey of St Germain-des-Prés in Paris, it was confiscated during the Revolution and is now in the Bibliothèque Nationale. The album would appear to have been compiled from sketches in which Villard de Honnecourt had jotted down items that interested him on the spur of the moment. Several drawings are specifically mentioned as being drawn from life (*contrefais al vif*). This would explain the fact that the drawings on some pages are upside down, which would be unlikely if they had been executed at leisure, but quite understandable if done in haste (Plate 84).

85 *Right* Presumed self-portrait of the sculptor Nicolaus Gerhaerts of Leyden, probably from the demolished choir-stalls of 1467. *Strasbourg, Musée de l'Œuvre Notre-Dame*

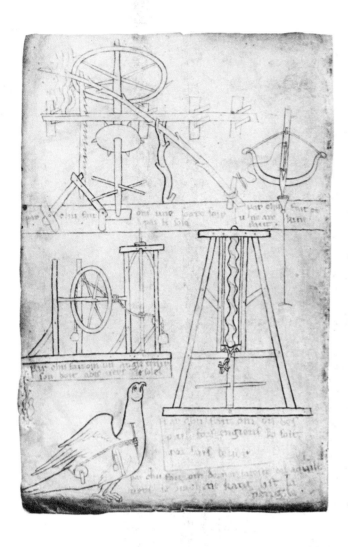

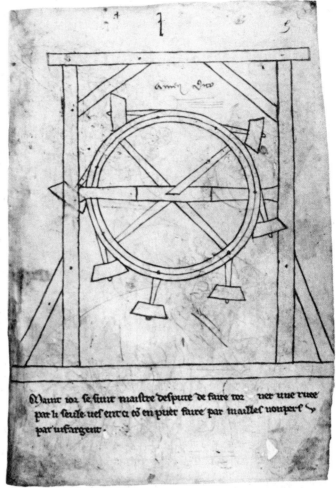

It would seem that the explanatory notes were only added later, perhaps when Villard decided to turn the sketchbook into a manual. Such manuals and pattern books are mentioned in wills as valuable legacies left by master-craftsmen, and Villard's seems to have been so used, for there are several additions by a so-called 'Magister II', also in the thirteenth century and entries in a fifteenth-century hand. Villard de Honnecourt was a native of the small village of that name near Cambrai in Picardy and writes in the local dialect. He announces himself in the preface: 'Wilars de Honecourt salutes you and implores all who labour at the different kinds of work contained in this book to pray for his soul and hold him in remembrance. For in this book may be found good help to the knowledge of the great art of masonry, and of devices in carpentry. It also shows the art of drawing, the outlines being regulated and taught in accordance with geometry.' (17)

The subjects cover an almost encyclopaedic range and testify to a most lively curiosity and intellect. There are plans, sections and elevations of buildings, details of masonry and

86 *Left* Detail of foliage carving. *Lincoln*

87 *Above* Designs for mechanical devices including a semi-automatic saw mill, a machine for lifting heavy weights and 'a crossbow that cannot miss'; from the Sketchbook of Villard de Honnecourt.

88 *Above right* Design for a perpetual motion machine from the Sketchbook of Villard de Honnecourt.

89 *Right* Design for a *poupée* or end standard of a choir-stall from the Sketchbook of Villard de Honnecourt, about 1235. *Paris Bibliothèque Nationale*

carpentry construction, geometrical solutions to such problems as 'How to take the diameter of a column when only a portion is visible', 'How to measure the breadth of a stream without crossing it', or 'How to find the height of a tower (from a distance)'. There are designs for church furnishings, including an elaborately ornamented lectern and two alternative designs for the *poupée* or end standard of a choir-stall, the first 'easy to make', the second the best that money could buy, disregarding the cost of labour or material (Plate 89); also designs for a siege machine catapulting rocks, and for 'a crossbow that cannot miss', for a machine based on the principle of the screw for lifting heavy weights and that, previously mentioned, for sawing off the tops of piles under water.

Villard de Honnecourt, like so many men of his day, was intrigued by automatons and perpetual-motion machines. 'How to contrive a wheel that shall turn of itself by means of an uneven number of mallets or by quicksilver' runs the optimistic caption to one design; 'How to make a saw saw by itself', the caption to a very crude design for a semi-automatic saw-mill, operated by hydraulic power. Mechanical saw-mills probably existed in his day. In 1303 the canons of St Sernin in Toulouse bought such a machine, while a decree of 1333 prohibits their use (which must, one presumes, have become quite common), and by the end of the century there are numerous documents relating to the licensing of such machines. The rather unconvincing drawings of machinery in the sketchbook should not blind us to the fact that Europe had already achieved some success with clockwork automatons. The oldest surviving example is the cock from the famous astronomical clock in the cathedral of Strasbourg, dating from 1354, which crowed three times and flapped its wings on the hour for nearly 300 years, and which is preserved, together with its mechanism, in the Musée Rohan in that city (Plate 91).

Our thirteenth-century master from Picardy was as fascinated and obsessed with labour-saving devices and cute gadgets as any modern American, and would perhaps have felt quite at home in the United States. The recto of leaf number 9 shows two such gadgets (Plate 84): 'If you want to make a hand-warmer, construct a kind of apple of brass in two halves which fit together. Inside the apple place six brass

circles. Let each circle have two pivots, and in the middle place a little brazier with two pivots. The pivots must be placed in contrary directions, so that in all positions the brazier may remain upright, for every circle supports the pivots of the next. If you make this contrivance exactly as indicated, you may turn it about in any way you please and the cinders will never fall out. It is excellent for a bishop, for he may boldly assist at High Mass, and as long as he holds it in his hands they will be kept warm so long as the fire remains alight. This machine requires no further explanation.' Known as a *calefactorium* or simply as an 'apple', such a hand-warmer was to be found in nearly every important church. Incidentally, the principle involved in keeping the brazier upright is the same as that used to keep the mariner's compass level.

'This is a contrivance that may be made in a drinking-cup,' writes Villard de Honnecourt of the object with the eagle standing on a small tower (Plate 84) and goes on to describe a 'Tantalus Cup', a popular source of amusement at banquets. 'In the midst of the cup is fixed a little tower, and in the middle of the tower is a tube that extends to the bottom of the cup . . . there must be also three small cross-pieces to the tower touching the bottom of the cup, so as to allow the wine in the cup to enter the tube . . . When the cup is filled, the wine will run through the tube, and through the foot of the cup, which is double.' The wine is thus siphoned out and disappears inexplicably into the hollow base as the unsuspecting guest raises the cup to his lips, or worse still – in another variation of the cup where the hollow base is omitted – spills over his clothes.

Considerably more than half the entire book is devoted to

90 *Above left* 'How to Train a Lion' from the Sketchbook of Villard de Honnecourt. *Paris, Bibliothèque Nationale*

91 *Above right* The iron cock from the original Astronomical Clock of Strasbourg, which flapped its wings and crowed three times on the hour. Dating from 1354 it is the oldest automaton in Europe; its mechanism is also preserved. *Strasbourg, Musée Rohan*

92 *Right* Detail of the rose window of the south transept, known as the 'Bishop's Eye'. *Lincoln*

freehand drawings of the world of nature and of art. There are monumental figures of prophets and other Biblical personages drawn with great style, which might well be intended to serve as models for the sculptor (perhaps Villard himself, for the impression we gain is of an artist-craftsman of many parts). There are copies of Roman remains, then far more numerous than now; lively sketches of men wrestling and playing dice and of a minstrel-fiddler with his dancing dog serenading a great lady with a tame parakeet on her arm. The animal world is singularly well represented by insects, a crustacean, eagles and ostriches, dogs and horses, a hare, a boar, even a porcupine (18). In an interesting sketch he explains the current method of training lions (Plate 90). The trainer brings two dogs and issues his command to the lion. If the lion growls or disobeys, the trainer beats the dogs. The lion then grows afraid (presumably he has previously been beaten and therefore associates the dogs' punishment with his own) and obeys the command – except when he is really enraged, in which case, 'he will do nothing for anybody'.

The geometrical framework superimposed on the freehand drawings, specifically mentioned by the artist in his preface, seems to function as a mnemonic aid rather than a significant system of measurement, but does furnish yet another example of the medieval obsession with geometry. The sketchbook also furnishes evidence of the extensive travels of master-masons even at this early date. 'I have been in many lands . . . as this book shows,' writes Villard, and among the surviving pages are sketches of work in France, Switzerland and Hungary. Villard seems to have seized on features that could possibly be adapted to his own use, rather like his modern counterpart taking clippings from the latest architectural magazines.

Particularly interesting for its deliberate deviations from the original is the drawing of the great western rose at Chartres, admired but, no doubt, already considered a trifle old-fashioned by Villard de Honnecourt. The ratio of solid to void has been substantially decreased; the relationship between the radiating arcade and the outer circles has been altered completely (the outer circles being placed on an axis with the radiating spokes

rather than with the openings); an extra series of quatrefoils which does not occur at all in the real window has been added, and trefoils, which break up the solid surface more completely, have been substituted for the existing outer circle of quatrefoils (Plates 93 and 95).

A drawing of the cathedral of Cambrai, destroyed during the Revolution, has a note 'this is the plan of the choir of *Madame Saint Mary* of Cambrai as it is now rising from the ground', and is quite possibly Villard's own design. Other details of the same church are alluded to and may well have been on some of the missing pages. The most elaborate architectural drawings in the sketchbook are, however, of the Cathedral of Rheims, architecturally the *dernier cri* at the time and which must have been of additional interest to the architect of Cambrai since the town was ecclesiastically dependent on Rheims. One drawing combines exterior and interior elevations of a nave bay (Plate 132), another shows a section through the system of flying buttresses, and above one of the drawings of the choir chapels is the note: 'This shows the elevations of the chapels of the Church at Rheims – like them will be those at Cambrai if they be built right.' Villard's exterior view of the chapels, a perspective of sorts rather than an elevation, shows the sculptured angels with outstretched wings, surprisingly enough shown nude rather than in their long robes (Plate 94). The battlements, to which he draws particular attention, seem to hark back to the earlier concept of the Church as the 'Fortress of God'. The present high pierced balustrade and the impressive

93 *Left* Western rose, Chartres; page from the Sketchbook of Villard de Honnecourt.

94 *Above* Drawing of the choir chapels, Rheims, by Villard de Honnecourt. *Paris, Bibliothèque Nationale*

95 *Right* The western rose. *Chartres*

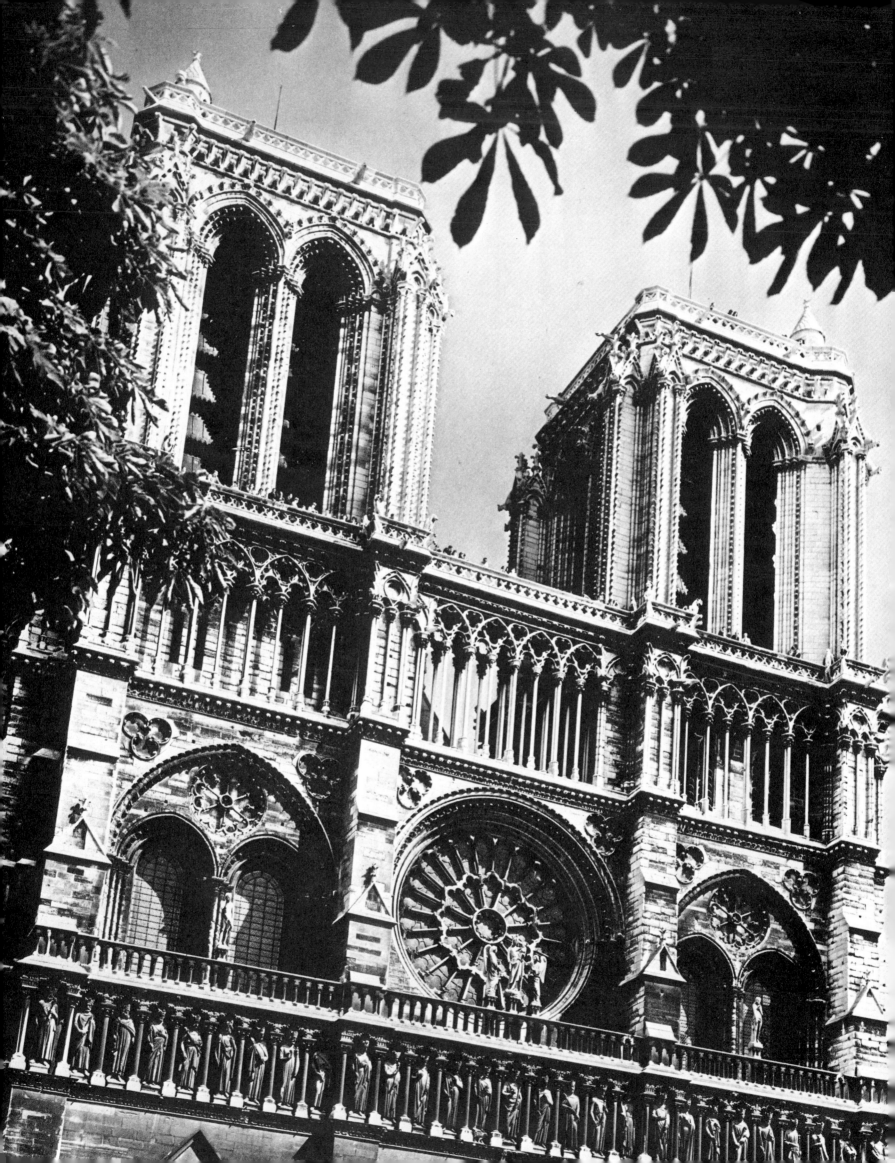

sculptured beasts are a mid-nineteenth century contribution by Viollet-le-Duc.

At Rheims Villard de Honnecourt did not fail to sketch the bar tracery of the aisle windows, truly revolutionary for their period, adding 'when I drew this, I was under orders to go to Hungary and therefore I like it all the better' – presumably as a reminder of a great moment in his professional career. But why to Hungary? Lassus, the nineteenth-century architect who translated and commented on the *Sketchbook*, has suggested a plausible connection, in that the Landgravine Elizabeth of Thuringia, sister of King Bela of Hungary, was particularly devoted to Our Lady of Cambrai and had, indeed, donated the funds for the reconstruction of the choir, commenced in 1227, and this was done, possibly under the direction of Villard de Honnecourt. (After her death in 1231, Elizabeth was canonized as Saint Elizabeth of Hungary and a fine Gothic church was built to enshrine her tomb at Marburg in Germany.)

For whatever reason Villard went to Hungary, it is certain that he must have had a great reputation to be specifically commissioned to travel that far. He states that he was in Hungary 'many a day' (*maints jours*). Unfortunately, his name has not been conclusively linked with any surviving work in Hungary (19). Indeed, in the whole sketchbook only a single architectural drawing, the plan of the chevet of a very monumental church with double aisles and chapels is mentioned specifically as his own design, and then, 'contrived in collaboration with Pierre de Corbie'. The most abiding impression of the *Sketchbook* is probably of its astonishing variety: ranging from a complex figure composition of the 'Deposition' iconographically very advanced for the period, to a simple hint on how to brace the spokes of a wheel without cutting into the shaft and, on the last page, a treatment for the cuts and bruises to which building workmen are prone.

The primary purpose of Villard de Honnecourt's architectural drawings seems to have been to refresh his memory. They could hardly be called working drawings. In 1838 the Gothic enthusiasts, Didron and Lassus, paging through a thirteenth-century obituary of members of the Chapter of Rheims Cathedral, noticed beneath the writing almost obliterated traces of architectural drawings which it proved possible to decipher. Apparently, several large architectural drawings on parchment had been erased and the sheets cut up and re-used for the obituary. There are elevations, sections and details, including a design for the west front of a cathedral which combines features of both Rheims and Amiens. Precisely set out to scale with compass and rule, we have here true working drawings whose author was no 'drawing-board architect' concerned with pretty pictures, but a busy man whose only interest lay in the building itself. Not a single unnecessary line has been put to paper. For example, in the case of symmetrical features, a centre line has been drawn and detail only given for one half. The 'Rheims Palimpsest' not only conclusively refutes the Romantic notion that the Gothic cathedrals just grew haphazardly without accurate drawings, but also provides a very plausible reason why so few drawings have survived. Drawn on expensive parchment for which a

body such as the chapter would constantly have use, it is quite probable that the drawings were erased when the building was completed and they apparently served no further purpose.

The fourteenth-century drawing of the west front of Cologne Cathedral, rediscovered in the early nineteenth century and serving as the model for the completion of the building later in the century, was drawn on a sheet of parchment ten feet long and three feet wide. Of comparable scale is the drawing of the west front of Strasbourg Cathedral attributed to Master Michael Parler of Freiburg and dating from about 1385 (Plate 192). Drawn in ink with accents such as the figures of the Apostles heightened in gouache, this is perhaps the most beautiful Gothic architectural drawing to have survived. It is, however, but the most spectacular specimen among a uniquely rich collection of drawings relating to the design of the Cathedral and ranging from about 1275 to the end of the fifteenth century, preserved by the lodge or *Œuvre* of the Cathedral.

Such large and elaborate drawings presuppose accurate drawing instruments. Although no ruling pens have survived, the perfectly even lines and the variation in thickness of different lines point to the use of pens with screw adjustments

96 *Left* Upper part of the west front. *Paris*

97 *Right* The fan vaulting of the retrochoir by Master John Wastell; the boss has the arms of England. *Peterborough*

such as are still used today. Drawings were produced in a drafting room, a *chambre de traits* or 'tracing house' as it was called. No designs for complete buildings have, however, survived. Probably drawings were only produced section by section as the work proceeded and were never numerous. They were supplemented by many large-scale or full-size details

98 *St Cecilia,* patroness of the cathedral, holding a hand organ and the palm of martyrdom, presides over the choir from the back of the *jubé. Albi*

commonly set out on a 'tracing floor'. A slab of plaster-of-Paris was convenient for this purpose. Wood boards were also used and, on occasion, even a level stone surface as, for example, at Limoges Cathedral, where geometrical constructions set out with a stylus remain engraved on the granite roofing slabs over the aisle. Wood was also used for making templates and stencils. Constructional models, surprisingly, appear to have played an insignificant part in the medieval period according to the experts. The effigy of Master Hugues Libergier, however, shows him holding what appears to be a model of a church (Plate 81).

There is always a temptation to credit stupendous achieve-

ments of an alien age to some esoteric secret. In the case of the Gothic cathedrals the temptation was irresistible. Was it not common knowledge that the society of honorary freemasons with its numerous secrets and mysterious rites was a latter-day offshoot of the associations of medieval masons? Besides, were there not specific references in the records of the medieval guilds to secrets which their members were forbidden to divulge? 'Point Three' of the Regius Poem, for example, dating from the fourteenth century, enjoins the apprentice 'to keep and guard his master's counsel and that of his fellows and tell no man whatsoever he has seen or heard in the lodge . . . lest he bring blame on himself and shame on his craft.' In 1459 a meeting of all the lodges of Germany, Switzerland and Alsace was held in Regensburg to codify lodge statutes. Paragraph 13 of the document listing the resolutions taken, states: 'Also no workman, nor master, nor parlier, nor journeyman shall teach anyone, whatever he may be called, not being one of our handicraft and never having done mason work, how to take the elevation from the ground plan.' (20)

What was meant by the expression 'to take the elevation from the plan' (*den Uszug us dem Grunde zu nemen*)? The answer was provided nearly thirty years later, when Matthäus Roriczer, the architect of the Cathedral of Regensburg, who had attended the meeting of 1459 but had, perhaps significantly, not signed the Resolution, revealed the secret which the masters had guarded for so long in a small treatise with the disarmingly simple title *On the Ordination of Pinnacles* (21) dedicated to the Bishop of Regensburg:

'My very good Lord . . . As your princely grace . . . is an amateur and patron of the free art of geometry . . . I have undertaken, with the help of God, to expound somewhat of the art of geometry and from the very commencement of the drawn-out stonework, to explain how, and in what proportions, out of the very grounds of geometry, with division by compasses, it ought to be deduced and brought into right sizes'. (22)

The designation of the Prince-Bishop as an amateur and patron of the art should be noted. Later, outsiders with common interests would be admitted to the lodges, and with the Renaissance 'amateurs' would eventually predominate, and play an important rôle in the transition from actual to honorary freemasonry.

Matthäus Roriczer goes on to explain the method of taking the elevation of a pinnacle from the plan. Most nineteenth-century historians saw merely the solution to a specific problem. As Professor Frankl has pointed out this was only a particular example of a general method; Roriczer had in fact revealed fundamental information on how the cathedrals were built and also an explanation – albeit only partial – for the harmony of their proportions. The successive steps in Roriczer's method of constructing a pinnacle are shown in Plate 99. First, draw a square the size of the base of the pinnacle. Join the centre points of the four sides, thus obtaining a smaller square placed at 45° within the main square. (Since the length of the side of the smaller square is equal to half the diagonal of the larger square, the area of the small square is half that of the larger square.) The process is repeated to obtain the requisite number of proportionately smaller squares. The final step is to rectify the squares and place them one within the other with their sides parallel. The lengths of these proportionate squares may now be used to determine the salient vertical measurements of the pinnacle. Thus, instead of the architect telling the mason to construct a pinnacle so many feet high, he says

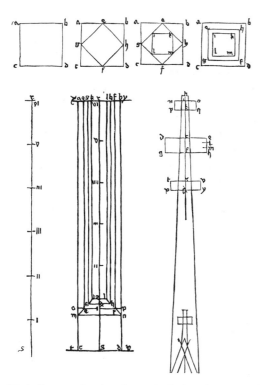

99 A diagram showing the method of setting out a pinnacle, by Matthäus Roriczer; redrawn from *Das Büchlein von der Fialen Gerechtigkeit, Regensburg,* 1486

instead: 'Make the height so many multiples of the length of the basic square.' (23) This same length may also be used to determine the precise disposition of decorative features; since the nest of squares may also be interpreted as a series of ground-plans at various levels, the angle of recession of the pinnacle can conveniently be defined by the difference between two of the proportionate squares. Provided by the architect with the basic square, armed with the master's sketch elevations, and informed of the salient height relationships, the mason could construct the pinnacle—or any other element—step by step 'out of the very grounds of geometry with division by compasses', relying on proportional relationships, rather than on numeral (arithmetical) measurements.

An addition to the sketchbook of Villard de Honnecourt by the so-called 'Magister II' shows that the method of doubling the square was already familiar to the masons of the thirteenth century. Beneath a diagram showing a smaller square athwart a larger (the first stage of Roriczer's method) is written 'Thus one divides a stone so that each of the halves is equal.' Another diagram on the same page shows the smaller square placed within the larger with sides parallel, this time with the cryptic caption: 'Thus one lays out a cloister with its galleries and cloister garden', the corollary, '. . . so that the two areas are equal', being omitted as self-evident to the masters of his day.

One of the most puzzling features of medieval architectural drawings, even the most elaborate and highly finished, is the absence of a figured scale. This occurs so consistently that one is forced to the conclusion that medieval architects did not favour the scaling of drawings. Research has confirmed that the medieval builders favoured the use of a module, that is, a convenient, if arbitrarily chosen unit of length used consistently as the basis for the planning measurements of the structure. The Cistercian builders, for example, used a 'great unit' varying from approximately five to seven feet long, depending on the length of the 'foot' prevailing in the particular district (24).

At the Abbey of St Denis a module consisting of five (or possibly ten) 'Royal' or 'Parisian' feet each approximately 13 inches, was used. At Milan Cathedral the plan was set out on the basis of an eight-*braccia* unit (the Milanese *braccio* being approximately 2 feet), while in England the standard length of the pole or perch (16½ feet), sometimes furnished a convenient unit. Simple fractions of the module provided a series of smaller dimensions.

As used by the cathedral builders, the module, whether 'great unit' or 'basic square', not only provided a practical substitute for a 'yardstick', but played an important aesthetic rôle. With the salient dimensions of the plan determined by the module, and the superstructure in turn 'taken from the plan' by a geometrical construction such as revealed by Roriczer in which the areas are in geometrical progression, all dimensions relate back to the module which provides a kind of common denominator. If, in addition, the major features of the design, such as height of nave, width of nave and width of aisles, conform to some simple proportional relationship which can be sensed intuitively by the eye (the Golden Section, or the elementary ratio of 2:1) then such a proportional scheme, if used consistently, can go far towards establishing an harmonious relationship of the various parts, each to the other, and to the whole. Though the essence of a great work of art must always remain a mystery, perhaps we have here at least a partial explanation for that compelling sense of unity that informs the myriad details of the cathedral. The same sense of unity also prompted the young Goethe, overwhelmed at the first sight of Strasbourg Cathedral, to write:

'A sensation of wholeness and greatness, filled my soul; which, composed of a thousand harmonious details, I could savour and enjoy, yet by no means understand or explain. So it is, men say, with the bliss of Heaven . . . The cathedral rises like a sublime wide-arching Tree of God, that, with a thousand boughs, a million twigs, and leafage like the sands of the sea, proclaims the glory of the Lord.' (25).

France

4 France

Laon

The Cathedral of Laon has one of the most magnificent situations in all France. Dominating the great hill that rises abruptly from the plain, its fantastic but dignified silhouette recalls a medieval coronet – and fittingly, for this little town, deprived even of its bishopric after the Revolution, was the last stronghold of the Carolingian monarchs and capital of France from 895-988.

Laon was already a bishopric at the end of the fifth century, its first bishop being a nephew of St Remi, the famous archbishop of Rheims. A flourishing commune, the city was in 1112 the scene of an extremely bloody uprising by the citizens against their imperious lord-bishop, Gaudri. Furious against his annulment of their charter, they set fire to the cathedral treasurer's house; the flames spread to the cathedral, still decorated with hangings for the Easter celebrations, which had been attended by the king himself a few days previously. Half the town had burned to the ground before the flames could be quenched.

Bishop Gaudri himself was beheaded by a serf in his own cathedral. It is not related what happened to Laon's many students in this turmoil, for the Cathedral School of Laon still attracted students from all over Europe, for the illustrious Anselm was at this time still alive. It was after these events that the canons took their sacred relics on tours of France, and later England, to collect funds to restore the ravaged cathedral.

Bishop Gautier de Mortagne (1155-1174) demolished the restored cathedral, then barely fifty years old, in order to build in the new Gothic style. Commenced between 1155 and 1160, only a few years before Notre-Dame in Paris (1163), Laon is the first complete cathedral to have been built in the Gothic style and among the most perfect realizations of twelfth-century ideals. Completed by 1230, with only minor later additions (1), it is a remarkably harmonious and unified structure.

The west front with its magnificent, deep-set rose window is one of the most original and beautiful, and perhaps the most powerful of the entire Gothic period (Plate 101). Here Suger's theme of the 'Gateway to Heaven' finds its first fully successful expression in the three great portals, preceded by porches which project boldly and extend across the entire façade in a supremely dramatic gesture.

The sculpture was, unfortunately, terribly mutilated during

101 The west front of Laon from a 19th-century print after a drawing by Émile Boeswillwald.

the Revolution when the monumental figures of the jambs were completely destroyed. The reliefs of the tympana and archivolts have been very indifferently restored – the new heads, for one thing, being too large for their bodies – but even so some idea of the grandeur, nobility and at the same time almost barbaric vitality of the original work can be gained

from the work visible today (Plate 102). Dominating the composition, from far and near alike, are the superb towers with their tall, canopied niches from which, against all expectation, emerge enormous stone oxen. There are few more powerful three-dimensional forms in all European architecture than these great towers, at once rugged and delicate. Like pierced abstract sculpture they compel one to move around in order to see them fully. With every few steps the composition changes; clefts open and close in the honeycombed cliffs and the great beasts seem one moment hieratic and immobile like their distant, winged cousins from Assyria; the next, poised almost impudently, with their hoofs on the very edge of the precipice, peering down from their cloud-swept eyrie at the lichen-covered roofs and narrow, twisting streets of the old citadel straight below, and on over the fertile cornfields to the horizon.

The towers of Laon made an enormous impression on

contemporaries. Villard de Honnecourt in his sketchbook noted, 'I have been in many countries, as you may see by this book, but in no place have I seen a tower equal to that of Laon,' and he devoted two detailed drawings to a plan and a perspective-elevation (Plate 105). He was particularly impressed by the buttresses, the 'grans pilers forkies', as he called them, and counselled all who would construct such great towers to study them attentively. His sketch showed the towers crowned by tall, crocketed spires, a large one over the central core and four small ones over the angle turrets. At the

102 *Above* The tympanum of the central portal, dedicated to the Virgin. Here she is shown already crowned; later Gothic artists favoured the moment when Christ places the crown on her head. In the archivolts are royal ancestors fitted into the branches of a tree of Jesse. *Laon*

103 *Right* View from the tribune gallery towards the nave. *Laon*

beginning of the nineteenth century one of these spires still stood, leaning crazily as the result of an earthquake in 1691.

Laon inspired many a church tower elsewhere, including those of the Cathedrals of Bamberg and Naumburg, none, however, so successful as the originals. The oxen remained unique, fittingly, since they commemorated that most unique of events: a miracle. Many thousands of loads of stone had to be hauled by the patient, plodding beasts up the long, wearying slope from the plain below; one day one of the oxen fell exhausted in its tracks and the journey would have had to be delayed if another had not appeared, helped to haul the waggon to the summit and then, as suddenly, disappeared – or so the story goes.

The light-flooded interior, of a grandeur that belies the moderate dimensions (the vaults are 78 feet high), amply fulfils the expectations aroused by the west front. As we remarked earlier, the thrust of the nave vaulting was customarily counteracted by tribune galleries before the invention of flying buttresses. This is the system employed at Laon (Fig. 6 and Plate 103). While the perfect solution of the classic *quadripartite* vault over an oblong bay was still being sought, a variant form something in the nature of a compromise was widely used in some of the greatest cathedrals of France including Laon, Notre-Dame de Paris and Bourges. Sexpartite vaulting retains as the vaulting unit a square or near-square, corresponding to two bays of the nave, and introduces an intermediate transverse rib, cutting the diagonal rib-vaults at their point of intersection and helping to support them (Plates 104 and 64).

Sexpartite vaulting transmits an unequal load to alternate piers. In obedience to the Gothic concept of giving linear expression to structural forces – and also to the typically French demand for *clarté* – this unequal loading is expressed by vaulting shafts in alternate clusters of three and five, which continue the line of the vaulting ribs downward over the surface of the nave wall (Plate 103). Strict logic demanded that this differentiation be continued to ground level, and, initially, each alternate monocylindrical pier, too, was customarily surrounded with a cluster of shafts. This, however, tended to disrupt the continuity of the nave arcade and was later abandoned for shafts terminating above the pier capitals. A survival of the earlier system with the encircling shafts carried down to ground level can be glimpsed round one of the piers in the background of Plate 104. The detail of mouldings and architectural sculpture alike has an exquisite purity and a wonderfully refreshing spontaneity. The earlier capitals, and intrinsically the most beautiful, still show a strong Romanesque feeling (Plate 106); the later already approach the standardized French-Gothic 'crocket type'. The original polygonal apse was demolished early in the thirteenth century, when the choir was extended to accommodate an unusually large number of canons, and was then terminated in a square east end. Favoured by the Cistercians and in England generally, this form is very unusual in France.

The combination of the creamy-white Chermizy stone (2) and the glowing glass of the east windows is enchanting (Plate 104). The glass of the great rose is much restored but that of the three lancets is original and of superb quality (Plates 21 and 77) (3).

105 *Above* A drawing of the towers of Laon from the sketchbook of Villard de Honnecourt. *Paris, Bibliothèque Nationale*

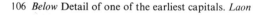

106 *Below* Detail of one of the earliest capitals. *Laon*

104 *Left* The interior looking west. *Laon*

Paris

When the Normans sacked Paris in 857, the cathedral dedicated to St Stephen and a church dedicated to the Virgin occupied the eastern tip of the *Île de la Cité* in the very heart of the city. Only the cathedral was spared by paying a great ransom, but after this date the restored church of the Virgin gradually attained pre-eminence. In 1160 a new bishop was enthroned in Paris. Maurice de Sully, son of a humble peasant, was a celebrated orator and professor of theology. Like Suger he had enormous energy and ambition, and like Suger was a great builder. In 1163 the foundation stone of a vast new Gothic cathedral, occupying the sites of both the existing churches was laid by Pope Alexander III, on a visit to Paris. Within twenty years the choir was in use and when Maurice de Sully died in 1196, only the westernmost bays of the nave and the west front were unfinished. By 1250 even the twin western towers had been completed.

Only slightly later than the Cathedral of Laon, Notre-Dame de Paris occupies a pivotal point in the history of Gothic architecture. One of the first cathedrals of truly colossal scale – the vaults of the nave have leapt from a height in the 70s to nearly 110 feet in one bound – it is also not only the last and greatest of the line of cathedrals with tribune galleries, but the probable birthplace of the true flying buttress, introduced over the nave aisles in about 1180.

The Parisian plan was of startling simplicity, the double-aisled, cruciform basilica without chapels being inscribed within a simple rectangle from which only a continuous

whole, a subtractive process from unity, as it were, rather than the characteristically additive Romanesque design principle: building up to unity by juxtaposing quasi and often assertively independent elements.

The absolute clarity of the original Parisian concept did not, however, survive for long. Various modifications were carried out even before the building was completed in 1250. The design of the clerestory lighting of the nave was altered in an effort to get more light into the very dark interior that resulted from the combination of tribunes and double aisles (5), but the resulting improvement was then cancelled out by inserting a row of chapels between the nave buttresses—a most unfortunate addition which also detracted greatly from the appearance of the lateral façades.

The original transeptal fronts, now recessed in relation to the walls of the chapels, were extended by one bay between 1250 and 1267. Erected by the two great master-masons of the day, Jean de Chelles and his successor, Pierre de Montreuil (responsible for the monumental inscription in honour of Jean which we have already noted), the new fronts with their glazed triforia have been virtually reduced to walls of glass. This period marks the perfection of the Gothic structural system, the almost complete dissolution of the wall surface and that ultimate degree of refinement that comes just before – or, perhaps, already indicates – decline. With the second half of the thirteenth century the end of the truly expansive era of Gothic culture has been reached and a period of consolidation gradually sets in. In architecture, even pyrotechnic displays of virtuosity – often for its own sake – cannot conceal an underlying conservatism.

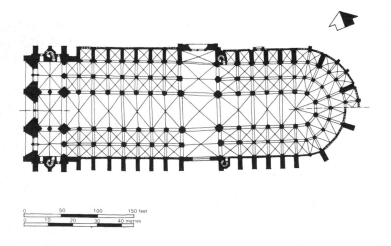

Fig. 8 *Above* Ground plan, *Paris*. The southern half shows the plan of 1163 before chapels were inserted between the buttresses and the transepts extended. Note the irregularities, typical of Gothic construction.

107 *Right* The double aisles of the nave showing the strengthening of alternate piers to take the extra load transmitted by the sexpartite vaulting. *Paris*

hemicycle projected (Fig. 8). The lantern over the crossing at Laon and the prominent transepts have both been suppressed, and the seven towers projected for Laon (4) reduced to two. There is a new sense of continuous space in the interior, a convincing statement of that essential 'oneness', that synthesis advocated by the scholastic philosophers. At Notre-Dame we have a single spatial entity broken down into units which have no autonomous existence except as parts of a

108 *Right* Detail of the *rayonnant* tracery of the great rose of the south transept, 42 ft 8 ins in diameter. *Paris*

109 The chevet with its graceful flying buttresses. *Paris*

110 Detail of the relief of the *Assumption of the Virgin. Paris*

to compensate for the uniform monocylindrical piers of the nave arcade (6) and to satisfy the French demand for *clarté*. In the thirteenth century the prototype flying buttresses of the nave were replaced by the present advanced design, leaping over both aisles in a single, daring flight.

The chapels of the choir, begun by Pierre de Montreuil, were only completed in the fourteenth century by Jean Ravy who was also responsible for the incredibly light flying buttresses of the choir, spanning almost 50 feet. Combining pure engineering and sheer poetry, these buttresses have the soaring grace of the finest modern bridges and contribute largely to the fairytale appearance of the chevet, which has been compared to an enchanted forest or a great galleon under full sail (Plate 109).

A series of superb bas-reliefs incorporated in the plinth of the north façade of the choir and dating from the end of the thirteenth century, depicts scenes from the life of the Virgin (Plates 110 and 120). According to the Apocrypha, the funeral cortège of the Virgin, with all twelve Apostles as pallbearers,

The new transeptal fronts of Notre-Dame are among the most splendid examples of the *Style Rayonnant*, so-called from the characteristic 'radiating' tracery of the enormous roses and rosettes that are such favoured motifs (Plate 108).

It is only in the two great roses of the transepts and that of the west front that Notre-Dame has retained any of its original glass. That of the western and southern roses has been much restored, but the northern rose has come down to us virtually intact (see front of jacket). The filigree delicacy of the tracery and the glorious colour of the glass, predominantly blue and incorporating no less than eighty subjects from the Old Testament, are both outstanding; their combination is unique and overwhelming in its emotional impact.

The original flying buttresses of the nave transferred some of the thrust of the sexpartite vaulting to the piers separating the double aisles and this variation in loading was expressed by surrounding each alternate monocylindrical pier with a cluster of small shafts, creating a fascinating rhythmic sequence (Plate 107). This subtle indication of the alternate stressing associated with sexpartite vaulting was, no doubt, introduced

111 *Right* Interior, showing the rhythmic sequence of compound piers alternately round with four octagonal attached shafts, and octagonal with four round shafts. *Chartres*

112 *Overleaf* Detail of the great north rose with kings of Israel and St Anne, donated by the royal family of France. *Chartres*

was intercepted by the High Priest of the Jews. Attempting to seize the body in order to burn it, his hands withered and stuck fast to the coffin. The bas-relief would seem to show two persons, but they are in reality one; the figure rolling on the ground in agony minus hands, representing a subsequent episode – prior to the happy ending with the High Priest converted and healed. This simultaneous depiction of a sequence of events occurs frequently in medieval art and was characteristic also of the Mystery Plays.

After the choir chapels had been completed around 1330, the cathedral remained virtually untouched until the very end of the seventeenth century, when a disastrous series of 'improvements' was initiated. The Gothic high altar was replaced by a pompous Pietà group in white marble, flanked by kneeling statues of Louis XIII and Louis XIV (7); the ancient tombs in the choir were demolished, and also the choir-stalls and the *jubé*, and the stained glass in many of the windows gave way to colourless glass. This process of destruction continued right through the eighteenth century. In 1771 the *trumeau* of the central doorway and its sculptured lintel were destroyed to permit the passage of a huge processional canopy.

During the Revolution an actress in a phrygian bonnet impersonating the 'Goddess Reason', mounted on a pedestal in the choir, and attended by young girls strewing flowers and chanting her praises, was worshipped with solemn ceremony, while everything of metal – bells, statues, chandeliers, grilles and reliquaries – was carted off to be melted down at the mint. Later the cathedral was used as a store for provisions and fell into complete disrepair.

The twenty-eight colossal statues of the Kings of Israel forming a continuous frieze over the portals of the west front (the theme of the Precursors initiated at St Denis) were unfortunately mistaken for Kings of France. 'With ropes around their necks they were pulled from their niches and, amidst wild acclaim, smashed to smithereens on the cobbles below. The present statues – as indeed every free-standing sculpture on the cathedral, with the sole exception of the Madonna on the *trumeau* of the north cloister doorway – are replicas produced under the direction of Viollet-le-Duc during the restoration of the fabric in the second half of the nineteenth century. The panels of the fourteenth-century choir-screen which had survived the changes of the eighteenth century and the vandalism of the revolutionaries were also then restored and repainted (Plate 117).

It is important to remember that much medieval sculpture, like that of Classical Greece was painted. Many of the great

117 *Below The Risen Christ appears to the three Marys,* Detail of the 13th-century choirscreen, re-painted in the 19th century under the direction of Viollet-le-Duc. *Paris*

113 *Previous page* Detail of St Mark the Evangelist carried on the shoulders of the prophet Daniel. *Chartres*

114 *Far left top* Reliquary of Sant' Anita. *Toledo*

115 *Far left bottom* Bishop's crozier. *Cologne*

116 *Left above and below* (a & b) Reliquary of the Holy Thorn, with the Angel which held the Thorn inside the Reliquary. *Rheims*

figures of the western portals, now soot-black on a soot-black background, were originally polychrome on a background of goldleaf, the sumptuous effect commented upon by visitors as late as the fifteenth century. To modern taste the idea is almost as repellent as that of a polychrome Parthenon, but we should bear in mind that our preference for natural stone is quite foreign to the spirit of the Middle Ages. Where medieval sculpture has retained its colour, the effect is generally very successful (8) and quite different from that of nineteenth-century restorations. One must not imagine the whole of Notre-Dame painted from plinth to pinnacle. Colour was concentrated around focal points, such as portals and rose windows. On towers, for example, small accents at most would be coloured or gilt.

The west front of Notre-Dame is one of the supreme architectural achievements of all time. The proportions are based on a sequence of four squares determined 'according to true measure', that is, each twice the area of the smaller square, developed geometrically in the manner revealed by Matthäus Roriczer. These squares are used to build up an overall rectangle in the proportion 2:3, the rectangle consisting of two interlocking or semi-superimposed squares: the façade proper, excluding the projection of the towers constituting one square; the upper two-thirds, from the top of the 'Gallery of Kings' to the summit of the towers, the second. In this façade, if anywhere, St Augustine's ideal of an architecture whose proportions are based on musical consonances, which themselves reflect the harmonious ordering and stability of the cosmos, could claim to have been realized. Here, an alliance of architectural genius and mathematics (in that order of importance) has given us a work whose perfection is admitted even by critics most hostile to the Gothic style.

118 *Below* View of Notre-Dame from the south across the Seine. *Paris*

119 *Below right* The west front. *Chartres*

120 *Opposite top* Bas-relief illustrating the *Funeral of the Virgin* and the legend of the withering of the hands of the high priest of the Jews. *Paris*

121 *Opposite bottom* Detail of the southern tower. *Chartres*

Chartres

The site of the Cathedral of Chartres has been a goal of pilgrimage from very remote times. Here, in an artificial grotto, stood an image of the Virgin adjoining a sacred well into which the bodies of the first Christian martyrs of Chartres are said to have been thrown, imparting miraculous healing properties to the waters. Indeed, until the Revolution, nuns attended the sick who had journeyed to the sacred well in the hope of a miraculous cure in a portion of the crypt. At Chartres the cathedral was, thus, also a hospital.

This legend of martyrdom can only be traced back to the twelfth century and it is more than likely that we have here another case of the familiar expedient in the early, struggling days of Christianity, of appropriating a celebrated pagan shrine and its tutelary deity to the new faith. This is supported by archaeological evidence of such a shrine on the site of the cathedral, by the frequent juxtaposition of sacred well and image at Gallic sanctuaries and, above all, by the fact that the original wooden image of the Patroness of Chartres, the *Virgo paritura* or 'Virgin about to Bring Forth' – ceremoniously burnt during the Revolution, but well-known through descriptions and copies – bore a striking resemblance to the Mother-Goddess figures of the Gallo-Roman era; it was also traditionally claimed to predate the Christian era, this curious fact being explained as an example of the prophetic worship of the Virgin.

This age-old association with the Virgin may have been the decisive reason why Charles the Bald in about 876 transferred

to the cathedral from the treasury at Aix-la-Chapelle the most sacred relic of the Virgin, given to his grandfather, Charlemagne, by the Emperor of Constantinople. This was the 'Sacred Tunic' or *sancta camisia* which she was said to have worn at the birth of Christ. From then on Chartres would have a double claim to be 'the preferred residence of the Virgin on earth'.

Successive churches on the site of the first cathedral, probably dating from the mid-fourth century, were destroyed by fire, twice deliberately, by order of the Duke Hunald of Aquitaine (743) and by Danish marauders (858). After this last disaster, Bishop Gislebert rebuilt on a far more ambitious scale, for the first time extending beyond the Gallo-Roman walls. To make up the considerable fall in the ground, he constructed a chamber at a lower level covered with extremely heavy vaults and used as a treasury for valuables. It still exists far beneath the present high altar (9) and was to play an important part in the history of the cathedral. In 1020 fire again razed the cathedral to the ground.

The new basilica built by Bishop Fulbert was renowned throughout Christendom for its splendour. The feature which concerns us particularly was the enormous crypt, which consisted of two long, parallel corridors joined at the apsidal end by an ambulatory. Three radiating chapels opened off this, the whole forming a horse-shoe shape encircling a largely unexcavated core. In 1134 a great fire destroyed the greater part of the town but the cathedral escaped relatively unscathed. There is evidence, however, that shortly afterwards a new freestanding tower was being built some little distance in front of the existing building, possibly to replace an existing north tower which may have been damaged in the fire. Incorporated in the later building and surmounted by an elaborate spire dating from the sixteenth century, the tower stands to this day (Plate 119). Soon afterwards (about 1145) a companion south tower was built, complete with its inimitable stone spire (Plates 119 and 121). Simultaneously the side aisles of the basilica were extended as far as the towers and a narthex constructed to mask the old façade, positioned more or less level with the back, or east side, of the towers. (Abbot Haimon's wonderful description of prince and peasant alike voluntarily harnessed to carts, relates to this rebuilding.) Work had not continued long on the narthex and its sculptured portals – the magnificent *Portail Royal* through which we still today enter the cathedral from the west – when there was a change of plan. The narthex was dismantled stone by stone, and the façade, incorporating the Portail Royal, was re-erected in its present position in line with the front of the towers. This was most fortunate, for on June 10, 1194 the great basilica of Fulbert was reduced to ashes, all except the west towers and the façade between them, probably protected from the heat by their great bulk. The great crypt also survived, thanks to its enormously thick groin vaults.

The initial reaction to the disaster was utter despondency. Then came consolation when it was discovered that the Sacred Tunic and the image of the *Virgo paritura* had survived. When the fire had broken out, some priests had carried them down into the Carolingian treasury of Bishop Gislebert and clanged down the iron trapdoors. Soon after, the entrance had been blocked by falling masonry. The priests and the precious relics were discovered unharmed several days after the fire. Despair now gave way not merely to equanimity but to a strange feeling of confidence approaching elation. The fact that the Virgin

had suffered her 'palace' to be destroyed was now interpreted not as a sign that she had abandoned Chartres but rather, as the chronicles inform us, 'that she desired a new and even more splendid church to be built in her honour'. To comprehend this dramatic change of heart, we have to bear in mind, as von Simson points out, that 'the religion of mediaeval man

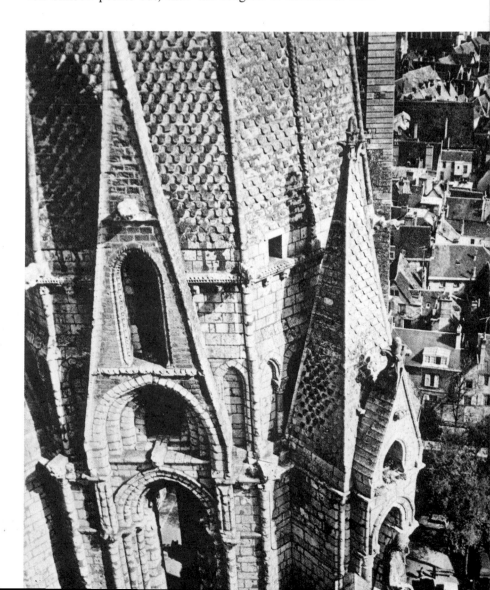

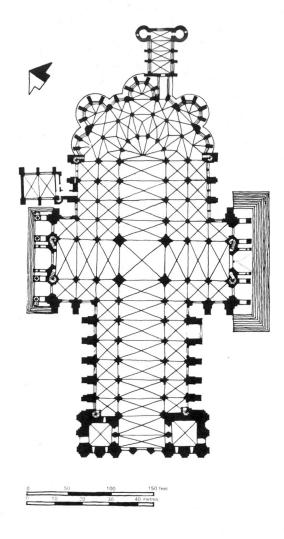

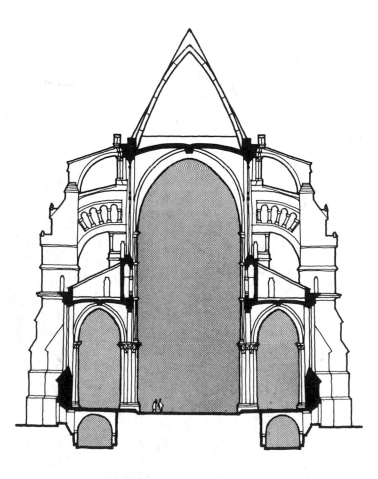

was a communication with a sacred reality that was invisible, yet immediately and continuously present. The veneration of saints and their relics, and the repercussions that this cult exerted upon nearly every phase of mediaeval life . . . are unintelligible unless the immediacy of this relationship with the supernatural is properly understood' (10). One of the most significant of these repercussions was economic, not only directly, but through the great fairs associated with the religious feasts that attracted crowds of pilgrims. It is no coincidence that the four great annual fairs with which the prosperity of Chartres was linked, coincided with the four Feasts of the Virgin. The loss of the relics that attracted the crowds to these feasts was, therefore, a major economic catastrophe; their recovery demanded a splendid new cathedral to house them.

The rebuilding project again awakened the greatest enthusiasm from rich and poor alike. Contributions for 'Our Lady of Chartres' poured in from all over France – and even beyond. King Richard the Lion-Heart, although at war with Philip Augustus, personally welcomed emissaries from Chartres soliciting donations and authorized them to travel freely throughout England. A stained-glass window is recorded as being donated by the Archbishop of Canterbury. One of the most charming stories in the 'Book of Miracles' is of an English student who had been studying in France and who, on the eve of his return to England heard such an impassioned appeal for funds that he donated his one valuable possession, a gold necklace he had bought to take back to his fiancée. The next night he was granted a vision of the Virgin, wearing his necklace.

Rebuilding started almost immediately, commencing with the nave, and by 1220 the main structure was completed. The side porches date, for the most part, from the second third of the century, and every detail of sculpture and glass was in position for the dedication ceremony of October 24, 1260.

It was decided to retain Fulbert's crypt and this predetermined the disposition of many elements of the new church. The great width of the Romanesque nave, which had been covered with a wooden roof, established a span of 54 feet for the stone vaulting as compared with 40 feet at Notre-Dame in Paris and must have posed severe technical problems. It was at the apsidal end that the complications were most critical, for the walls of the three radiating Romanesque chapels on which the columns of the ambulatory had to bear, did not converge to a single point, nor did they divide the hemicycle into equal parts. A comparison between the plans of the crypt and upper church reveals sound reasoning behind such apparently capricious anomalies as the irregular spacing of columns and the different sizes of chapels, and compels admiration for the ingenuity with which the architect reconciled two seemingly incompatible systems.

These enforced links with the past seem in no way to have intimidated the architect of the new cathedral. Far from a compromise solution, he produced a revolutionary design. At Chartres the tribune galleries were dispensed with from the start and bold flying buttresses in double tiers (11) used to ensure the equilibrium of the high vaulting which here assumed

Fig. 9 *Above left* Ground plan. *Chartres*

Fig. 10 *Left* Transverse section. *Chartres*

122 *Right* Flying buttresses of the choir. *Chartres*

were at the prospect of admitting yet more 'light of Divine essence' through these greatly enlarged windows, it would seem that they were also a little apprehensive lest the religious atmosphere of the interior be disturbed by too much light, and so we find a marked deepening of the tones of the glass, particularly of the blues, compared with the twelfth-century glass of the west windows, a preoccupation with the quality rather than the mere quantity of light transmitted; this approach has a parallel in our day by first creating entire window walls and then muting the excessive light, not by cutting down the area, but by using tinted, 'glare-proof' glass.

The modern concept of transparency was entirely foreign to the Gothic builders. To them the window still enclosed rather than defined space and in this sense remained a wall; a disembodied, glowing, translucent wall but, nevertheless, an optical barrier shutting out the profane world. If anywhere on earth, it is at Chartres that one experiences the strange sensation of being transported half-way to heaven experienced by Abbot Suger. The impact of the jewel-like radiance suffusing the interior is overwhelming and initially all-engrossing; the architecture seems but a frame for the glass.

The glass of Chartres covers an area of some twenty-two thousand square feet. The three windows under the west rose and the justly famed figure of *Notre-Dame de la Belle Verrière,* now in the ambulatory of the choir, were salvaged from the fire and date from about 1150; virtually all the rest of the glass dates from the period between 1215 and 1240. The artists are generally unknown but one signed piece of thirteenth-century glass, a medallion in the Cathedral of Rouen, bears the words 'Clemens vitrearius carnotensis m(e fecit)' – (Clement, glass-maker of Chartres made me).

Monumental figures of Prophets, Apostles and Martyrs, executed with an almost savage boldness, appropriate to work seen from such a distance, preside from the great clerestory lancets. The medallion windows, composed of a myriad tiny fragments of glass, were placed in the aisles and ambulatory, where their small scenes from the lives of the Saints could easily be 'read' in the prescribed manner: from left to right and from the bottom upwards – and never, surely, have religious ideas and instruction been presented in so palatable a form as in these brilliantly illuminated 'slides'.

Almost all these medallion windows were donated by the guild corporations of the town; by the goldsmiths, masons, carpenters, butchers, bakers, tanners, etc. Nowhere is the pride and joy of the medieval craftsman in his work more clearly illustrated than in these scenes, elaborated far beyond what any contractual obligation could have demanded. These windows provide a forceful reminder of the unity of medieval society within the Church. Every stratum of society contributed to the building of the cathedral; every stratum was represented, if not in the vignettes depicting the work of the donor corporations, then in the lives of the Saints, an elect, enjoying an honour no mere monarch could aspire to, but who in life had been anything from shoemaker and peasant to common labourer.

The last part of the structure to be completed was the north transept where the glass of the rose was donated by the royal family and dates from between 1223 and 1236 (Plate 112). The arms of Castile accorded equal prominence with the

123 St Thomas Becket cut down by Norman knights, detail from the *Martyr's Pillar* of the south porch. *Chartres*

its classic quadripartite form (Plate 122). The pier also assumed its characteristically Gothic form at Chartres, where the cylindrical supports of the nave arcades at Laon and Paris were replaced by compound piers or *piliers cantonnés* which permitted the line of the vaulting ribs to be carried right down to plinth level in a structurally logical and aesthetically satisfying manner. With quadripartite vaulting, the alternate stressing associated with sexpartite vaulting disappeared, but its echo lingered on at Chartres in a subtle decorative detail: the compound piers are alternately round with four octagonal attached shafts and octagonal with four round shafts (Plate 111). The mass is in both cases equal, so that the effect is of a mere ripple of variety and interest on the surface of unity.

As we have said, at Chartres the four-stage, early-Gothic interior elevation has been reduced to the three stages of classic high-Gothic: nave arcade, triforium passage and clerestory window (Fig. 10). These clerestory windows, in the form of twin lancets surmounted by an elaborate rose, are altogether some 44 feet high and stretch the full breadth between piers. Fascinated as the builders of Chartres obviously

124 *Right* South portal. *Chartres*

Golden Lys of France, recall the rôle of Blanche of Castile during this period, at first as Queen and then as Regent of France. The central of five great lancet windows under the rose – as also the sculptured *trumeau* of the north porch – is devoted to St Anne. The unusually high honour accorded her at Chartres is probably explained by the fact that her skull had

125 Decorative bas-relief from the 13th-century *jubé* of Chartres. *Paris, Musée du Louvre*

been among the relics looted by the Crusaders from Constantinople, and that this had but recently (1205) been bequeathed to the cathedral, where, in the words of the cartulary 'the head of the mother was received with great joy in the church of the daughter' (12). The other lancets are occupied by four great personalities from the Old Testament, Melchizedek, David, Solomon and Aaron. Time has affected the glass at Chartres in one unexpectedly curious way: many of the flesh tints have darkened considerably, imparting a bizarre but extraordinarily compelling effect to these hieratic figures with their glaring, white eyeballs and cocoa-coloured skin. The chivalric image of Solomon was quite possibly inspired by the future St Louis, then a young man, described by Fra Salimbene of Padua as '*gracilis, macilentus et angelica facie*'. Beneath the four figures are four connected anecdotes: the idolatry of Nebuchadnezzar, the suicide of Saul, the madness of Jeroboam, shown worshipping his golden calves (Plate 145), and Pharaoh falling headlong from his horse into the Red Sea.

The Church's claim that the New Testament rested firmly upon the foundation of the Old Testament, was given its most audacious visual expression in the lancets of the southern rose, where the four Evangelists are shown sitting on the shoulders of the four greatest prophets (Plate 113). The disparate scale of the two figures – aesthetically so effective – no doubt reflects the teachings of the Scholastics and, particularly, Bernard of Chartres, who had compared the men of his day to dwarfs, only able to see further than the intellectual giants of antiquity

by virtue of being borne upon their shoulders.

The decision to retain the existing *Portail Royal* and the towers must have rather cramped the style of the architect of the new cathedral. Deprived of an opportunity to design a west entrance in the new style, he, perhaps, lavished all the more love on the transepts where, well beyond the former church and encumbering substructures, he had a relatively free hand (Plate 124). The model for the magnificent triple porches of both north and south entrances was obviously Laon, recently completed and universally acclaimed. At Chartres both the architecture and the sculptural programme have been greatly elaborated. The gracious breadth of the portals at Laon has been increased still further, and the triple porches interconnected, creating a far more complex spatial effect.

The sculpture of the *Portail Royal* (*c*. 1150), closely related to that of St Denis and possibly even the product of the same workshop, is not only the best preserved and finest example of this transitional style, but ranks among the greatest sculpture of all times (Plates 26 and 126). Never has there been a more perfect integration of sculpture and architecture than in these hieratic column statues. No longer Romanesque, despite the attenuated proportions and the highly stylized but superbly decorative treatment of drapery, not yet quite Gothic, these serene and confident figures, with their very human expression, have most aptly been described as *l'avant-printemps de la sculpture gothique* (13).

The emancipation of sculpture from subservience to architecture is already far advanced in the sculpture of the north and south portals executed a little less than a century later (14). The figures have assumed natural proportions and a natural stance, and stand almost clear of the wall, but are still sensitively related to their architectural setting. Among the finest figures are the Old Testament prophets from the central portal of the north porch. St John the Baptist is also particularly beautiful (Plate 128). Never has the ascetic ideal been portrayed more poetically. Plate 127 shows, from left to right, Melchizedek, Abraham, Moses and Samuel. Especially poignant is the group of Abraham and Isaac, the father with hand poised to strike the fatal blow; the bound Isaac calmly resigned to his fate; both looking Heavenward as they hear the Redeeming Voice. The restraint of the figures even at this dramatic moment reflects the chivalric ideal of moderation in joy or anguish: in thirteenth-century art even scenes of martyrdom are balletic rituals, with the emphasis on the triumph of the spirit, not the death of the body. A mawkish delight in gruesome details only came much later and reflected a very different outlook.

Sculptured on the corbel bracket supporting Abraham and Isaac is the substitute sacrifice: the ram caught in the thicket, carved with consummate artistry. Brackets were commonly so decorated. Under the Queen of Sheba a crouching negro slave bears gifts for Solomon, and under St Gregory, dictating the words that a dove whispers in his ear, his secretary, pen in hand, looks up in astonishment. Charming and beautiful, these little figures may also have provided an additional means of identification for the unlettered.

All four 'Mirrors', of Nature, of Instruction, of Morals and of History, are expounded at Chartres in more than 10,000 surviving figures in glass and stone. A few cathedrals may rival

126 *Right* The 'column statues' of the *Portail Royal* – a perfect integration of sculpture and architecture. *Chartres*

its architecture, one or two, perhaps, its sculpture, none its glass, let alone the incomparable ensemble of architecture, sculpture and glass. Chartres, as it has come down to us, is the most complete and most perfect expression of all that is finest in the mind and the spirit of the Middle Ages.

There were only minor additions (15) to Chartres after 1260 until, on the night of July 26, 1506, lightning destroyed the lead-covered, wooden spire over the north tower. The chapter entrusted Master Jean Texier, or Jean de Beauce, with the design of a worthy stone spire and this was completed by 1513. Building in a creative era that scorned imitation of the past, his design is in the very late *flamboyant* Gothic style of his day (Plate 119) (16). The restless movement and broken silhouette of Master Jean's spire consort strangely with the serenity of the older sister; strangely, but not unsuccessfully, for great care was taken to balance the *mass* of the two towers, the lighter mass of the new compensating for its greater height, which certainly bears a better relationship to the height of the façade than the southern tower, built, as we recall, for a recessed west front.

The major act of destruction at Chartres came in the eighteenth century when the interior of the choir was transformed in the neo-classical style. The inner surface of the elaborate choir-screen commenced by Jean Texier and but recently completed (1715), was sheathed with marble reliefs of the most indifferent quality. Fortunately the exterior of the screen with its two hundred figures and exquisite tracery, survived. The greatest loss was the simultaneous destruction of the thirteenth-century *jubé*. Fragments of its sculpture, buried under the paving, were discovered by chance and rank among the finest work of the entire Gothic era (Plate 125).

127 *Left* Figures from the Old Testament in the sunless north portal; from left to right: Melchizedek, Abraham with Isaac, Moses and Samuel. *Chartres*

128 *Below* St John the Baptist in the north porch. *Chartres*

Rheims

It was at Rheims, on Christmas Eve of the year 496, that the Bishop, St Remi, baptized Clovis, leader of the conquering Franks, and a large number of his warriors, thus reconfirming the authority of the Church and establishing the tradition of Rheims as the preferred site for the consecration of the kings of France.

In 1210 the Carolingian cathedral was reduced to ashes by a fire which destroyed the greater part of the city, and already the following year, on the anniversary of the disaster, the foundation stone of the present cathedral was laid. Pope Honorius III granted a special indulgence to all who should

129 From their high vantage point on the nave buttresses a choir of angels keep watch over the Celestial Jerusalem. Note the lively corbel heads—human and animal—at the base of the crocketed spires. *Rheims*

contribute to the construction of the new church: '*structura egregia et adeo dispendiosa*'. By 1241 the canons had taken possession of the choir, and work on the splendidly decorated west façade had begun. The courtyard of the Archbishop's palace, still cluttered with stone and building equipment, was specially cleared for the coronation of Philip IV of Valois in 1328, but during the Hundred Years' War work proceeded very slowly, so that the cathedral had not yet been quite completed at the time of the consecration of Charles VII in the presence of Joan of Arc in 1429. By 1481 only the spires of the towers, on bases ready prepared to receive them, were lacking, when a fire destroyed the roof, the bell tower and the tall *flèche* over the crossing. By the time the damage had been repaired, both the means and the will to build the spires had gone.

The labyrinth of the nave, with the names of the first four

architects, was preserved until 1778, when one of the canons, annoyed by the constant commotion caused by children and idlers following the twisted path, donated 1,000 *livres* to have it replaced with plain paving slabs. Fortunately, most of the details of the inscriptions of the plaques had been recorded. To Jean d'Orbais, master until 1231, 'who began the chancel of the Church' goes the major credit for the initial design. He was followed by Jean le Loup (1231-1247), who completed the choir and laid the foundations of the west front; Gaucher de Rheims (1247-1255) is mentioned as working on the great portals and was, perhaps, primarily a sculptor, while Bernard de Soissons (1255-1290), shown tracing a circle with his compasses with the caption '*qui fit cinq voûtes et ouvra à l'O*', raised five bays of the nave vaulting and worked on the 'O', the great rose. A fifth master, familiar from other sources, and who may also have been included in the inscription was Robert de Coucy (1290-1311) who continued work on the west front and the towers (17).

Despite the extended period of construction, the Cathedral of Rheims is exceptionally homogeneous stylistically, for the later masters adhered to the original design. The west front which probably comes closest to the popular image of the

'ideal' Gothic cathedral, is of great beauty, and successfully combines a great variety of elaborate decorative elements into a convincingly unified ensemble, with an assurance that marks the beginning of a new epoch. The great porches of Laon, relegated to the lateral façades at Chartres, return triumphant to the west front at Rheims. On the debit side, such details as the gable of the central porch, literally dripping with sculpture, show a tendency towards 'stage décor' rather than pure architecture, and the whole façade lacks something of the strength and nobility and the impeccable proportions of Paris or Amiens.

The 'Gallery of Kings' fittingly achieves its most monumental expression at the Coronation Church with fifty-six colossal figures; each 14 feet tall and weighing 6-7 tons, they form a massive frieze at the base of the towers which continues around the lateral façades and back as far as the roof (Plate 131). The central place of honour has been accorded to Clovis, flanked by his wife, Clotilde, and St Remi. Below them, across the entire central bay, stretched a narrow balcony from which, on Palm Sunday, the choir boys accompanied by musicians, formerly sang the *Gloria*, while the clergy and the faithful, assembled on the steps 150 feet below, chanted the responses.

The lateral façades have not been impaired by the addition of nave chapels, and constitute one of the special glories of Rheims. The buttress piers terminate in aedicules crowned with elaborate crocketed pinnacles. Within the aedicules stand angels with outstretched wings keeping guard over the image of the Celestial City of Jerusalem (Plate 129). The buttress system of Rheims is exceptionally stable and together with the sturdy vaults, ensured the survival of the cathedral during the prolonged bombardment of World War I (18).

The classic formula of Chartres was further developed and refined by the master of Rheims. Unhampered by having to conform to earlier work, he could regularize the layout of the chevet, which was broadened to embrace the transepts, providing the large space required for the coronation ceremony.

Perhaps the most significant contribution made by Jean d'Orbais was his treatment of the windows. At Chartres the

130 *Left* Detail of the nave triforium. *Amiens*

131 *Right* Detail of the roof over the nave with its cresting of gilded *fleur-de-lis* and the upper stages of the south west tower; the figures of the kings are 14ft high. *Rheims*

Fig. 11 Ground plan. *Rheims*

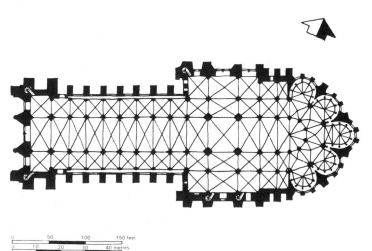

aisle walls had only been pierced with single lancets, leaving a considerable area of wall on either side, but at Rheims the lancets have expanded to twin lights taking up the same width as the clerestory windows whose shape they echo. Villard de Honnecourt, as we have noted, visited Rheims while it was under construction, and Jean d'Orbais, no doubt, proudly explained his revolutionary ideas to the visiting master, who made a sketch of the interior and exterior elevations of a nave bay (Plate 132). Apart from the new treatment of the aisle windows and developing the same line of thought, the wall below the aisle windows has been given an arcaded treatment providing a visual analogy with the triforium, where the column below the central mullion of the clerestory window has become much thicker than its neighbours, anticipating the perfect integration of clerestory and triforium at Amiens (Plate 130). Villard de Honnecourt's record is of all the greater historical importance since the version actually executed at Rheims was far more conservative (19).

At Chartres the shapes of the lancet and rose had been punched out of the solid wall surface, as from a plate. At Rheims they are separated by light members, constructed independently, and the 'plate tracery' of Chartres has given way to the first 'bar tracery', opening a world of new possibilities: in the dexterous hands of the Gothic stone-mason tracery would be bent and twisted to trace the filigree outline of a multi-petalled flower, to branch into a thousand twigs, or flicker like tongues of flame.

If the architecture of Rheims shows remarkable unity, the sculpture, on the contrary, embraces a great diversity of styles (20). The early figures (about 1220) follow the Chartrain tradition. From about 1235 onward two workshops were active, one evolving along traditional lines, the second showing an extraordinarily strong Graeco-Roman influence, no doubt inspired by Roman remains in the vicinity, which were then far more numerous than now. The spirit of classical antiquity seems to live again in the *Visitation* of the central portal (Plates 135 and 138). The aged Elizabeth is a Roman matron, and only the introspective expression of the Virgin distin-

guishes her face from that of an Aphrodite. From the middle of the century a third school asserted itself. Representing a return to medieval traditions, it effected a synthesis, as it were, of all that had gone before, in singularly elegant and gracious works exemplified by the famous 'Smiling Angel' of Rheims (Plate 136). Widely acclaimed, the sculpture of Rheims was imitated as far afield as Germany, Italy and Spain, and served as the preferred model for small-scale sculpture in ivory, wood and metal. At Rheims sculpture has assumed an autonomous existence. Intrinsically superb, the figures of Rheims are no longer truly integrated with the architectural setting.

The interior of Rheims and especially the view looking down the nave towards the west is ravishing and unique (Plate 148). The great rose inscribed within a pointed arch – erasing the last faint memory of its Romanesque antecedent (21) – is echoed by a similar rose over the central doorway, instead of the usual stone tympanum; for the first time we find a lavish sculptural programme inside a French Gothic cathedral on the great west wall, honeycombed with niches, with decorative trefoil-cusped heads containing figure sculpture. The seven tiers are separated by panels carved with sprays of foliage of exquisite delicacy. Below, a dado of cloth, hanging in heavy folds, is simulated in stone – complete to the pins by which it is tacked to the wall, so that the Coronation Cathedral was always ready for its most festive occasion (22). Most celebrated of the scenes is the so-called 'Communion of the Knight' (Plate 137). This actually represents Melchizedek, that mysterious figure from the Old Testament, foreshadowing Christ in his dual rôle of King and High Priest. He is shown offering consecrated bread and wine to Abraham, who is dressed as a knight of the period of St Louis.

132 *Below left* The interior and exterior elevations of a bay of Rheims cathedral. Drawing from the Sketchbook of Villard de Honnecourt. *Paris, Bibliothèque Nationale*

133 *Below* Detail of the pier capitals and vaulting ribs of the nave aisle; in the distance can be seen the triforium with its slightly thicker colonnette. *Rheims*

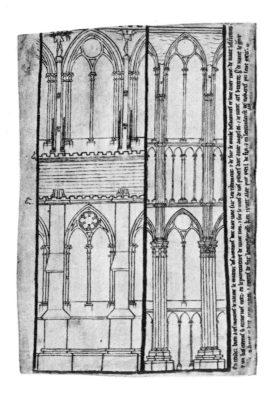

134 *Top* The central portal of the west front. The inscription on the lintel replaced the Revolutionary dedication to the 'Temple of Reason'. *Rheims*

135 *Bottom* The Virgin and St Elizabeth from *The Visitation,* sculptural detail from the west portal; the chevron pattern of the colonnettes, the remains of the original colour, was revealed by recent cleaning. *Rheims*

The pier capitals show the same fascination with the world of nature, and include vignettes of peasant life and fabulous beasts, interspersed amid foliage already too naturalistic for its architectural content, but so beautifully executed as to disarm criticism (Plates 133 and 139).

Outstanding among the objects in the rich treasury is the Coronation Chalice, of gold, decorated with filigree work, cabochons, pearls and cloisonné enamels (Plate 389). Known as the 'Chalice of St Remi', due to an error in the inventories, it actually dates from the end of the twelfth century and was used for the communion of the kings of France at their coronation. The inscription on the base invokes anathema on anyone who should steal the chalice – ironical, since only the theft and concealment of the chalice by a revolutionary

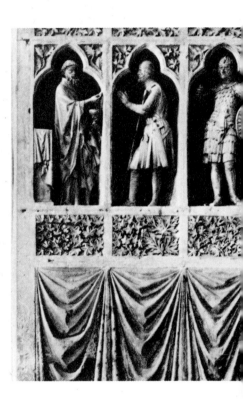

prevented its destruction during the Revolution. The Reliquary of the Holy Thorn is composed of an eleventh-century Fatımıd rock-crystal vase in a mid-fifteenth-century setting by the Parisian goldsmith, Guillaume Lemaistre (Plate 116). The gold armature and base are embellished with pearls and pink balas rubies and the reliquary surmounted by an exquisitely chased angel in gold with enamelled wings and robe, holding a crown of thorns. The tiny gold angel, now displayed next to the reliquary, formerly held the thorn and was placed inside the vase (23).

136 *Above* St Nicaise, who formerly carried the sliced top of his scalp, and the smiling *Angel of Rheims*; sculptures from the northern portal of the west front. *Rheims*

137 *Above right* Detail from the inner face of the west wall; on the left the so-called 'Communion of the Knight'. *Rheims*

138 *Overleaf* The introspective expression of the Virgin is all that distinguishes her from a classical Venus. Detail of *The Visitation* (see also Plate 135). *Rheims*

139 *Overleaf* Dragons are entwined with foliage on a capital in the nave arcade. *Rheims*

Amiens

In 1206 the Cathedral of Amiens acquired from Constantinople a portion of the skull of St John the Baptist which became the object of a celebrated pilgrimage and contributed greatly to the prosperity of the town, famed for its cloth, its dyes and particularly for a flourishing traffic in woad. The Romanesque cathedral was destroyed by fire in 1218 during the episcopacy of the highly intelligent and aristocratic Evrard de Fouilloy, and while the dean was the renowned theologian and preacher, Jean de Boubers or d'Abbeville, afterwards cardinal and intimate of Pope Gregory IX. We may be sure that the lofty idealism and the complex but coherent exposition of dogma in the vast iconographic scheme of the new cathedral owed much to these two exceptional minds.

Contrary to the usual practice, work started on the nave, in order to preserve as long as possible the Church of Saint Firmin on the site of the choir. The foundation stone was laid by Evrard de Fouilloy in 1220 and the nave completed by 1236. The construction of the choir and transepts was started soon afterwards. Held up for a while by lack of funds and also by a disastrous fire in 1258, the structure was completed by 1269 and in 1288 the metal plaque was inserted at the centre of the labyrinth in the nave, thanks to which we know the name of the architect who had conceived this masterpiece, Robert de Luzarches and his two successors (see p. 89). The chapels inserted between the nave buttresses were constructed between 1292 and 1375, while the uppermost stages of the two west towers date only from the late fourteenth and early fifteenth centuries. The eighteenth century saw the usual disfigurement of the choir in the taste of the time, but the cathedral escaped the ravages of the Revolution lightly, thanks to the concerted effort of a motley group of enlightened and influential local citizens, led by a judge, an architect, a librarian and the wigmaker, Jean Lescouve, mayor of Amiens.

The treasury was plundered, and, as elsewhere, the numerous bronze and copper sepulchral images were carted off to be melted down at the mint but, by a miracle, two effigies of bishops – the only two to have survived in all France – were spared at Amiens, including that of Evrard de Fouilloy (24). A superb example of bronze sculpture, cast in a single piece, the founder-bishop is shown in the act of benediction and treading down sin – rather gently it would seem – symbolized by the two endearing little dragon-like creatures (Plates 140 and 49) (25).

In the nave of Amiens, Gothic structure and the treatment of the classic, three-stage interior elevation established at Chartres, achieve perfection (Plate 141). In this work are united a majesty untainted by pompousness; refinement without a suggestion of effeteness; a clarity of structural and spatial definition which seems the embodiment of scholasticism in stone; and a triumphant but controlled vertical movement. A unique feature is the vigorously carved band of foliage below the triforium. Stretched like a garland across the vaulting shafts, it counters their soaring line with a powerful horizontal accent and maintains the opposing directional forces in a

142 *Right* The choir, with its glazed triforium. *Amiens*

140 *Above* Detail from the bronze effigy of the founder bishop, Evrard de Fouilloy (see also plate 49). *Amiens*

141 *Right* The nave, perhaps the supreme expression of the Gothic spirit. *Amiens*

143 View of the north transept with its later windows in the *style rayonnant*, 1325. *Amiens*

reassuring equipoise. This 'classical' balance becomes particularly apparent if one compares Amiens with Cologne (a post-'classical' design based on Amiens, where the vertical line is unchallenged) (Plate 260).

The triforium, which at Chartres had formed an independent element, has at Amiens been subtly integrated with the clerestory by continuing the central mullion of the window down to the base and organizing the arcade into three-light units, surrounded by a pierced trefoil and combined within a pointed arch, effectively echoing the shape of the great windows above.

In the later choir this tendency to unite triforium and clerestory was carried to its logical conclusion with the creation of a *claire-voie* or glazed triforium, achieved by covering the ambulatory and chapels not with the customary lean-to roof that abutted against the solid wall of the triforium, but with a series of double-pitched roofs, kept clear of the triforium, imparting a picturesque external appearance which in lesser hands could only too easily degenerate into fussiness (Plates 142 and 149). Internally, the dream of the glass church has become reality, but what has been gained in elegance, has been lost in plastic vigour with the disappearance of the very striking 'positive-negative' effect of the window tracery silhouetted against the radiant glass, and the light triforium arcade standing out against the shadowy passage.

The urge to reach the sky which had, successively, raised the vaults from 79 feet at Laon to 110 feet at Paris, 114 feet at Chartres and 125 feet at Rheims, culminated at Amiens in a height of 139 feet. Only once would the vault rise still higher

in France, to 157 feet 6 inches at Beauvais. Accompanied by a further paring down of the structural skeleton, the limit had been reached – and overstepped. Virtually completed by 1272, the great vaults of the choir of Beauvais collapsed in 1284 and in their fall crushed something, too, of the spirit of unbounded confidence of the early Gothic Age.

The west front of Amiens has an overwhelming grandeur (Plate 153). Based on Notre-Dame in Paris, it is more ambitious, richer, warmer but not quite so perfectly proportioned or controlled. The great portals are, however, incomparable. The almost hypnotic attraction exerted by the central portal, despite the *embarras de richesse,* is due not only to its dominant scale, but to the subtle stratagem – of which one is not consciously aware – of making it far deeper than the side porches. The major part of the façade, up to and including the Gallery of Kings, was raised at one sweep between 1220 and 1236. On the *trumeau* of the central doorway stands the well-known *Beau Dieu d'Amiens,* probably the finest medieval statue of the Blessing Christ to have survived unscathed, combining a truly regal authority with compassion, and devoid of any trace of sentimentality. The north portal is dedicated to St Firmin, the first bishop of Amiens. Among the Saint's guard of honour, occupying the splayed jambs of the portal, stand two martyrs nonchalantly holding their decapitated heads in their hands (Plate 152).

The magnificent bas-reliefs within the monumental quatre-foils of the basement include paired Virtues and Vices (Plate 29), each pair placed beneath the monumental figure of a saint or martyr considered to embody that particular virtue, and signs of the Zodiac paired with an appropriate occupation. Beneath the sign of *Pisces* (February), a bearded figure in winter clothes warms his bare feet before a fire on which he is roasting a fish on a spit (Plate 28). The composition, which includes shoes and a dresser, successfully evokes an atmosphere of cosy domesticity, secure from the rigours of the season. In the portal of the south transept stands the most popular of all French Madonnas, the *Vierge Dorée,* so-called from the original gilt finish which is still discernible despite the bird-droppings from the nest of starlings in her crown (Plate 150). What a world of difference between this elegant and captivating young mother (about 1250) and the aloof and regal Queen of Heaven of the west front dating from some thirty years earlier (26).

The front of the transept above the *Vierge Dorée* has become a gigantic 'window-wall'. Around the upper half of the great rose, seventeen animated figures illustrate the concept of 'The Wheel of Fortune' deriving from the *Consolation of Philosophy* by Boethius. The figures on the left, well-dressed and seemingly about to mount the wheel, culminate in a motionless, crowned figure apparently immune to the whims of Fortune. The figures on the right, however, indicate that the triumph of the crowned figure will be short-lived, as they

144, 145 *Right above* Classic examples of 13th-century glass: in grisaille from Salisbury and in colour from Chartres (showing Jeroboam worshipping his golden calves).

146 *Right below* Early 15th-century detail from the east window, *York;* the transparent yellow is obtained by the 'silver stain' technique.

147 *Far right below* Mid 14th-century canopy detail of unusual colouring from the choir of the *Stephansdom. Vienna, Historisches Museum*

149 *Left* The double pitched roofs of the chapels have been kept clear of the triforium, thus enabling it to be glazed. *Amiens*

150 *Below* The *Vierge Dorée*, nicknamed the 'soubrette picarde' by Ruskin. *Amiens*

plunge to earth dishevelled, barefoot and in rags (Plate 154).

Amiens has preserved a uniquely beautiful ensemble of 110 choir-stalls in the *Style Flamboyant*. Carved between 1508 and 1522 by a whole team of craftsmen, the stalls and their misericords incorporate 4,700 figures, mostly from the Old Testament. One of the stall-ends shows a craftsman at work with his mallet and chisel and is signed Jehan Trupin (Plate 155). The canopies over the stalls reserved for the king and the dean – when officiating in the absence of the bishop – can be seen towering to a height of 40 feet over the *Louis Quinze* grille that now encloses the choir (Plate 142), the oak seeming, in Ruskin's words, 'to grow like living branches, to leap like living flame . . . canopy crowning canopy, pinnacle piercing pinnacle . . . and wreathing itself into an enchanted glade, inextricable, imperishable, fuller of leafage than any forest, and fuller of story than any book' (27).

151 *Above right* Flying buttresses taking the thrust of the high vaults of the choir. *Amiens*

152 *Above left* The portal of St Firmin; on the left two martyrs nonchalantly hold their decapitated heads. *Amiens*

153 *Overleaf* West front. *Amiens*

154 *Overleaf* The southern rose surrounded by the 'Wheel of Fortune'. *Amiens*

148 *Left* Interior looking west. *Rheims*

Bourges

The sleepy little town of Bourges is situated in the very heart of France – the geographical centre being twenty miles away. Singularly unspoilt, it has preserved many relics of its past as the capital of the Dukes of Berri. Especially evocative are the glimpses of the cathedral from the twisting lanes, and completely overwhelming is the grandeur of the west front seen from the *parvis* – so small that one must crane one's neck to take in the view. Here at Bourges the concept of the church as 'Gateway to Heaven' received its ultimate expression in no less than five great portals (Plate 156).

Several churches dedicated to St Etienne (Stephen), have succeeded each other on the site of the present cathedral, occupied, according to tradition, by the palace of Léocade, 'first senator of the Gauls', who towards the end of the third century assigned one of its halls to Saint Ursin as a chapel. During the second half of the twelfth century, certain new structures were commenced in the high-Romanesque style; it is doubtful whether these amounted to a total reconstruction of the existing church. Parts, however, including the fine north and south portals, probably originally intended for the west front, were incorporated in the subsequent Gothic church.

The palace of Léocade had been situated just inside the Gallo-Roman walls, which crossed the present cathedral one

bay west of the hemicycle of the choir. As the ambitious design of the new Gothic cathedral envisaged an eastward extension beyond the city walls, the architect was faced with the problem of bridging a substantial change in the levels. This was solved by the construction of a magnificent crypt – in France second only in size to Chartres – which is not really a crypt at all, but a lower church whose perimeter is completely above ground level and pierced by large windows (Plate 158). The proportions and the detail, particularly of the foliate capitals, are exceptionally fine. Work proceeded without a break on the choir and by 1232 it was in use, with the two Romanesque portals serving as entrances while work continued on the nave. This was probably completed by 1266 and the great west front with all its sculpture by 1285. At the end of the fourteenth century Guy de Dammartin, architect to Jean, Duke of Berri, inserted the vast west window with its *Rayonnant* tracery which takes up the full width of the nave and which consorts so strangely – but rather effectively – with the older work (Plate 164).

The twin towers of the west façade were ill-fated. The south tower which was to have had an octagonal spire similar to Chartres, was never completed. Towards the end of the fourteenth century there were signs of settlement and the great buttress on the south was built to support it. The north tower stood until early in the sixteenth century when it began to show signs of failure, and on December 31, 1506, collapsed, bringing down with it several bays of the northern aisles. Between 1508 and 1540 it was reconstructed in the *Flamboyant* style. Several of the thirteenth-century statues of the porch were re-used for its portals, others placed in niches high on the tower where their inaccessibility saved them from the greatest

155 *Left* A woodcarver at work, detail from the choir-stalls. *Amiens*

156 The church as the 'gateway to Heaven': the quintuple portals of *Bourges*

disaster to befall Bourges, its occupation for several weeks of 1562 by fanatical Calvinist forces who smashed all the free-standing sculptures and mutilated the bas-reliefs. Thanks, perhaps, to the Calvinistic preoccupation with hell and damnation, we have been spared the magnificent *Last Judgement* of the central portal. Dating from the second half of the

157 *Below left* Decorative detail from the west front. *Bourges*

158 *Below* The magnificent crypt which as a result of different levels is really a lower church, built in the purest Gothic style. *Bourges*

159 *Right* Part of the west front with the northern tower in the *flamboyant* style. *Bourges*

thirteenth century, it has come down to us in a state of almost perfect preservation, as if the sculptors had only just laid aside their chisels (Plate 163).

In the lowest of the three registers of the tympanum the dead rise from their tombs, seemingly dazzled by the light after their long sleep. They are naked, for as much as the medieval age disliked portraying the nude, the Bible was explicit on this point. In accordance with medieval theory resurrected man lives for all great Eternity at the perfect age of the Redeemer's Resurrection, whatever might have been his age at death. All exult in a state of bodily perfection. There are no children or aged, blind or crippled. After the Resurrection comes the Judgement. In the centre of the second register stands the Archangel Michael, a serene and lovely figure. He holds the fateful scales in which are weighed man's good and evil deeds (28), and protectively shepherds a soul – represented in the accustomed manner as a child – away from a persistent leering demon.

On the left, or inauspicious side of Christ and the Archangel, the damned are hustled towards the Gate of Hell by hideous demons, some with talons instead of feet, one with pendant breasts sporting the features of voracious monsters, another

with a tail ending in a serpent's head which spitefully nips the leg of his victim. Grotesque heads are engraved upon the lower part of their bellies or behinds, a detail for which Emile Mâle offers an extremely plausible explanation: that having descended to the level of the brute, the fallen angels displaced the seat of their intelligence and put their souls at the service of their lower appetites – an interpretation which finds support from the wings which sprout not from the shoulders but the backside of one demon. The Gate of Hell was almost always represented in the form of the gaping mouth of the monster, Leviathan, drawn from the Book of Job, which Old Testament commentators equated with Satan and his works. The passage 'out of his mouth go forth flames like torches of fire . . . out of his nostrils smoke like that of a pot heated and boiling', was taken literally, and at Bourges demons fan the flames with bellows while the damned, including a bishop, are hurled into the cauldron. Here sit two pathetic figures, their stoic resignation underlining the hopelessness of resistance, plagued not only by the flames but by giant toads which cling tenaciously to tongue and breast.

To the right of the Archangel the elect move in decorous procession towards Paradise, their state of grace perfectly

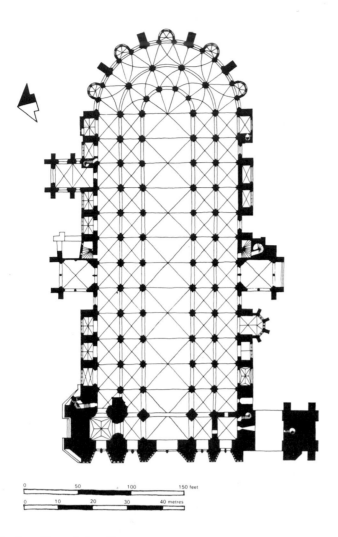

Fig. 12 *Above* Ground plan. *Bourges*

160 *Right* The rhythmic gradation of heights achieved by the Bourges master; note the enormous height of the nave arcade. *Bourges*

expressed by the suave harmony of line, just as the riotous *mêlée* of demons and damned – viewed as an abstract arrangement of forms alone – spells dissonance, revolt and chaos. At the Gate of Heaven, depicted as an aedicule within which sits the patriarch Abraham with the souls of the righteous gathered to his bosom, stands Saint Peter, keys in hand, greeting the elect. A monk wearing a thrice-knotted cord, probably inspired by Saint Francis of Assisi, and a king lead the procession, ideal representatives of *Sacerdotium* and *Imperium*.

Presiding over the scene, strangely remote from the proceedings and seeming to address his appeal to the living rather than the dead, sits the Risen Christ as Judge, displaying his wounds, while four angels hold the Signs of the Passion – cross, crown of thorns, lance and nails – symbols of ignominy transmuted to symbols of glory. Closing the composition, the Virgin Mary and St John kneel in humble supplication as if, in defiance of all that the doctors of the church had said of the impossibility of influencing the irrevocable decision at this ultimate stage, their prayers might still aid the repentant sinner. Finally, a minor but exquisite touch: two angels carry away the sun and the moon, dimmed to the insignificance of candles at noonday by the light emanating from the Throne of Grace.

It was at Chartres that one of the two classic solutions to the French Gothic cathedral was evolved; the second is to be found at Bourges. The plan of Bourges bears a significant

resemblance to that of Paris, perhaps not surprising since the Archbishop of Bourges at the time of the inception of the design was a brother of the Bishop of Paris (29). There are, however, two striking differences not apparent from the plan. The transepts at Paris are still important features both externally, with their gable-fronts and great roses, and within, where the vault is the same height as that of the nave. At Bourges there are no transepts whatever and the double aisles of the nave continue without interruption around the apse as a double ambulatory. When Notre-Dame de Paris was first built, tribune galleries were still necessary, to take the thrust of the nave vault, but by the time the Bourges master conceived his section they had been superseded by flying buttresses.

At Bourges the tribune gallery has been omitted, but instead of following the pattern at Chartres and reducing the height of the inner aisle to give a high clerestory window above, the Bourges master left the inner arcade at a great height so that his section resembles that of Notre-Dame with the omission of the floor of the tribune. The rhythmic gradation of the heights of the outer and inner aisles and nave, respectively 29 feet 6 inches, 69 feet and 123 feet, and the even distribution of light ensured by three sets of windows, together with the tremendous height of the nave arcade, combine to create an interior that has no rival in its spaciousness and in the monu-

161 *Right* Vision of Christ with the two-edged sword between his teeth, the book with the seven seals in his right hand and the seven stars in his left, standing against the seven golden candlesticks, symbols of the seven churches of Asia; detail of the window of the Apocalypse. *Bourges*

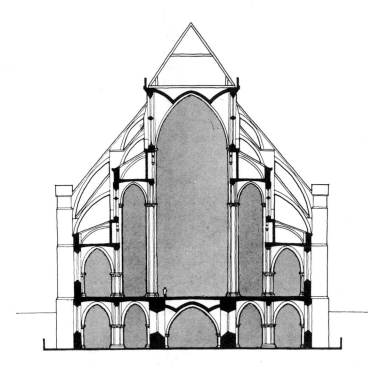

hardly surprising perhaps, as it would appear that many of the same craftsmen worked at both cathedrals. As at Chartres there are monumental Biblical figures in the clerestory lancets and medallion windows below, which here, too, include lively vignettes showing the work of the donor guild-corporations (Plates 12, 17 and 18). Totally different in character from these everyday scenes is the unique *Window of the Apocalypse,* sombre in colour and seemingly illuminated by flashes of lightning as befits its theme. The finest of the three great quatrefoils depicting the Risen Christ shows him in his rôle of Judge, bearing the two-edged sword between his teeth, holding the seven stars in his outstretched left hand, the book with the seven seals in his right and standing in the midst of the seven golden candlesticks, symbols of the Seven Churches of Asia – a truly majestic figure (Plate 161).

162 *Opposite* Three German emperors from the 14th-century windows of the north aisle. *Strasbourg*

Fig. 13 Transverse section. *Bourges*

163 *Below The Last Judgement* from the west front. *Bourges*

164 *Overleaf* The sculptured rose of the central gable provides a telling contrast to the precision of the *rayonnant* tracery of the west window inserted at the end of the 14th century. *Bourges*

mental grandeur of the general vista. As fine as that of Chartres, the Bourges solution was, however, less flexible and less frequently adopted. Its influence can be seen in the cathedrals of Coutances, Le Mans, Toledo and even Milan.

The large amount of thirteenth-century glass that has survived at Bourges is of equal quality to that of Chartres,

Coutances

Coutances, which was named after the Roman Emperor, Constantius Chlorus, fell to the Norman invaders in the tenth century and was only reunited to France by Philip Augustus in 1204. The present cathedral was commenced soon after and, not surprisingly, shows some typically Norman characteristics. Coutances is, in fact, the masterpiece of Norman Gothic.

Using some portions of the existing Romanesque cathedral, which can even now be traced (30), the cathedral as it stands was built after the fire of 1218. Work commenced with the nave which was constructed very rapidly. There was then a pause, probably while additional funds were collected, and the

165 The apse and lantern from the bishop's palace. *Coutances*

166 The twin west towers. *Coutances*

remainder of the work, including the great towers, was completed about 1250. The result is an almost uniquely homogeneous structure. The only subsequent additions were an apsidal chapel and a series of chapels in the nave, added in the fourteenth century, the latter separated from each other by beautiful open tracery, and furnished with charming altars and piscinas incorporated in the design.

At Coutances the Norman preference for soaring towers, already seen in the façade of the Abbaye-aux-Hommes at Caen and now allied to the Gothic emphasis on verticality, has given birth to twin west towers that thrust skyward with the energy of rockets leaving the launching pad (Plate 166). Higher towers

there may well be, but none that pierce the sky with quite such vehemence as these clusters of conical turrets. The effect must have been apocalyptic on that day, in June 1944, when the city was on fire and the roof of the great lantern of the cathedral smoked like a gigantic torch. This lantern tower over the crossing, a tall octagon with four turrets containing spiral stairs at the angles, echoing the square lower stage, is one of the most elegant of its type.

Even allowing for the great destruction wrought first during the Hundred Years' War, then by a Huguenot Army during the Religious Wars and finally by the Revolutionaries, the sculpture at Coutances does not seem to have a very important rôle in the architectural scheme, which is perhaps surprising when one considers that it was built in the same period as Chartres and Amiens. Almost the only sculptural ornament on the lantern façade are the bold crockets which emphasize the vertical continuity of the adjacent, and perfectly plain, shafts; this again is a purely architectonic use of sculptured detail.

The lantern never received its intended spire but this is perhaps no great loss for the octagon composes very happily with the chevet, particularly when seen from the gardens of the bishop's palace (Plate 165). The vaulting of the chevet steps down in three tiers, over the double-aisled ambulatory, following the pattern of Bourges. The coupled columns of the main arcade of the choir are a favoured Norman device (Plate 168): with twin arches rising from the capitals and separated by a deep cleft, the effect is of an independent structure sweeping round the nave–an extraordinarily dynamic and sophisticated effect.

The *pièce de résistance* is provided by the breathtaking interior view of the lantern (Plate 169). Riding high on the arches of the crossing, it has been likened by Viollet-le-Duc to the Christ Child carried on the shoulders of St Christopher. The enormous mass of the supporting piers is belied by the ranks of matchstick-thin shafts, attached by only a narrow neck to the masonry, which soar without interruption to the springing of the arches. The genius of the designer is strikingly evident in the gently restraining accent of the shaft capitals which the late-Gothic masters would have been tempted to omit. Their diagonal line provides a perfect prelude to the parallel sides of the octagon above. The view downwards from the twin, superimposed galleries in the lantern is awe-inspiring, but definitely not for anyone suffering from vertigo.

The architecture of Coutances is notable for its purity of style. Of singular beauty is the detail of the interior arcading of the lantern, meticulously executed even where barely visible from the ground. The carving throughout is extremely lively; the crocket buds of the capitals and the superb frieze, where they alternate with fern-like fronds, seem only to await a warm spring day to open (Plate 167).

Coutances preserves some fine glass of the thirteenth and fifteenth centuries. Of particular interest is a window in an attenuated lancet in the high clerestory of the choir showing St Lô, the celebrated bishop of Coutances, in the act of benediction, surmounted by a composite of the seraphim with its three pairs of wings and the cherubim with its wings patterned with enigmatic eyes (Plate 13). The wheel is the symbol of the strangely-named 'Thrones', third of the nine orders of heavenly beings, according to the medieval 'science' of angelology. Patriotic Normans claim their green countryside as the inspiration for the extremely unusual and successful colour scheme.

167 *Above right* Detail of the interior of the lantern, showing carving of the capitals. *Coutances*

168 *Right* Detail of the coupled columns and vaulting of the ambulatory of the choir. *Coutances*

169 *Opposite* High above the arches of the crossing the lantern was compared by Viollet-le-Duc to the infant Christ carried on the shoulders of St Christopher. *Coutances*

Rouen

Rouen, capital of Normandy, had particularly close connections with England and was a favoured residence of the
first Plantagenets. Richard I so loved the city that he left his
'Lion Heart' to the cathedral, where it was interred in the
choir (Plate 171) (31). The cathedral is a heterogeneous
structure of many styles and periods, with a very complex,
and much disputed, early history. A few elements, such as the
lower stages of the northern tower, survive from the twelfth
century, the rest post-dates a great fire in the year 1200.

Typically Norman (and also English) is the magnificent high
lantern over the crossing (Plate 170). Characteristic of the

The windows in the background form part of the series containing thirteenth-century glass, one of which, as we noted,
was signed by the glass-painter Clement of Chartres.

Normandy was conquered by Philip Augustus in 1204 and
French influence became dominant as the century progressed.
From the very end of the thirteenth century date the unique
and justly celebrated series of bas-reliefs of the *Portail des
Libraires* or Portal of the Booksellers. The top register is
devoted to Biblical History ('The first Harvest' and 'The
Death of Abel' appear in Plate 175); the other sculptures,
except for a few oblique references to the Liberal Arts and
Virtues and Vices, are given over to figures of utter fantasy
and invention: vigorous carvings of tumblers, bearded dwarfs,
amazing hybrid creatures, whose only function is to fill the

barbed quatrefoils with strikingly original and decorative
compositions. Ruskin divided grotesques into two types, 'the
sportive and the terrible'. These genial sirens and centaurs
definitely belong to the former category together with a comic
cynocephalus in buskins, a boar-headed man striking a
philosophic 'Thinker' pose and a grave doctor intently con-

unexpected, and, therefore, all the more rewarding, features
of the architecture of this formative phase of Gothic, before
the discovery of the 'perfect' solutions had somewhat dampened
the spirit of experiment, are the enchanting heads that peep
out from the crocketed capitals of the choir piers, effectively
terminating the vertical line of the vaulting shafts (Plate 172).

170 *Above left* View up into the great central lantern in the Anglo-Norman
tradition. *Rouen*

171 *Above* Ambulatory of the choir; on the left the effigy of King Richard I of
England who bequeathed his 'Lion Heart' to the cathedral. *Rouen*

172 *Right* Detail of arches in the choir. *Rouen*

templating a specimen in a flask, unaware, it seems, that his torso has been changed into a bird with a dolphin's tail. Knowing the medieval fondness for symbolism, it is tempting to read esoteric meanings into these carvings, but it would appear that they are simply a spontaneous expression of that innocent delight in the marvellous, characteristic of the age (32);

173 Grotesque from the *Portail des Libraires. Rouen*

an outpouring of that irresistible urge to decorate that filled the margins even of serious prayer-books with playful drolleries and arabesques.

The circumstances of the Hundred Years' War saw another wave of English influence. This is particularly evident in the upper part of the new west front, started at the end of the fourteenth century and continued by the master-masons of the Duke of Bedford during the English occupation of Rouen (1419-1449). It was not completed until the sixteenth century. Spectacular in the extreme, the new front stretches across the old façade like a great reredos or, better still, a festive hanging – for there is something eminently 'painterly' rather than sculptural about the disposition of the superimposed tiers of sculpture (33). A magnificent frontispiece, it gives no indication of the structure behind. In this respect it resembles English screen façades and is the very negation of French *raison*.

In this façade several new stylistic elements make their appearance, heralding the characteristic Continental style of the late-Gothic period known in France as the *Style Flamboyant* from its flickering, flame-like forms. The characteristic of the style is the undulating reverse-curve which had already

appeared in the 'Decorated Style' of the first two-thirds of the fourteenth century in Britain. Applied to the head of an opening it results in the ogee arch, with its outline alternately convex and concave; while in tracery one finds such sinuous shapes as the *mouchette* and the *soufflet* (34). All three forms appear in the 'English' work at Rouen (Plate 174). *Mouchettes* and *soufflets* adorn the gable fronts, and in the heads of the two left-hand arches, the tracery describes ogee arches. In the later full-flowering of the *Flamboyant* style the rigid peaked line of the gables also melted into the ogee form.

The imported forms were quickly 'naturalized' and developed to give effective utterance to the elation that swept over France at the successful conclusion of the disastrous Hundred Years' War. A particularly splendid example is the south tower of Rouen, commenced in 1487, the so-called 'Butter Tower' since it was paid for by indulgences to eat butter during Lent. The new style was also enthusiastically received (with native variations) in Germany and Spain, but, paradoxically, rejected in Britain in favour of the severity of the 'Perpendicular Style'. The restless and highly emotive forms of *Flamboyant* Gothic reflect the changed spiritual climate of the fifteenth century. The fervent faith and serene confidence of the thirteenth century had given way to nagging doubts and only too often, to a superstitious pietism, while the Black Death and the recurrent plagues that decimated Europe, produced both a morbid preoccupation with death and a frantic, almost hysterical escapism.

Classical scholasticism, culminating in the philosophy of St Thomas Aquinas with its emphasis on the unity of truth and the compatibility of Faith and Reason, had succumbed to two diametrically opposed currents: an anti-rationalist, ecstatic mysticism, epitomized by Master Eckhart and his followers; and the Nominalism of the school of William of Ockham, with its emphasis on the evidence of the senses, experiment and logical thought. Opposites though they were, they had this in common: 'Both cut the tie between reason and faith . . . Mysticism in order to save the integrity of religious sentiment, Nominalism to preserve the integrity of rational thought' (35).

The 'classical' architecture of the thirteenth century had been characterized by order and clarity and the clear definition of structural members. In fifteenth-century Gothic we find a preference for 'baroque' forms, for ambiguous spatial effects, for continuous mouldings that unite such different structural elements as pier and arch, and for a capricious and increasingly luxuriant ornamentation that threatens to engulf the entire structure.

174 *Right* The spectacular 'English' screen of the west front. *Rouen*

175 *Overleaf* Detail of the *Portail des Libraires* with its unusual grotesques. *Rouen*

Albi

The southern provinces of France which had seen such a magnificent flowering of Romanesque art are not particularly rich in Gothic cathedrals. Unquestionably the most magnificent is the unique, red-brick cathedral of Albi. Poised on an escarpment over the River Tarn, above the rhythmic arches of the *Vieux Pont,* dating from 1030, and the picturesque houses straggling up the hill, the imperious bulk of the Cathedral of Ste Cécile and the bishop's palace create a unique and compelling townscape (Plate 78). This peaceful scene witnessed one of the grimmest episodes in all European history, with the rise of Catharism during the twelfth century and the sub-

survived, not more than fifty in all Languedoc according to a frank admission of the Dominican Inquisitors, but this did not prevent Bernard de Castanet from continuing to combat heresy. Not a week passed without some citizen being arrested, tortured or thrown into prison. A large proportion of the confiscated wealth invariably found its way into the bulging coffers of the bishop. Fear and hatred were rife and increasing opposition to Castanet was voiced, even by the canons (36). Such was the turbulent background against which the design of the new cathedral took shape: a portrait in brick of the imperious and justly feared bishop.

Over a cliff-like plinth, affording no foothold for an assailant, the walls rose unbroken to a height of some 45 feet from the floor of the cathedral and far higher still above the outside

176 *Above* General view of the exterior. *Albi*

177 *Right* The west front, no elegant doorway but a medieval *donjon,* stout enough to withstand a siege. *Albi*

178 *Overleaf* View of the *flamboyant* Gothic porch from the fortified gateway. *Albi*

sequent suppression of the Albigensian Heresy, involving the most diabolical cruelty and the wholesale massacre of men, women and children, over a wide area in southern France.

Resistance had already been crushed when in 1277 Bernard de Castanet was enthroned as the new bishop, and immediately set about building a new cathedral to replace that 'undermined by the wars and the heretics'. Few of those unfortunates had

ground. Nowhere was the fortress-like character of the church more evident than in the great west tower confronting the castle of the House of Montfort (37), beyond the jurisdiction of the bishop, and a potential source of danger (Plate 176). Here is no gracious belfry echoing the welcome of the great, sculptured portals of northern France, but a medieval *donjon,* starkly unadorned, its walls unpierced save for the meanest arrow-slits and reinforced at the angles by circular buttresses stout enough to withstand a siege (38). The tower rises sheer above the roof of the nave, but sets back in stages on the west, giving an extraordinary impression of pulsating energy only just held in check.

A single, unpretentious doorway on the south opened into the hostile outer world (39). In happier days (1519-1535) this

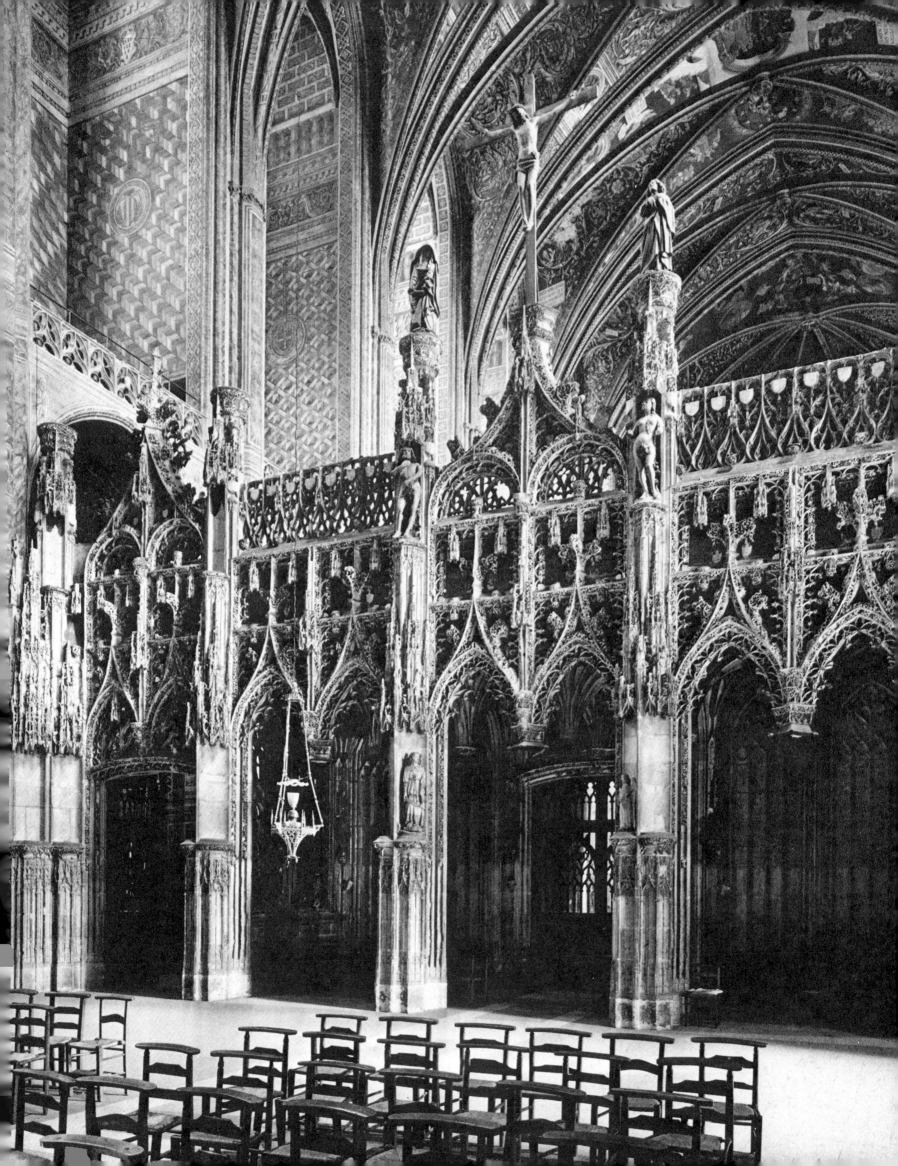

and wealthy patron capable of embellishing the vast, but probably rather austere interior; and he did not disappoint them. Even in an age when the private lives of princes of the church were not subjected to close scrutiny, that of Bishop Louis was so scandalous as to enforce his abdication in 1502. This was not, however, quite as disastrous a fall as one might have imagined, for he had managed to arrange for his nephew

179 *Previous page* The *jubé* or rood-screen closing off the choir. *Albi*

180 *Left* One stronghold viewed from another: the apse of the cathedral from the watchtower of the Abbey of St Salvi. *Albi*

Fig. 14 Ground plan. *Albi*

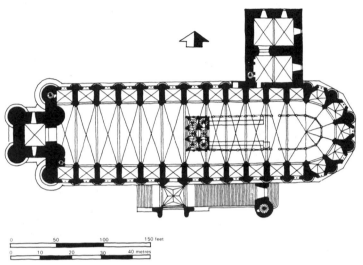

was enlarged and dignified with a sumptuously decorated stone porch in the *Flamboyant* style, aptly referred to as the *baldaquin*. The approach, through a fortified gateway and up a monumental flight of steps, is dramatic in the extreme (Plate 178). A miracle of virtuosity, the vibrant, flickering forms of the decoration, becoming richer and more complex as they ascend, are set off to perfection by the stark wall of brick behind, giving the effect of a precious *objet d'art* displayed in a modern museum setting. There is something particularly appealing to the modern architect about the bold and simple massing of this southern style of Gothic (40).

The first sight of the interior is astonishing. In place of the spatial complexity of the great cathedrals of the North, we have a concept of audacious simplicity: that of a single great space in the form of a nave 100 feet high and with vaults almost 60 feet wide, flanked by chapels inserted between enormous buttress walls, 5 feet thick and 20 feet deep. There are no aisles and no transepts. The emphasis is on the preaching-hall favoured by the mendicant orders and one can almost hear the Dominican Grand Inquisitor fulminating against heresy although the elegant decorations convey a very different atmosphere.

The original church was substantially completed between 1282 and 1390. The second important building phase was inaugurated with the appointment of Louis of Amboise as bishop in 1473. Member of an eminent and wealthy family, brother of the chief minister of King Louis XII, and himself a confidant of the king, Louis was a *bon viveur*, a lover of luxury and a great patron of the arts. It would seem that the chief motive of the chapter in electing him was to have a powerful

Louis to succeed him. Between them, the two Louis were responsible for all the major additions to the original structure: the three upper stages of the great west tower, the porch (41), the enclosure of the choir, and the mural decoration, all of which are admirable. Most unfortunate, however, was the decision to divide the height of the chapels with a tribune gallery. Not only did this interrupt the soaring verticality, but created a lighting problem, particularly acute in the choir with the erection of the choir-screen. The solution was to punch the small windows in the brickwork of the apse which so detract from the external appearance (Plate 180). With electricity at our command, there is perhaps a case for their suppression now.

By good fortune the finest Gothic choir enclosure to have survived in Europe is to be found here in Albi. It is precisely in such a vast, box-like interior that the space-dividing function of the *jubé* is most justified and most effective. Instead of one monotonous view, one is now offered a great variety of spatial sensations. From the vast nave with its blue and gold vaults hovering far above, one moves into the intimacy of the *jubé* porch with its intricate star vaulting, or wanders round the shaded ambulatory with its figures from the Old Testament waiting impatiently, so it seems, to enter the choir where Apostles and Saints bask in the light of the New Testament, and the high windows (Plate 179). The architectural decoration, especially of the serried canopies, is unbelievably delicate and complex. Richelieu, on a visit in 1629, is said to have mounted a ladder and rapped the stone, before he could be convinced it was not stucco. Even if one disapproves of choir-screens on principle; even if one detests

Strasbourg

In 1176 the splendid Cathedral of Strasbourg, equalled only in all the domains of the German Emperor by the Imperial Minster of Speyer, burned down for the fourth time in a century. A few years later Bishop Heinrich I undertook a complete reconstruction, utilizing only the old foundations, which were strengthened to take the load of the stone vaulting envisaged for the first time. By 1225 the apse and crossing and the north transept, all substantially as we see them today, had been constructed in late-Romanesque style. Then, with the south transept complete to half its height, there was an abrupt change to the Gothic style.

As if to vaunt the possibilities of the new *opus francigenum,* the master of Strasbourg created one of the most sensational works in the entire repertoire of Gothic art, the unique Angels' Pillar (1225-1230). Ranged in three tiers are the Evangelists, Angels sounding oliphants and, on the highest tier, Christ and three Angels bearing the Signs of the Passion (Plate 182). The figures alternate with attached piers whose stark simplicity provides a perfect foil for the sculpture, and underscores the vertical line still further, so that the pillar, despite its substantial dimensions, seems to soar weightlessly upward into the dim penumbra of the vaulting. The sculpture is of the highest quality and reflects the influence of Chartres.

In the *Death of the Virgin* (after 1230) on the tympanum of one of the twin doors of the south portal, the primary influence

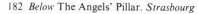

182 *Below* The Angels' Pillar. *Strasbourg*

the late-*Flamboyant* style, one is liable to be overwhelmed here, and like Prosper Mérimée, 'to feel ashamed of reason before this magnificent folly'.

The decade of Louis II's episcopacy (1502-1511) saw the triumph of the Renaissance style. Louis wisely completed the rood – and choir – screens in the Gothic style, but dismissed the French artists who had painted the enormous Last Judgement on the west wall, today in a much mutilated condition, and interesting rather than beautiful. They were replaced by a team of Italian artists who, within the short space of six years, covered the rest of the walls and the vaults with the most extensive and best-preserved Renaissance frescoes of the period to have survived in France. Confronted with the youthful vigour of the Renaissance *putti,* the angels of the *jubé* and choir-screen, incomparably more beautiful though they are, have an indefinable languor (Plate 181). Here, sadly, is the swan song of Gothic art.

181 *Above* One of the angels from the choir enclosure holding a monogram of Jesus; in the background, *putti* from the Renaissance frescoes. *Albi*

183 *Top* The Judgement Portal of the west front with the *Wise and Foolish Virgins* as symbols of the *Elect* and the *Damned. Strasbourg*

184 *Bottom The Death of the Virgin,* a fine synthesis of French grace and German feeling. *Strasbourg*

would seem to be that of Rheims, as interpreted by a German sculptor (Plate 184). The restless, eddying movement, underlined by the multiple folds of the drapery, and the emotional involvement of the participants in the drama, seem to reflect an innate German tendency to *Expressionism*. On either side of the twin portals stand the two magnificent figures of the *Synagogue* and *Ecclesia* (42). Holding a Cross and Chalice, the Church casts a proud but magnanimous glance at her vanquished rival, whose eyes are lightly bound, for the Old Law had, it was claimed, perceived only half the Truth. The ineffably appealing figure of the Synagogue, noble even in defeat, embodies the lofty idealism of the age (Plate 190).

The nave was built in high-Gothic style between 1240 and 1275. Its proportions, based on the stable equilateral triangle, compose very well with the Romanesque crossing and apse

but lack the exhilaration one associates with the loftier cathedrals. Much of the magnificent fourteenth-century glass has been preserved. The great lancets of the north aisle house nineteen heroic figures of German Emperors, attired with barbaric splendour and with their names, such as *Henricus Babinbergensis, Carolus Magnus Rex* and *Lotharius Romanorum Imperator,* emblazoned on their haloes. In striking contrast are the southern windows depicting scenes from the Life and Passion of Christ. Justly famed for their expressive, calligraphic line and brilliant colouring, they anticipate the narrative style of the fifteenth century (Plates 162 and 186).

The pride of Strasbourg is the superb west front (Plate 187), of especial interest since the unique series of drawings preserved by the *Œuvre Notre-Dame* (43) makes it possible to follow the evolution of the design from the last quarter of the thirteenth to the end of the fifteenth century. Work began on May 25, 1277 under Erwin von Steinbach along the lines of a drawing by his predecessor (44). On to a front in the tradition of Notre-Dame in Paris, Master Erwin appended a second free-standing, skeletal façade whose taut, attenuated, closely-spaced shafts have been compared to the strings of a harp. The incredibly rich, three-dimensional effect and dramatic *chiaroscuro* reach a climax in the gable over the central doorway (Plate 187).

Here, as at the south transept with its figures of the Synagogue and Church, the theme is the superseding of the Old Law by the New, a preoccupation supposed by some scholars to reflect the large Jewish colony in Strasbourg during the Middle Ages. Solomon on his throne is attended by twelve lions, the uppermost pair *rampant* and seemingly paying homage to the seated figure of the Virgin above, in her personification as *Throne of the New Wisdom.* The pencil-sharp pinnacles halo her figure and point to the heart of the great

185 *Above* A view of Strasbourg in 1630 by Wenceslas Hollar, engraved in 1645. *London, British Museum*

186 *Right The Entry into Jerusalem;* detail from 14th-century window illustrating the Passion. *Strasbourg*

rose window, proclaiming that this too should be regarded as a symbol of the Virgin, the fairest of flowers, the *super rosam rosida* of the chroniclers.

To the right of the south portal of the Last Judgement stand the elect: the Wise Virgins with their lighted lamps welcomed by Christ, the Heavenly Bridegroom. On the left the damned: the Foolish Virgins and the fascinating figure of the Tempter (Plates 183 and 191). In the flower of youth and dressed in the height of fashion down to the elegant, little pointed shoes, the seducer smiles beguilingly, holding out the apple of temptation to the nearest virgin. She glows with pleasure and prepares to unloosen her gown, unaware of the rotten core behind the seducer's fair front; his bare back gnawed by ghastly toads and adders (45). For the other two foolish virgins the pleasure of the moment has already given way to remorse. Distraught with grief at the prospect of eternal damnation, they sway precariously on their pedestals, ill-constrained within their niches (46).

Despite its complexity, the west front has compelling unity, which derives from its harmonious proportions, constructed 'according to true measure' (47). The twin towers of the third stage followed the traditional pattern but the construction of a vast cliff of masonry between them marked a radical change of conception. The magnificent drawing by Master Michael Parler (about 1385), from which the rose (Plate 192) has been reproduced, shows a single central tower in the German manner. This design was, in turn, superseded, and between 1399 and 1419 Ulrich von Ensingen, builder of the great tower of Ulm, erected the present tall octagon with its complex interpenetration of open forms characteristic of German late-Gothic. His successor, Johan Hültz of Cologne, produced new designs for the spire. An early proposal showed an open-work octagon strongly reminiscent of that at Freiburg-im-Breisgau (Plate 58). His later design, as executed, is original to the point of bizarre eccentricity with its aerial stairways contrived within the bristling pinnacles. Completed in 1439, the 466-foot spire of Strasbourg was the highest masonry structure of the Middle Ages and regarded as nothing less than the Eighth Wonder of the World (48).

The spire very nearly fell victim to the Revolution. In 1794 a municipal official demanded that it be demolished on the grounds that it offended the concept of Equality—a disaster mercifully avoided by the conciliatory gesture of crowning the *flèche* with an enormous Phrygian Bonnet in sheet-iron. The sculpture was less lucky and more than three hundred figures were destroyed within a week in 1793. Only the courageous efforts of the Minister of Public Works and a Professor Herman saved some of the finest masterpieces, including the *Ecclesia* and the *Synagogue* which they concealed in the Botanical Gardens.

190 *Overleaf* The head of vanquished *Synagogue* (after 1225). *Strasbourg, Musée de l'Œuvre Notre-Dame*

191 *Overleaf* Head of the *Tempter*, about 1280. *Strasbourg, Musée de l'Œuvre Notre-Dame*

192 *Overleaf* Detail of drawing by Master Michael Parler about 1385; ink on parchment with the figures of the Virgin and Apostles heightened in gouache. *Strasbourg, Musée de l'Œuvre Notre-Dame*

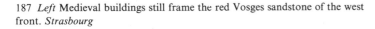

187 *Left* Medieval buildings still frame the red Vosges sandstone of the west front. *Strasbourg*

188 *Above* A 19th-century view of the façade. *Strasbourg*

189 *Right* Lateral façade of the south tower. The vertical line rules supreme. *Strasbourg*

England

5 England

In view of the extremely close, if not always cordial, relations between France and England after the Conquest, it is not surprising that the Gothic style should first have been exported to England. Acceptance of the *opus francigenum* was facilitated by the fact that, until the thirteenth century, some of the great English prelates still hailed from the mainland, and also by the fact that the development of the Gothic style owed much to the Normans. Indeed, as we have seen, the oldest ribbed vaults to have survived are those over the choir-aisles of the Norman cathedral of Durham, commenced in 1093, so that, technically speaking, England was ripe to receive the new style and might quite early have developed the Gothic style independently. The lead established at Durham was not, however, maintained; the Île-de-France became the cradle of the Gothic style, and it was a French designer, William of Sens, who introduced the new style to England in the rebuilding of the choir of Canterbury after the fire of 1174.

The English pupils, however, showed a singularly independent spirit and great originality almost from the start. There was far less interest in structure *per se* and, instead, an emphasis on elaborate decoration which reached a climax in the fantastic star and fan vaults, which, together with the ogee curve, were England's greatest contribution to the vocabulary of Gothic ornament(1) (Plate 256). Such characteristics as the fondness for overall pattern and that markedly linear quality which has been a feature of English art in almost every period, represented a reassertion of the Hiberno-Celtic, Anglo-Saxon heritage, temporarily driven underground at the Conquest.

The most striking feature of English cathedrals, that differentiates them so strongly from their continental counterparts, is their tranquil landscape setting in a close. In the Middle Ages there were nine secular cathedrals (including Lincoln, Salisbury, Wells and York) controlled by a dean and chapter of canons, and nine monastic cathedrals (including Canterbury and Ely) under a prior, which became secular cathedrals at the dissolution of the monasteries by Henry VIII; at that time five abbey churches (including those of Peterborough and Gloucester) were also raised to cathedral status. The layout associated with monastic establishments became so much the norm that they influenced those of the secular foundations, and so the largest cloister in England is found at Salisbury, where it was not strictly required at all, but was probably considered necessary to complete the architectural ensemble.

The English cathedrals do not attempt to emulate the soaring height of the French prototype but are, instead, remarkable

193 Detail of the pier capitals in the nave. *Wells*

for their great length, particularly that of the choir, which often includes a secondary transept – a feature taken over from the great Romanesque abbey church at Cluny – so that the eastern arm becomes a complete cruciform structure in itself. Whereas the classic French plan is compact and unified with barely projecting transepts, the typical English plan has boldly projecting transepts and tends to sprawl, while the internal space is often deliberately subdivided by such elements as screens, strainer arches, and organs, so placed as to offer only a tantalizing glimpse beyond (Plates 209 and 216). If the monumental grandeur of the French interior has been lost, we are consoled with an infinitely varied sequence of spatial sensations that is unique and, probably, the most rewarding feature of the English cathedral.

Classical architecture as epitomized by the Greek temple and the Italian Renaissance church on a symmetrical, centralized plan, makes an absolute and final statement expressed in a 'closed composition'. It is difficult, if not impossible, to add or remove anything without vitiating the integrity of the concept. Gothic architecture, on the other hand, of all the historical styles, is the most 'organic', in the sense in which Frank Lloyd Wright has made the term understood in modern architecture, including a capacity for expansion as need dictated. This is true of all Gothic, but just as the logical and coherent compositions of France and the partially classicized forms of Italy are the least receptive to additions, so half the charm of the English cathedrals, to a large extent designed on the additive principle, is the result of their straggling informality and the juxtaposition of dissimilar styles and periods.

English Gothic monumental sculpture cannot seriously be compared with that of France. The native genius found its perfect expression in a lighter vein: in foliage sculpture on capitals, corbels and roof bosses that, for variety, originality and sheer beauty has never been surpassed; in superb decorative heads and intimate genre scenes, and fine sepulchral monuments.

Equally irresistible are the illuminations of the East Anglian school of the first quarter of the fourteenth century. The stylized plant forms of the earlier manuscripts have sprouted luxuriant naturalistic foliage, providing a suitable habitat for the denizens of field and forest, the lively figures and the droll grotesques distributed with seeming abandon over the margins but, in the finer examples at least, with an unerring sense of design. The linear style, the delight in movement, the strong anecdotal element and the delicious sense of humour are characteristically English. Animal impersonations had already been a favourite theme in the Bible of William of Devon dating from the mid-thirteenth century (Plate 195). The Gorleston Psalter (*c.* 1310-1325) commences one page with an enchanting parody of a funeral procession in which rabbits dressed as priests and acolytes accompany a coffin borne by two pallbearer dogs (Plate 194). Bringing up the rear comes a rabbit carrying a reserve of candles. The relations between monk and nun also come up for comment: in one marginal illustration a nude man trundles away a wheelbarrow full of nuns; in several, monks expose their genitals before nuns.

This same period (the late-thirteenth and early-fourteenth centuries) was also the hey-day of English embroidered ecclesiastical vestments which contributed so much to the visual splendour of the offices in the great cathedrals. England's supremacy in this field was acknowledged throughout Western Europe and magnificent examples of *opus Anglicanum* are to be found as far afield as Sweden and Spain, with Italian collections particularly rich as a result of frequent gifts to the papacy by English kings, nobles and prelates (2).

Canterbury

In the year 597 St Augustine and his fellow missionaries from Rome were welcomed to *Cantwarabyrig,* or 'the borough of the men of Kent', by King Ethelbert of Kent and his Frankish queen, Bertha, already a Christian. The king was converted and baptized, together with thousands of his subjects, before the departure of St Augustine, who later returned as 'Bishop of the English'. The primacy of the Cathedral of Christchurch at Canterbury – hotly disputed by York – was again confirmed by the 'Accord of Winchester', attended by William the Conqueror in 1072, but the real fame of Canterbury dates from a century later.

194 *Above* Funeral procession of a rabbit from the Gorleston Psalter, East Anglian, 1310-25. *London, British Museum*

195 *Right* Humorous animal impersonations from the Bible of William of Devon, mid 13th-century. *London, British Museum*

196 *Above right* View of the west towers from the main gateway of the cathedral close. *Canterbury*

197 *Opposite* The west front. *Lincoln*

Henry II in his struggle to assert the supreme authority of the Crown, even over the clergy, had appointed his worldly friend, Thomas Becket, Archbishop of Canterbury, only to find him an uncompromisingly staunch supporter of the rights of the Church. The archbishop was exiled and a subsequent reconciliation in France was but a prelude to a new clash. Becket returned to England and Henry, in one of his notorious rages, thundered, 'Is there no one who will rid me of this low-born priest?' Four of his knights took his words at their face value, crossed the Channel so swiftly as to elude the couriers sent to stop them, and after a stormy interview with the archbishop, cut him down in cold blood before the altar in the north transept of the cathedral. The repercussions of the crime were momentous. In the archbishop's martyrdom and the sub-

Caen, appointed archbishop by William the Conqueror, and enthroned amidst the ruins resulting from a disastrous fire in 1067. His hasty and rather unambitious reconstruction in the style of the great *Abbaye aux Hommes* at Caen, soon proved quite inadequate, and by the beginning of the twelfth century the area of the eastern arm had been doubled in a new building programme. The vast Norman crypt with its labyrinthine forest of columns still survives today. The superstructure, designed by a master-mason named Blitherus, completed in 1126 during the time of Prior Conrad, was, according to the chroniclers, without equal for grandeur and beauty in all England. Its existence was, however, destined to be shortlived. Only forty-eight years later 'the Glorious Choir of Conrad' was destroyed by fire. The monk, Gervase of Canterbury, has

sequent humiliation of the king, who did penance by walking barefoot through the streets of Canterbury and submitting to a scourging at Becket's tomb, the Church had found a redoubtable weapon in its struggle with the secular powers. Becket was canonized and the cult of St Thomas purposefully fostered. Numerous miracles were reported at his tomb and the pilgrimage to Canterbury, immortalized in Chaucer's 'Canterbury Tales', became one of the most important in Europe; altars and chapels dedicated to St Thomas throughout the length and breadth of Christendom served as a permanent reminder of the results of rebellion against the authority of the Church.

No trace survives of the church used by St Augustine, and hardly a vestige from the time of Lanfranc, the aged Abbot of

198 *Left* Branches of the *Tree of Jesse* entwine Old Testament kings and prophets; detail from the 'Golden Window'. *Wells*

199 *Above left* View in the Trinity Chapel which formerly housed the shrine of St Thomas Becket; in the background a glimpse of the Corona Chapel. *Canterbury*

200 *Above right* The chevet and the tower-like termination of the Corona Chapel. *Canterbury*

201 *Overleaf* The high finish made possible by carving with a chisel instead of shaping with an axe; detail of the Corinthianesque capitals of the Trinity Chapel. *Canterbury*

left a vivid eye-witness account of the disaster and a detailed and accurate description of the rebuilding in the Gothic style.

On September 5, 1174, a fire destroyed three cottages near the cathedral, sending smouldering cinders, carried by the violent wind, to the cathedral, where they lodged between the joints of the roofing material and started a fire, 'concealed between the well-painted ceiling below and the sheet-lead above'. It was only when the lead started to melt that the alarm was raised:

'See! see! the church is on fire.

'The people and the monks assemble in haste, they draw water, brandish their hatchets, they run up the stairs, full of eagerness to save the church already, alas! beyond their help. But when they reach the roof and perceive the black smoke and scorching flames that pervade it throughout, they abandon the attempt in despair, and, thinking only of their own safety, make haste to descend ... and when the half-burnt timbers fell onto the choir below upon the seats of the monks, the seats caught fire and thus the mischief grew worse and worse. And it was marvellous, though sad, to behold how that glorious choir itself fed and assisted the fire that was destroying it ... And now the people ran to the ornaments of the church, and began to tear down the pallia and curtains, some that they might save, but some to steal them, while the reliquary chests were thrown down from the high beam and thus broken, and their contents scattered ... In this manner the house of God, hitherto delightful as a paradise of pleasure, was reduced to a despicable heap of ashes' (3).

The monks 'put together as well as they could, an altar and station in the nave of the church, where they might wail and howl rather than sing', and expert advice was sought in both England and France on how best to repair the burnt choir. Opinions differed: some masters thought the damaged piers could be repaired, others asserted that the entire choir would have to be demolished. Eventually the work was entrusted to a Frenchman, William of Sens, 'a man of lively genius and good reputation ... and as a workman most skilful both in wood and stone'. He seems also to have been a good psychologist. Realizing that the existing work would have to be demolished, he 'yet for some time concealed what he found to be done, lest the truth should kill the monks in their present state ...' Meanwhile, he started preparing for the rebuilding and when the monks had regained their spirits he told them the worst and they consented 'patiently if not willingly to the destruction of the choir'.

Since the stone was to be brought from Caen in Normandy, William of Sens 'constructed ingenious machines for loading and unloading ships ... delivered moulds and templates for shaping the stones to the sculptors ... and diligently prepared other things of the same kind.' Preparations for the new work took up the first year, but by the summer of 1178 several bays of the choir had already been vaulted. Then, while the master was up on the scaffolding superintending the construction of the vaults, the beams broke under his feet and he fell to the ground from the height of fifty feet. Crippled 'by the vengeance of God or spite of the devil', the master continued to direct building operations from his bed for some time, and several more vaulting bays were successfully completed. Then, seeing that he would not recover, William the Frenchman returned

to his homeland and was succeeded by William the Englishman, 'small in body, but in workmanship of many kinds acute and honest'.

Gervase seems to have been singularly sensitive to the radical departure from tradition in the new Gothic choir. In a passage remarkable for its acute analysis of style, he notes especially the comparative slenderness of the new supports and the new emphasis on height. Thus, while the cylindrical piers were of equal diameter to the old, the new piers were twelve feet higher and the new interior higher by the entire height of the clerestory windows. Exceptionally interesting is his awareness of a new aesthetic in which the structure itself affords satisfaction: the choir had formerly been covered with 'a ceiling of wood, decorated with excellent painting, but here is a vault beautifully constructed of stone and light tufa'. The greatly improved standards of masonry technique seem to have struck Gervase most forcibly. The limited amount of decorative sculpture in the old cathedral had, he notes, been cut with an axe, while the lavish new decoration was delicately chiselled. The contrast between the crudely executed work in the Romanesque crypt and the superb new Corinthianesque capitals, especially those of the coupled columns of the Trinity Chapel, is certainly astonishing (Plate 201).

Hardly surprisingly, the design of William of Sens follows contemporary French practice and in particular reflects the influence of the new Gothic cathedral of his home town. The extremely curious contraction of the Canterbury choir (Fig. 15) was due to the desire to preserve the two obliquely placed Norman chapels of St Anselm and St Andrew, while the typical French plan was modified to comply with the

202 *Previous page* The Corona Chapel, built to house the severed scalp of St Thomas Becket. *Canterbury*

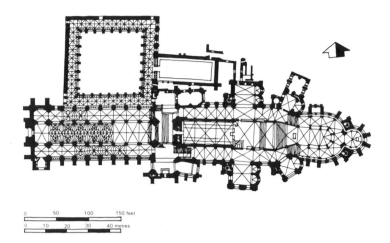

Fig. 15 Ground plan. *Canterbury*

English desire for length; this was particularly appropriate here in view of the many elaborate processions of both clergy and pilgrims to the tomb of St Thomas. Upon the completion of the choir the body of the martyr had been removed to a generous (and once again wider) space behind the high altar, where it was housed in a magnificent gold-plated shrine, richly adorned with precious jewels including the '*Régale de France*' donated by Louis VII in 1179. Reputedly the finest ruby in Europe, it was mounted as a ring for Henry VIII when the shrine of 'the traitor Becket' was demolished at his command. Today the climactic goal of pilgrimage is an empty space and only the marble pavement, deeply indented by the knees of the devout, testifies to the fact that this was once one of the holiest places of Christendom.

The *coup de grâce* dealt Becket by the assassins was delivered with such force that the top of his scalp was cut off. This relic was housed separately in a chapel further extending the east end, the appropriately-named and appropriately-shaped *Corona* or 'Becket's Crown' (Plate 202). Like the apsidal termination housing the shrine, it dates from the period of 'William the Englishman' but, as such authorities as Geoffrey Webb believe, might well represent the execution of a design already envisaged by William of Sens (4). The rather indiscriminate mixture of round and pointed arches is typical of this period of transition from Romanesque to Gothic. The use of dark shafts of Purbeck marble contrasts strikingly with the light stone. Although the ultimate origin of this decorative motif is disputed – earlier examples existing both in England and in northern France and Belgium – it was only in England that it became a really important feature of Gothic design, where it contributed to the incisive character which was so congenial to the English temperament. Equally English is the tendency to retain whatever can be salvaged from the past and to build piecemeal, so that instead of the relatively homogeneous character of the French cathedrals, at least conceived as a whole, we are usually confronted with an assemblage of elements of widely differing styles and dates, which gain in historic interest what they lack in unity. Another example, already mentioned, is to be found in the retention of the two Norman chapels which were allowed to compromise the whole new design.

Despite the wealth which poured into the cathedral coffers,

almost two centuries elapsed after the completion of the choir before the Norman nave of Lanfranc – by then in danger of collapse – was rebuilt in the late-Gothic, so-called 'Perpendicular' style. The name is particularly apposite when applied to the nave of Canterbury with its triumphant vertical line (Plate 203). The spatial unity so sought after at this period was here achieved by raising the nave arcade at the expense of the clerestory, so that there is a marked integration of the volumes of the nave and the aisles, whose high windows provide the main source of light; an effect approaching that of the German 'hall-church'. The designer was Henry Yevele (1320-1400), the royal mason, who also worked at Old St Pauls and Westminster and whose well-documented architectural career was one of the most successful, both socially and financially, of the entire Gothic period (5).

In 1493 work started on the splendid Bell Harry Tower which provided a sorely needed focal point for the straggling composition (Plate 204). Although the crossing piers had been strengthened to receive the additional weight, they soon showed signs of failure through buckling and John Wastell, the architect of the tower, erected the pierced strainer arches which contribute so much to the drama and mystery of the lantern with its beautiful fan-vaulting – the final triumph of the national Gothic style that was born here at Canterbury (Plate 205).

204 *Above* View of Canterbury in 1804 by J. Buckler showing the central Bell Harry tower which provided a much needed focal point for the straggling composition. Note the Norman north tower of the west front; it was demolished in 1834 and replaced with a replica of the south tower.

203 *Left* View up into the lierne vault of the nave, one of the greatest triumphs of the Perpendicular style. *Canterbury*

205 *Overleaf* The openwork strainer arches introduced to prevent the buckling of the crossing piers under the weight of the central tower. *Canterbury*

Lincoln

In 1185 an earthquake shook the hill which provides the cathedral of Lincoln with such a splendid site, necessitating the reconstruction of all but the monumental west front and west towers of the Norman minster. The new cathedral, in a style no longer transitional but Gothic, was commenced by Bishop Hugh, a Carthusian monk from Avalon near Grenoble, who was a rare combination of mystic, intellectual and able administrator. The man in charge of the works, Geoffrey de Noier, the *constructor a fundamentis* as he is referred to in documents, was equally remarkable. The name is French, and he is sometimes supposed to be a member of a Norman family domiciled for some generations in England. Certainly, as critics from Viollet-le-Duc to the present day have consistently noted, the work at Lincoln is a foretaste of the typically English approach to the Gothic style. Brilliantly inventive, Geoffrey seems to have taken an almost perverse delight in the unusual, culminating in the design of the vaulting of St Hugh's choir which the Rev. Robert Willis so aptly described as 'crazy' (Plate 206).

To the nineteenth-century critics, judging from the rationalist viewpoint of their day, there had to be some practical motivation behind this bizarre design, and various ingenious but unconvincing theories were produced to prove that the intention had been structural, or aimed at a more even distribution of light. With the twentieth century and a recognition, and a positive relish, of the irrational element in artistic creation, we no longer feel compelled to discover a practical motive, and are quite as likely to find Geoffrey's design stimulating, rather than disquieting, and to agree with Paul Frankl's contention that it provides 'a delightful note of dissonance in the melody and polyphony of the cathedral as a whole . . . the salt without which Lincoln Cathedral would lose so much of its savor' (6).

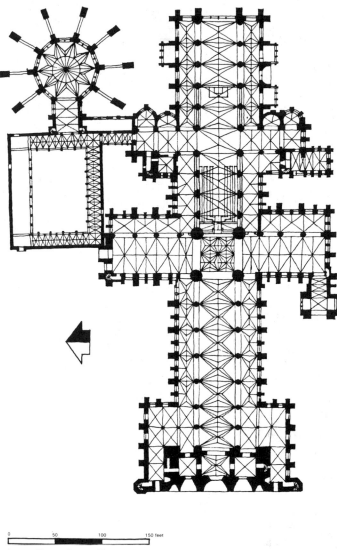

Fig. 16 Ground plan. *Lincoln*

206 *Below* The 'crazy vaults' of St Hugh's choir. *Lincoln*

Although the asymmetrical arrangement of the vaults of Lincoln had no successors, they are prophetic of many of the most characteristic developments of late-Gothic – and this in a structure contemporary with Chartres (7). Until this time vaults had been either quadripartite or sexpartite with the bay structure clearly defined. Here the definition of the individual bay is blurred and instead there is a continuous zig-zag movement in depth, stabilized, and at the same time accelerated by the longitudinal ridge rib. In the additional tierceron ribs which perform no structural function we have the first conscious exploitation of the decorative potentialities of vaulting ribs for their own sake, and in this sense all the gossamer patterns of lierne, star and fan vaults trace their parentage to the 'crazy vaults' of Lincoln.

Equally original is Geoffrey's double arcading of the aisle walls in which conventional blank-arcading in limestone has superimposed over it a second tier of trefoil arches supported on Purbeck shafts placed in the centre line of the back arcade (Plate 211). Again we have the syncopated rhythm propelling us forward irresistibly down the aisle, coupled with a sideward movement of illusory depth: the crisp contrast between the dark Purbeck shafts of the front tier and the light background into which the shafts of the further arcade blend almost imperceptibly, appears to increase the distance between the two tiers (8). Geoffrey's successor(s) returned to straightforward sexpartite vaulting in the main transepts and regularized and further elaborated his crazy vaults to create a superbly decorative tierceron star vault in the nave (Plate 209).

Construction had commenced, as was customary, at the east end; scarcely had the nave been finished and the magnificent Norman west front (Plate 197) enlarged on both sides and at the top, to create a spectacular, if inorganic screen-façade bearing no relationship whatever to the structure behind, when it was decided to rebuild the east end. The reason was to relieve the congestion resulting from the streams of pilgrims visiting the tomb behind the high altar of Bishop Hugh, canonized as 'St Hugh of Lincoln'. The original layout with its polygonal apse – as eccentric in detail as one would have expected from Master Geoffrey – was, nevertheless, basically a modification of the French chevet, but in the rebuilding a characteristically English square termination was substituted. The influence of the Cistercians who also favoured this treatment can, at most, only partly explain this deep-seated national preference for a square-ended chancel dating back to Saxon times. John Harvey (9) has advanced the interesting and plausible theory – although not accepted by all authorities – that the fundamental reason was a preoccupation with the correct orientation of chapel altars, and that this in turn stemmed from pagan customs which in some parts of the country only finally succumbed to Christianity in the ninth century. The sub-conscious memory of a solar-cult would, he maintains, also account for the seeming obsession with the rays of the rising sun falling on the altar.

Certainly, no more fitting setting for a paean to the sun

207 *Above* Silver chalice and paten with the *manus Dei* from the tomb of Bishop Gravesend, died 1279. *Lincoln*

208 *Above right* The Angel Choir seen from the triforium of the gallery; note the lavish use of crockets decorating even the ridge rib of the vaulting. *Lincoln*

209 *Right* The nave looking east. *Lincoln*

could be imagined than the new choir, although the brilliance of the light flooding the interior through the glorious, eight-light, traceried east window, no less than 59 feet high, must – the question of precise orientation apart – surely be simply another example of the Gothic preoccupation with light; at Lincoln this would probably assume especial sig-

The Angel Choir, so-called from the varied sculptured angels with outstretched wings in the spandrels of the triforium arcade, must be numbered among the very finest achievements of English Gothic, alike in its lofty spirituality, serene proportions and the variety, interest and exquisite quality of every detail of the exuberant, but perfectly controlled, decoration. Here too, the combination of Purbeck marble and light stone received its consummate expression in the triforium arcade (Plate 208). Equally fascinating is the treatment of the clerestory windows. Although the elegant bar tracery was an importation from Rheims via Westminster Abbey, the extraordinarily rich, three-dimensional effect of the double tiers of tracery must be credited to the national genius. Already at Canterbury the thick wall of the clerestory, a legacy from Anglo-Norman building practice, had been divided by a passageway into an outer and inner wall. In the early work at Lincoln this feature was further elaborated, the outer skin consisting of lancet windows pierced in the wall, the inner skin of an arcade, while here, in the Angel Choir, the two elements have been moulded into a compelling unity.

Geoffrey de Noier's original central tower had collapsed and had been replaced by a new tower erected between 1238 and 1255 by Master Alexander, elaborately decorated with the diagonal lattice or trellis pattern so favoured by this master. In the early fourteenth century the tower was extended according to the designs of Richard of Stowe to a height of 271 feet to form the highest, and certainly one of the finest, central towers in England (Plate 215). Towards the end of the fourteenth century a similar extension of the western towers was completed, and all three towers crowned with tall needle

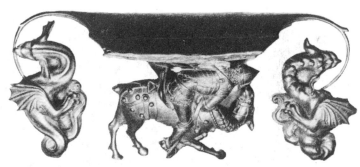

210 *Top* The main south transept and the 'Bishop's Eye'. *Lincoln*

211 *Above left* The staggered double arcading of the choir aisles by Geoffrey de Noier. *Lincoln*

212 *Above right* The sculptured angels with outstretched wings in the spandrels of the triforium arcade, which give their name to the angel choir. *Lincoln*

213 *Above* A wounded knight, probably intended as a symbolic fall of pride; 14th-century misericord from the choir. *Lincoln*

214 *Overleaf* Detail of the arcade of the angel choir; at the base of the richly carved corbel is the 'Lincoln Imp'. *Lincoln*

215 *Overleaf* The central tower: the lower half with its characteristic trellis pattern is mid 13th-century, the upper portion early 14th-century. *Lincoln*

nificance, for the bishop from 1235 to 1253 was the great Robert Grosseteste, scientist and scholar, pioneer in education and author of a celebrated treatise on optics, in which he extolled light as the 'most noble of natural phenomena . . . the mediator between bodiless and bodily substances: a spiritual body and embodied spirit'.

spires of wood covered with lead, forming what must have been a truly awe-inspiring composition. The spire over the crossing, reputed to have soared to 524 feet, was destroyed by a gale in 1584, those of the western towers surviving until 1807.

This has been but a sampling of the riches of Lincoln, ranging from the naive but impressive Norman bas-reliefs of

the west front and the earliest of the polygonal chapter houses that are the glory of English Gothic cathedrals, to the great northern rose facing the deanery and hence nicknamed the 'Dean's Eye', with its virile pattern stamped out of the plate tracery as though from dough; this window makes a pair with the 'Bishop's Eye' in the south transept, with its amazingly original pattern of flowing tracery in the 'Decorated' style inserted in about 1330 and filled with kaleidoscopic fragments of old glass salvaged from windows shattered by gun-fire during the Civil War (Plate 210). Equally outstanding are the stone *pulpitum* or choir-screen and the 'Easter Sepulchre' in the choir with its fine old stalls and misericords, including the celebrated figure of a knight pierced in the back by an arrow and falling from his stumbling horse, probably intended as a symbolic 'Fall of Pride' (Plate 213). All considered, Lincoln has, indeed, a strong claim to be the finest church in England.

216 The nave looking towards the crossing. *Wells*

Wells

The unspoilt little market town of Wells, which has changed so little since the Middle Ages that the cathedral is still but a stone's throw from the open countryside, is the tranquil setting for one of the smallest but most beautiful of English cathedrals, which, in all Europe, best preserves the subordinate buildings of a secular cathedral: cloisters, chapter house and chapter library, fortified gateways leading to the close (like the evocatively named 'Penniless Porch' where alms were distributed to the needy), the walled and moated precincts of the bishop's palace, the fine houses of the dean, archdeacon and chancellor (10), and, most exceptional of all, the Vicar's Close, built in 1348 by Bishop Ralph of Shrewsbury for the accommodation of the vicars or deputies of the canons. Facing each other in two rows, the dwellings each had an upper and a lower chamber and a small private garden, while a tiny chapel at the northern end and a dining hall and kitchen at the south completed the facilities for the virtually self-contained model village. Direct access to the cathedral – avoiding the perils of the public way by night – was later provided by a covered bridge over the 'Chain Gate', connecting with the chapter house.

Tradition credits the foundation of the first church dedicated to St Andrew, near the springs which have given the city its name, to King Ina of Wessex at the beginning of the eighth century. The present cathedral, the earliest Gothic cathedral in England to be built entirely with pointed arches, was begun under Bishop Reginald de Bohun in about 1186. The choir and transepts and the easternmost bays of the nave were completed soon after 1200 and the west front and towers were well under way when the church was consecrated in 1239.

The English fondness for treating a façade as a great screen or reredos for the display of sculpture found its grandest expression at Wells; the 147 foot wide west front created by placing the western towers outside the line of the aisles, together with the sides and returns of the towers, still shelters within niche and marble-shafted *aedicule* 300 of the original 400 figures, constituting the finest ensemble of medieval sculpture in England. Over 150 figures are life-size or larger, and all truly monumental in concept, to a degree rare in England, particularly the alert figures of kings, seated with elbows akimbo – an idiosyncrasy also found in the gallery of kings at Lincoln. The upper stages of the west towers, singularly sensitive and sympathetic additions in the Perpendicular style, were only completed in the fifteenth century, terminating the façade in a worthy manner (Plate 218). The sight must have been even more spectacular in the Middle Ages – if less to our taste today – when enriched with metal ornaments and resplendent with gilt and bright colour, traces of which remain to this day.

'What a contrast between the pitiful little pigeon-holes which stand for doors in the west front . . . looking like the entrances to a beehive or a wasps' nest, and the soaring arches and kingly crowning of the gates of Abbeville, Rouen or Rheims. . .'(11) Ruskin's comments *à propos* the west doors of

217 *Right* The scissor arches introduced at the crossing. *Wells*

218 *Overleaf* The west front. *Wells*

Salisbury apply equally to Wells. The great west portals of France with their richly sculptured jambs and archivolts seem to have exercised singularly little influence on English Gothic. During the Middle Ages the space to the west of Wells Cathedral was occupied by a graveyard and the west doors were rarely opened. The ceremonial entrance, and a worthy one, was by the lavishly-decorated north porch, one of the most notable features of the entire cathedral.

The view that greets the eye on entering the nave from the West is unique, but also characteristically English in its moderate height and the emphatic horizontality achieved by the extraordinary design of the triforium (Plate 216). At Lincoln the vaulting shafts had been carried down over the triforium and the spandrels of the main arcade to terminate in corbels immediately above the pier capitals (Plate 209). In the nave of Wells the shafts terminate above the triforium openings which form a continuous arcade affording no indication of the bay structure. Below, the knife-sharp definition of the string-course further underscores the linear, horizontal emphasis and, as if to stress their purely decorative character, the lancet openings of the triforium have continuous mouldings uninterrupted by capitals.

Around 1320 the central tower in the Decorated style was raised to its present height (12) and almost immediately the crossing piers showed signs of failure. The remedy, in the form of scissor-shaped girders bracing three sides of the crossing – the fourth being sufficiently strengthened by the stone screen shutting off the chancel–has given this cathedral perhaps the most bizarre and sensational structure in all Gothic architecture. Since the cathedral is dedicated to St Andrew, a reference to the saint's diagonal cross of martyrdom was probably intended, but the most potent associations are rather with the dynamic forms of industrial architecture. Disquieting, and certainly not beautiful, the brutally massive strainer arches of Wells, nevertheless, exert an uncanny fascination, contribute enormously to the drama and mystery of the interior, and afford the most exciting and unexpected spatial sensations (Plate 217). They are also of the greatest significance in showing the effect when the English tendency to compartmentalize space is carried to its ultimate conclusion.

In the beginning of the fourteenth century the eastern arm was remodelled and extended in the Decorated style. Extra bays were added to the choir, terminating in a square end with a high east window – the so-called 'Golden Window' from the dominant gold and green colour scheme of the superb original glass of about 1330, in a rare state of preservation but seldom reproduced in detail, for the simple reason that the photographer takes his life in his hands on the narrow triforium gallery (Plate 198). The singularly complex but unattractive vault, overloaded with ornament, may have been a translation into stone of the wooden roof designs found in Somerset, although these can now only be seen in churches of a later period.

219 *Left* View towards the Lady Chapel from the retrochoir. *Wells*

220 *Above right* Stealing fruit in an orchard; a scene carved on a capital in the south transept. *Wells*

221 *Right* Salamander on a corbel bracket. *Wells*

222 *Overleaf* The stairs leading to the chapter house and to the covered way over the Chain Gate. *Wells*

At the same time, a Lady Chapel in the shape of an elongated octagon was built further to the east. Originally intended to be virtually free-standing, three sides of the octagon were later integrally linked with the main structure by the addition of a low retrochoir supported on six slender piers (Plate 219). Surveying the resulting suavely-flowing space – an architectural masterpiece – it is difficult to believe that this extremely complex interpenetration of vaults and volumes was, in a sense, an afterthought. But then, it must be remembered that the very need to improvise and even to compromise, has so often brought forth the best results from the English designer, in art and architecture alike, and that this was the one period when English architecture was in advance of anything in Europe. The final touch of magic is given by the fine sepulchral monuments and the magnificent glass, here a kaleidoscopic patchwork of fourteenth-century fragments whose very abstract character reinforces the timeless atmosphere.

The same very high standard of artistry and workmanship displayed in the sculpture of the west front and the north porch is also maintained in the interior. Particularly remarkable are the magnificent foliage capitals, no two alike, free of the least suggestion of stiffness. In a light vein are such vivacious *genre* scenes as those of the 'Vine Thieves'. In the first of four vignettes, depicted on the four sides of a capital, two thieves steal furtively from an orchard (Plate 220); in the second a farm hand armed with a pitchfork is despatched after them; in the third he has caught one of the thieves red-handed and twists his ear, and in the final sequence administers a thrashing with the pitchfork – all depicted with the clarity and conciseness of a comic strip.

An undercroft with barred windows and stout double doors preserving their original iron fittings, and formerly serving as a treasury, supports the detached chapter house, approached from the north transept by an exceptionally beautiful stairway (Plate 222). Footworn treads trace out the safest path along the steps which casually branch off from the rising flight to the richly traceried archway opening into the little vestibule of the chapter house. These superb polygonal chapter houses are only found in England, usually vaulted in stone to a central pier. The earliest example at Worcester, dating from the twelfth century (though subsequently modified externally) was circular, with the vaulting divided into ten bays. In the thirteenth century came the decagonal chapter house of Lincoln with a span of 59 feet, the second largest built. At Westminster Abbey an octagon, which, among other advantages, gave a greater width for the windows, was adopted, and also used in about 1275 at Salisbury and Wells, where the undercroft determined the layout, while the chapter house itself only dates from the end of the century. At Salisbury structural considerations still dictate the layout of the ribs; at Wells the addition of intermediary ribs, so that altogether there are 32 closely packed ribs spreading in the manner of a palm frond from the central pier, is indicative of a new approach to design in which the decorative element is dominant. The effect at Salisbury is starker, at Wells more elaborate – both are equally beautiful and unsurpassed of their type (Plates 223 and 237).

223 *Previous page* Thirty-two closely packed ribs spread in the manner of a palm frond from the central pier of the chapter house. *Wells*

Peterborough

In 1116 a servant kindling a fire in the great Saxon monastery of St Peter at Peterborough is said to have become impatient and exclaimed, 'May the Devil kindle you!' – the obliging response being so vigorous that church and monastery went up in flames. The present building was erected during the following eighty years and, Durham apart, possesses the most splendid Romanesque interior in England with its stately nave of ten bays, its magnificent wooden ceilings and the original apsidal termination of the choir. At the end of the twelfth century work started on an extension to the west end in the Gothic style. Two additional bays were added to the nave,

224 *Above* The turrets and spires of the west front seen from the north-east. *Peterborough*

225 *Right* The west front with its strange but compelling proportions based on the classical musical consonances, *diapason, diapente,* and *diatesseron. Peterborough*

the second in the form of a west transept surmounted by towers. Further west still, a new front was provided in the form of a portico consisting of three great arches soaring to a height of 82 feet and flanked by buttressing towers surmounted by spirelets (Plate 225).

The truly monumental conception of the Peterborough front – Gothic England's most notable essay in the 'Grand Manner' – is confirmed by the dimensions: the three great arches and the flanking buttresses taking up as great a width

226 View of the predominantly Norman interior looking towards the Gothic west front; the Perpendicular style wooden ceiling over the choir dates from the late 14th century. *Peterborough*

227 Retrochoir with the finest late-Gothic fan vaults in any cathedral. *Peterborough*

as the west front of Wells with its myriad statues, and almost one-and-a-half times the width of the Norman west front of Lincoln before it was extended by the Gothic additions. As Geoffrey Webb has so ably demonstrated in his fascinating essay on the Peterborough design (13), it was this Norman work at Lincoln which was the primary source of inspiration (Plate 197). The most puzzling feature of the Peterborough design is that the central arch, which might have been expected to be wider, or at least as wide, as the side arches is, in fact, far narrower. Such a deliberate flouting of an almost universally accepted canon of proportion in a design of this calibre seemed so extraordinary that most critics have felt the only explanation could lie in a modification of the original design which, for example, might have envisaged two smaller side arches occupying the space now taken up by the single wide arch.

Geoffrey Webb has, however, produced a most original but convincing theory that the arrangement, 'far from being a chance expedient, formed part of a highly intellectualized and

ambitious design.' According to his interpretation, the central archway surmounted by its gable was intended to be seen as a narrow link between two dominant masses comprising the side arches, gables and turrets, the flanking buttress towers and their spires *and the higher towers over the western transepts*. The strange outward displacement of the turrets on either side of the central gable should, Webb maintains, be considered not as a belated effort to give greater breadth and dignity to the central entrance, but rather as a means of stressing their intended relationship with the very similar turrets of the towers above.

The fact that the transept towers can *not* be seen as an integral part of the composition of the façade, that the gables acting alone are out of scale with the great arches below, and that the front as it stands must in some respects be judged a failure – albeit a glorious one, infinitely superior to a petty success – is the result, not so much of inherent defects in the conception, but of the fact that only the northern of the two transept towers was ever built and even that has lost its spire. In the mind's eye add the missing tower and two tall crowning spires and, as Geoffrey Webb showed by trick photography, the balance of the composition is restored and the true potentialities of the design realized, particularly if one also effaces the inappropriate late-fourteenth-century porch whose squat proportions and hard, insensitive detailing contrast so sadly with the vigorous plasticity of the thirteenth-century work. One of the most fascinating features of the west front is its proportional scheme. The height of the façade, to the string-course over the arches, is exactly half the overall width (the favoured double-square relationship also used at Wells); the width of the central arch is two-thirds that of the side arches, in turn three-quarters that of the side arches plus the buttress tower, which is half the width of the central arch. The entire

228 *Right* Detail of the powerful yet elegant mouldings of the huge piers of the west front. *Peterborough*

scheme is, therefore, governed by the ratios 1:2, 2:3 and 3:4 which correspond to the classical musical consonances, *diapason* (octave), *diapente* (fifth) and *diatessaron* (fourth) which, as we have seen, were credited with a profound mystic significance. Only towards the end of the fifteenth century was work commenced on 'The New Building', an extension to the east end in the Perpendicular style. Large windows were pierced in the central Norman apse, the lateral apses removed and the aisles extended and joined by a square-ended retrochoir, covered with the finest of the late-Gothic fanvaults to be found in any cathedral (14) (Plate 227). This is hardly surprising since the designer, John Wastell, was also responsible for the incomparable vaults of King's College Chapel at Cambridge.

The earliest manuscript in the fully mature, East Anglian style is the Psalter in the *Bibliothèque Royale* in Brussels, produced about 1300 for Peterborough, then an important centre of art production. The *Beatus* title page (from *Beatus vir*, the opening words in Latin of Psalm I) is wonderfully opulent, decorative and crowded with enchanting incidental details (Plate 79). Small wonder that these East Anglian manuscripts enjoyed such a vogue throughout Europe, where they provided one of the formative influences in the development of Flemish and Netherlandish illumination. The 'Peterborough Psalter' has an additional interest since some of the religious figures and scenes are considered to have been inspired by the twelfth century paintings formerly in the choir of the abbey church. Dissolved by Henry VIII, the monastery of Peterborough was reconstituted as a cathedral on September 4, 1541.

229 *Below* Thirteenth-century piscina, where the priest washed the sacred vessels during mass; north choir aisle. *Peterborough*

Salisbury

Salisbury is the sole example in England of a Gothic cathedral built without interruption to a uniform plan and on a virgin site. The seat of the see had formerly been at Old Sarum, a couple of miles to the north, within a fortified *enceinte,* successively Roman, Saxon and Norman. The wind howled around the exposed hill-top site, 'so that the choristers could often hardly hear each other sing', and there were other and more serious disadvantages such as a constant water-shortage and friction with the military garrison. These finally induced Bishop Richard Poore in 1217 to petition the Pope for permission to move the cathedral. This was granted in 1219 and a new cathedral commenced the following year on a spacious level site in the plains, bounded on two sides by the River Avon. The inhabitants of Old Sarum followed their bishop and a new town, neatly laid out on a grid pattern, arose alongside the cathedral.

Unhampered by existing work or the exigencies of a restricted or difficult site, and with adequate financial resources, the plan of the cathedral may reasonably be taken to represent

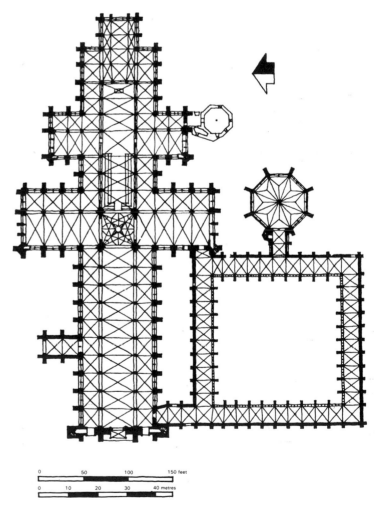

Fig. 17 Ground plan. *Salisbury*

230 *Right* Detail of the west front: a sculptured cliff. *Wells*

the 'ideal solution' as conceived by an English mind working within the high-Gothic Scholastic tradition. It proved to be an uncompromisingly lucid and orderly solution, symmetrical except for the northern porch and later cloister and chapter house, and entirely free of those picturesque irregularities which we are apt to attribute to the medieval mentality, but which were so often enforced by external circumstances. National preferences and the requirements of ritual have been given free expression in the great length, the boldly-projecting double transepts and the square-ended, eastern terminations, producing a completely different composition from Amiens, commenced in the same year. A leading rôle in the conception of the design is generally attributed to the artistically inclined canon, Elias de Dereham, who is known to have worked on the shrine of St Thomas at Canterbury and to have been connected with several building projects; the actual master-mason was Nicholas of Ely. Rising in dignified isolation from a lawn dotted with great trees, Salisbury presents the classic picture of the cathedral in a pastoral setting, at the opposite remove from the bustle surrounding those on the continent. Equally English is the arrangement of box-like mass added to box-like mass, building up into a stepped pyramidal composition, given coherence by the focal point of the superb tower and spire added a century later by Master Richard of Farleigh in the Decorated style – an addition infinitely more monumental and aspiring than anything the original builders could have contemplated. This is truly the crowning glory of Salisbury, proportioned with impeccable care and in its lively and exuberant detail providing a perfect foil to the rather cool, prim, reserved forms of the Early English style (Plate 232).

Rising to 404 feet, the stone spire ranks second in beauty only to the southern tower of Chartres (Plate 234). In both cases a convincing sense of scale has been conveyed, even at a great height, by vigorous texture: at Chartres by the bold, overall fish-scale pattern which somehow escapes any suggestion of coarseness; at Salisbury by the even more daring alternation of plain and diagonally diapered segments, each of which enhances the other.

Architecturally, the finest view of Salisbury is undoubtedly that from the North-East (Plate 232), but for romantic ambience the vista from the South-West is unsurpassed, although the wide-spreading front, modelled on Wells but falling sadly short of that masterpiece, has little to recommend it except the glorious colouring of the weathered, lichen-encrusted Chilmark stone, the architectural elements lacking co-ordination and little of the original sculpture surviving (Plate 231). Building operations had commenced at the east end, and by 1226 the Lady Chapel (15) had been completed. This opens off a retrochoir of the same height and is itself divided into a nave and narrow aisles of equal height, thus constituting a miniature 'hall-church'. The supports are

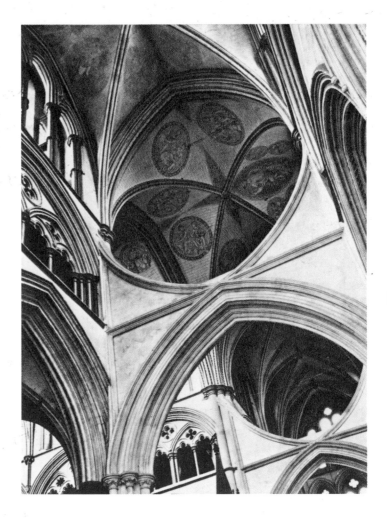

231 *Left* The cathedral in a landscape setting. *Salisbury*

232 *Top right* View from the north-east with the pyramidal composition dominated by Richard of Farleigh's tower and spire. *Salisbury*

233 *Bottom right* The scissor arches introduced to strengthen the piers of the eastern transepts; the figure paintings on the ceiling are Victorian restorations of 13th-century originals. *Salisbury*

234 *Overleaf* Detail of the great tower. *Salisbury*

entirely of Purbeck marble, clusters of detached shafts in the retrochoir, and in the Lady Chapel, incredibly slender, single shafts which have been compared rather unkindly, but with some justice, to stove pipes (16). Together with the acutely pointed arches of the vaulting, the effect is one of buoyant weightlessness.

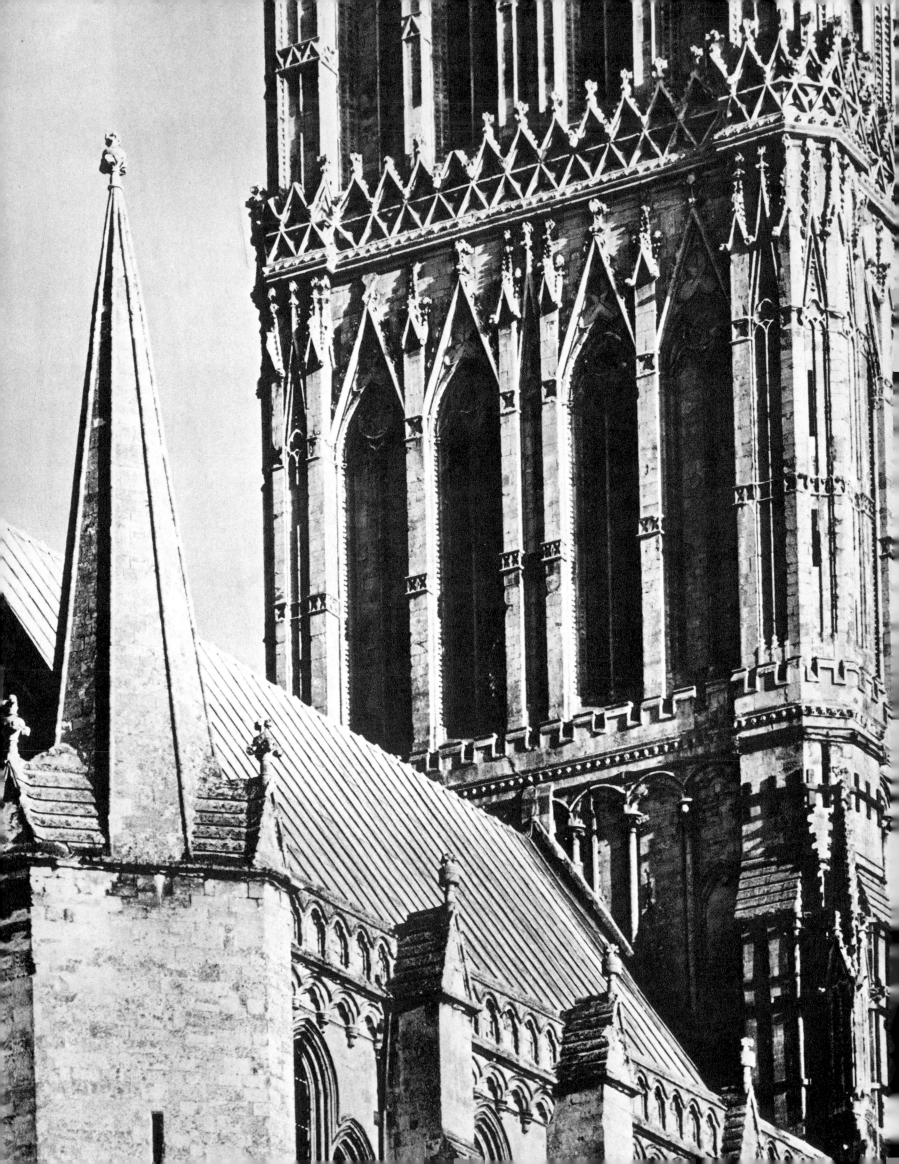

Purbeck marble is everywhere in evidence at Salisbury, even being used for the great drums of the nave piers (Plate 235). The most unfortunate feature of the interior is the triforium in the form of a 'false-tribune' opening into the roof space over the aisles – that strange English compromise between the transitional tribune gallery (of Laon, for example) and the developed French triforium. Lack of sufficient height for the design adopted dictated the unattractive expedient of causing the arches to spring obliquely from the clustered piers, the squat effect being further aggravated by the exclusive use of dark marble shafting for the colonnettes, so that their valuable vertical accents are lost against the dark void, and the heads of the arches with their elaborate plate tracery appear suspended in space. It need hardly be pointed out how typically English is the emphatic horizontal subdivision that ensues.

By 1258, thirty-eight years after work was commenced, the interior was complete and the only subsequent structural changes were the sealing off of the later central tower with an elaborate lierne vault, the insertion across the main transepts of pierced strainer girders (similar to those at Canterbury) and the singularly successful scissor arches strengthening the eastern transepts, an example of English improvisation at its most brilliant (Plate 233). The cool perfection of Salisbury is nowhere more evident, or less attractive than in the nave, where the effects of the loss of the old glass which must so effectively have warmed and softened the interior, have been aggravated by the worst feature of James Wyatt's restoration: the ruthless removal of the chantry chapels and any other features which compromised the neatness or obstructed the vistas so dear to the eighteenth century, and the marshalling

of the tombs he deemed worthy to survive on the podium joining the nave columns, thereby drawing further attention to this original but unhappy feature (Plate 235) (17).

The cloisters, completed in 1284, are the earliest to survive unchanged and also the largest of any English cathedral even though strictly speaking fulfilling no practical function in a secular cathedral, except the minor convenience of covered access to the chapter house (Plate 237), which could easily have been arranged at a fraction of the cost of the cloister.

The tunnel-like proportions of the cloister walk are rather oppressive despite its spaciousness, due to the same excessive ratio of width to height which marks the triforium. The four-light openings with their rich Geometrical-Decorative tracery above are, however, superb in their sturdy strength and elegance, equally attractive seen in silhouette from the shady walk or from the garth with its two vast and magnificent cedars of Lebanon, which contribute greatly to the charm of the ensemble; the trees and cloisters provide a further example of the English gift for integrating architecture and nature, which is the special lesson of Salisbury (Plate 236).

235 *Previous page* View of the nave from the south aisle. *Salisbury*

236 *Below* The geometric tracery of the cloister walk seen through the branches of a cedar. *Salisbury*

237 *Right* Detail of the vaulting of the chapter house. *Salisbury*

York

It was at York, an important Roman city, that Constantine the Great was proclaimed Caesar, and in a wooden church on the site of the *praetorium* that Edwin, King of Northumbria, was received into the Church in the year 627 after his conversion through the efforts of his Christian wife, Ethelburga, daughter of that Ethelbert of Kent who had been baptized by St Augustine. Under the celebrated scholar, Alcuin (735-804), York became one of the greatest centres of learning in Europe.

The oldest part of the present minster, excepting the Norman crypt, is the south transept with its over-scaled wheel window, constructed under Archbishop Walter de Gray between about 1220 and 1241, and immediately followed by the north transept with the *pièce de résistance* of the entire cathedral: the five slender lancet windows 53 feet high and only 5 feet wide, known as 'The Five Sisters'. They provide a superb frame for the finest ensemble of thirteenth-century *grisaille* glass in Europe (Plate 242). In addition to the generous endowments of the archbishopric, pilgrims to the tomb of St William of York, a former archbishop and great-grandson of William the Conqueror, provided an important source of revenue. Given this strong financial basis the new transepts were conceived on an unprecedented scale. The 102 foot high vaults, the highest in England, Westminster Abbey apart, and their wide span, posed considerable problems and the structurally unenterprising designer(s) opted for a simple solution, imitation vaults in oak, originally painted to simulate stone, but left in their natural colour after the last restoration, creating a striking effect (Plate 240).

The fine vista across the transepts, culminating in 'The Five Sisters', was only opened up at the beginning of the fifteenth century, when the far smaller Norman lantern tower was replaced by the present monumental structure – also the largest of its kind in England – admitting a flood of light and with its vault hovering 180 feet above the pavement. The work was carried out under the direction of the king's mason, William of Colchester, lent to the chapter by Henry IV in an attempt to regain favour at York after his execution of Archbishop Scrope following an unsuccessful rebellion. The strong feeling against the king as much as the promotion of an outsider, may account for William's initially hostile reception at York, where his assistant was killed and he himself barely escaped, and had to appeal for protection to the king.

In the Decorated style chapter house completed in about 1296, the desire for unimpeded space took the form of dispensing with the customary central pier and this enforced the use of a wooden vault. The rippling movement of the elaborate stone canopies of the stalls ranged round the perimeter is typical of the plastic, three-dimensional forms favoured at this period. Remarkable are the numerous whimsical and humorous carvings. Adjoining the entrance door is a Latin inscription, '*Ut rosa phlos phlorum sic est domus ista domorum*' (As the rose is the flower of flowers, so is this the (chapter) house of (chapter) houses) – a charming tribute, but one which could surely only have been made by someone unfamiliar with, or deliberately blind to, the claims of Lincoln, Salisbury or Wells.

The nave, commenced at about the same time, is remarkable chiefly for its size and such stylistic trends as the integration of clerestory and triforium into one unit which look forward to later developments. In this case high stone vaults do seem to have been intended originally, despite the span of over 45 feet, but the York expedient of wooden vaults was again used. Only completed around the middle of the fourteenth century, and possibly as late as 1370, the wood vaults and, particularly, the junction with the stone springers, are singularly unhappy visually. The finest feature is the great west

238 *Above left* View from the south-east. *York*

239 *Left* Detail of the tracery of the great west window, popularly known as 'The Heart of Yorkshire'. *York*

240 *Right* View of the interesting triforium and clerestory of the north transept covered with oak vaulting. *York*

window of 1338 where the regimented rows of saints beneath elaborate canopies characteristic of the glass of the period are effectively relieved of monotony by the exuberant curvilinear tracery of the head (Plate 239).

In the choir, too, rebuilt between 1361 and 1400, it is the windows that are the most memorable feature and fittingly so, for despite being the largest medieval church in England (after the destruction of Old St Paul's), York Minster is not, with the exception of the transepts, chapter house and central lantern, particularly distinguished from an architectural point of view. Its true claim to fame derives rather from its great collection of medieval glass, reputedly totalling half of all that survives in England.

Intrinsically the finest specimens are a few twelfth-century panels from the Norman church and the thirteenth-century *grisaille* of 'The Five Sisters'. Typical of the Decorated style glass of the early fourteenth century are the series of windows of the nave aisles in which bands of colourless glass, decorated with the heraldic shields which begin to feature so prominently even in the ecclesiastical art of the period (18), separate a double row of figure compositions in full colour (Plate 243). Beautiful borders, many with lively sketches of birds and animals, outline each light, unifying the composition and preventing too emphatic a horizontal tie between the lights. Another subtle refinement is that the border of the central light is always different from the matching borders of the side lights.

The great east window of the Lady Chapel in the Perpendicular style, 72 feet high by 31 feet wide, dates from the beginning of the fifteenth century and retains virtually all its original glass. Although the glass covers approximately the same area as a tennis court, it is composed entirely of small scenes and figures, executed with great delicacy and verve and full of lively incident and detail (Plate 146). The window is exceptionally well documented. Even the contract between the Dean and Chapter and the artist, John Thornton of Coventry, has survived, whereby he undertook to finish the work within the three years from 1405 to 1408, 'painting the histories, figures and other things with his own hand'. In return he was to receive a wage of 4s a week, an extra £5 each year and a bonus of £10 on completion of the work. The cost of the materials and the wages of his assistants were to be borne by the Chapter. John Thornton made his reputation and later set up his own shop at York, at this time an important centre of stained-glass design, although to the end of the medieval period only white glass was produced in England, all the coloured glass being imported.

In the topmost panel of the window God the Father holding open a book with the words, 'I am the Alpha and Omega', presides over a convocation of angels and saints filling the traceried head of the window. Below, 117 panels, each a yard square, depict episodes from the Old Testament and the Apocalypse – a stupendous achievement, even if the consistently fine craftsmanship seldom rises to the level of greatness.

Ely

The guiding spirit behind the foundation of the great Abbey of Ely was that extraordinary woman, St Etheldreda, who managed to survive two marriages – the second, of twelve years' duration, to Ecgfrid, King of Northumbria – and remain a virgin. Having finally obtained her husband's permission to become a nun, she returned in 673 to the Isle of Ely which she had inherited from her first husband, founded a monastery and, as abbess, became in the words of the Venerable Bede, 'the virgin mother of very many virgins dedicated to God'.

After her death, her sister Sexburga succeeded as abbess, translated Etheldreda's body to the church, and there occurred the first of many miracles at the tomb which made it a famous goal of pilgrimage. Rebuilt after the destruction and carnage of the Danish invasion of 870, the monastery surrounded by virtually impenetrable fen country became the focal point of Hereward the Wake's last stand against William the Conqueror. Before the end, the monastery made its peace with the Conqueror and was duly recompensed: not only was it spared, but the great Norman church which still today survives in large part, was commenced in 1083 and completed in 1189, the whole being carried out in the Romanesque style.

The first addition in the Gothic style was the elegant Galilee Porch (19) at the base of the single, central west tower, erected at the beginning of the thirteenth century (Plate 244). This was followed between 1239 and 1259 by the demolition of the Norman apse and the extension of the choir by six bays, terminating in a flat east end, in a style that anticipated many of the features of the Angel Choir of Lincoln, commenced soon after. In 1321 work started on an ambitious new Lady Chapel to the north of the choir, but when scarcely under way, a new and far more pressing task presented itself. The piers supporting the Norman lantern tower over the crossing had long shown signs of failure, but beyond the precaution of no longer holding services in the choir, then located beneath the crossing, nothing was done. In 1322 the piers crumbled and the tower collapsed, falling towards the east and destroying several bays of the choir. From the disaster stemmed the great glory of Ely: the sensational octagon and lantern.

It may possibly have been the sight of the monumental space created when the debris of the crossing piers was cleared away which inspired the revolutionary idea of doing without these piers and forming a great octagonal central space, the

241 *Below* Fourteenth-century carvings over the south door of the nave; in the centre Samson dressed as a knight fights a bear; on the left he subdues a lion but is unaware that his hair has been cut by Delilah, who on the right makes fun of him. *York*

242 *Right* 'The Five Sisters' window. *York*

width of nave plus aisles, a concept credited in the chronicles to the sacrist, Alan of Walsingham. After the usual delay in finding suitable stone and arranging for its transport, which here also involved strengthening the roads and bridges along the route – described at length in the Fabric Rolls – the walls of the irregular octagon, with four short and four long sides, corresponding to the main axes, were soon under way. It was, however, one thing to conceive such a monumental space, quite another matter successfully to roof it. The enormous weight of a stone vault spanning almost 70 feet pointed rather to the use of timber, a material in which the skill of the English Gothic masters was unrivalled. Indeed, in many secular buildings particularly the great halls with their magnificent exposed wooden roofs, it was the master-carpenter rather than the master-mason who was in charge of building operations.

Even in wood, however, the problems posed at Ely were formidable and unprecedented, and the Chapter was forced to consult an expert, one Master William de Hurle (or Hurley) of London, who must have had a great reputation to command the very considerable retaining fee of £8 a year. His solution was as audacious as it was original: a wooden vault surmounted by a smaller high octagonal lantern, the eight angle posts of which form the hammer-posts of eight modified hammer-beam roof trusses which transmit the load of 400 tons outward to the piers of the octagon. These eight oak posts consist of timbers 63 feet long and 3 feet square. Merely to find eight beams this size proved a great problem; to transport and raise them into position, more than 90 feet above the pavement, using the primitive equipment of the times, constituted a tremendous engineering achievement.

The view up into the octagonal lantern is extraordinarily beautiful (Plate 246). What little sense of direction was still implicit in the lower octagon was dispelled by rotating the octagon of the lantern in relation to the octagon below, so that one has the feeling of being encompassed within a truly centralized space – by what has been called 'the only Gothic dome'. Although William Hurley's solution exercised considerable influence on wooden roof construction, the octagon of Ely remained unique and without apparent influence until the Renaissance brought a new preoccupation with monumental central spaces. Both the method of support and the layout of the crossing piers of Sir Christopher Wren's St Paul's reveal the influence of Ely, with which he was familiar, as his uncle was the bishop.

The Fabric Rolls of the cathedral contain a great deal of information on the decoration of the octagon. The timbers were first whitewashed and templates or stencils with the various sham tracery patterns prepared from parchment and canvas. Several artists are mentioned by name, including 'Ralph, the gold beater', who prepared gold leaf for the gilding of the bosses and other focal points from florins supplied by the prior. The final stages of the decoration of the lantern were

243 *Left* With the 14th century, heraldry plays an important rôle even in ecclesiastical art in England. *York*

244 *Above right* View from the west showing the fine double storeyed Galilee porch appended to the base, and the central Norman tower and the late 14th-century lantern which crowns it; the north-west transept collapsed and was never rebuilt. *Ely*

245 Detail of the east window of the Lady Chapel in the curvilinear Decorated style *Ely*

entrusted to Master Walter the painter, who spent forty-two weeks on the work at a wage of 9*d* a week, his keep and a robe. When the later colour-wash was removed in the nineteenth century, traces of the original decoration were revealed. The patterns were geometrical and the predominant colours stone-beige and green with accents in black and bright red. The

present elaborate *décor* dates from the Victorian restoration. While the painting is hardly to our taste today, it is at least acceptable, which is more than can be said for the glass, particularly that in the huge windows in the oblique sides of the stone octagon, which must surely rank among the most atrocious legacies of that artistically benighted epoch.

Concurrently with the construction of the octagon between 1322 and 1346, the new Lady Chapel was also completed and the damaged bays of the choir replaced by an almost cloyingly rich design of which the most successful feature is the lierne vault, the prototype of the stellar vaults which were to become

246 *Left* The view upwards into the octagonal lantern. *Ely*

247 *Above* Decorative head disgorging foliage; from the arcading of the Lady Chapel. *Ely*

248 *Above right* The elaborate lierne vaults over the westernmost bays of the choir (1322-1336) are of great historic significance as the prototype of the stellar vaults which were to become an important feature of late Gothic design, especially in Germany and Spain. *Ely*

such a feature of late-Gothic design, especially in Germany and Spain (Plate 248).

It was the 'Decorated Style', which flourished during the reigns of Edward II (1307-1327) and Edward III (1327-1377), with its elaborate ornamentation, its emphasis on movement, variety and surprise, and its partiality for the reverse-curved ogee arch that, as we have seen (20), provided one of the formative influences in the genesis of the late-Gothic, Flamboyant style of France. The only cathedral in England constructed in large measure during the period is Exeter; but probably the best example of the style at its most exuberant is the Lady Chapel at Ely (Plate 249).

The space itself, a single volume covered with the widest stone vault in English Gothic (46 feet), is comparatively simple, reflecting the spatial unity so sought after at this period, but the effect is anything but dull, thanks to the almost perversely complex scheme of decoration. Particularly remarkable are the ogee arches of the wall arcade and the double tiers of niches that ornament the piers above, which curve outward as they rise, creating what are known as nodding ogee arches. Used in combination with rigid vertical gables which accentuate the three-dimensional movement of the sinuous curves by contrast, the effect is one of extraordinary – almost too much – richness. The interior must, indeed, have been quite overwhelming in its heyday, before the niches were denuded of their sculpture, the bas-reliefs mutilated by the iconoclasts, the glass destroyed, and when the white stone was painted in brilliant colours, judging from the traces which still remain.

The stone used for the sculptured decoration was 'clunch', a type of chalk, which is soft and easily worked when freshly quarried and hardens on exposure, and which is ideally suited to deep undercutting (Plate 247). In the Decorated period the fresh and vigorous 'stiff-leaf' ornament of the Early English phase gave way to ranker growth, with the emphasis on rippling surface texture rather than incisive outline. Especially favoured were knobbly, bloated forms reminiscent of bladder-seaweed.

249 *Right* The interior of the Lady Chapel. *Ely*

250 Detail of the head of the alabaster effigy of King Edward II. *Gloucester*

Gloucester

The uninhibited 'Baroque' exuberance of the Decorated style could not long be reconciled with the English temperament and succumbed after some seventy years to the severity and rigid linearism of the 'Perpendicular' or 'Rectilinear' style, in which, as the names imply, there is a dominant vertical line, but with subordinate horizontals, constituting a shallow rectilinear framework. When applied to blank walls, the effect of Perpendicular decoration is often strongly reminiscent of wood panelling, a fact that has prompted suggestions of a possible timber origin.

The new style apparently first made its appearance in London, where the major early examples, notably the Royal Chapel of St Stephen in the Palace of Westminster and the Chapter House of Old St Paul's, have, unfortunately, disappeared and are known only through drawings (21). The earliest surviving example is the remodelling of the Norman work at Gloucester Abbey which, therefore, has great historic significance, apart from its intrinsic merits. The transmission of the style to Gloucester (22) can at least partly be explained by the

bury the putrefying corpse. The Chronicle of Gloucester Abbey relates how the abbot, moved by pity, bore the body of the king to Gloucester, where it was received with fitting pomp and ceremony and buried in a place of honour just north of the altar in the Norman choir. Abbot Thokey's courageous deed bore richer fruit than he could ever have foreseen. The course of events turned against the conspirators; the dead king's son, Edward III, achieved his independence from his mother, and so the weak and incompetent Edward II, whose public and private life alike had hardly been a model of propriety, in time came to be worshipped as a martyred saint.

Over his miracle-working tomb arose a splendid monument, largely paid for by Edward III. Resting on a base of Purbeck marble and surmounted by an elaborately sculptured canopy in freestone, fairly bristling with pinnacles, lies an effigy in alabaster, the earliest and the finest English example of the use of this material for large-scale tomb sculpture. The head is particularly fine (Plate 250). Although dating from about 1331, only four years after Edward II's death, it was not conceived as a portrait, but rather, as Joan Evans has pointed out, as an idealized, 'Christ-like' image (23). The royal favour bestowed on Gloucester and the contributions of the pilgrims

close connections existing at the time between that city and the court – connections which were further strengthened by the aftermath of one of the most lurid episodes in English history: the murder of Edward II at Berkeley Castle in 1327.

Fear of the Queen and her accomplice, Roger Mortimer, led the nearby abbeys of Bristol and Malmesbury to refuse to

251 *Above left* Detail of the intricate lierne vaulting over the choir with its elaborate angel bosses. *Gloucester*

252 *Above* Detail of the great east window commemorating the victory of the Battle of Crécy erected between 1347 and 1349. *Gloucester*

to Edward II's tomb, placed large funds at the disposal of the abbey, which initiated an extensive building programme. The south transept was first remodelled and attention then devoted to the eastern arm. Here, except for the reconstruction of the east end and the construction of a high new clerestory, raising the height of the vault some 20 feet above that of the nave, the

and prominent members of the nobility who fought in the campaigns in France, culminating in the victory of Crécy (1346). Completed about 1350, the window may be regarded as the first in the long line of war memorials which form so unique and characteristic a feature of English churches (Plate 252).

The remodelled presbytery was roofed with a close-meshed,

253 *Left* The vaulting over the crossing with the bow-shaped skeletal arch which transmits the load of the pendant ribs to the crossing piers; the circular opening permitted building materials to be hoisted into the tower above. *Gloucester*

254 *Above* View from the nave aisle towards the transept; the pierced screens of masonry create an extraordinary effect of depth and transparency. *Gloucester*

Norman structure was retained and its massive forms merely pared down and sheathed with Perpendicular style panelling. Possibly the work of William Ramsey, the royal mason, and author of the new chapter house of St Paul's, the design has been likened to 'an amazing work of carpentry in stone' (24).

The east wall was filled with the largest medieval window in England, 72 feet high and 38 feet wide – wider, in fact, than the choir itself, since the three sections of the window are canted to form a shallow bow, thereby increasing the resistance to wind pressure, and the walls of the easternmost bay made to slope outward, so that the effect from a distance is of a complete window-wall extending beyond the projecting piers. The predominantly white glass, flooding the interior with light, includes the heraldic shields of Edward III, the Black Prince,

lierne vault resembling a net, knotted at the intersections with bosses. These are of exceptional interest and beauty, particularly over the altar, where they take the form of a choir of music-making angels (Plate 251). The vaulting was extended westward without interruption to include the crossing, effectively unifying the two areas. This involved the removal of the eastern arch supporting the face of the tower and its reconstruction at a higher level, concealed above the vault, and also the transmission of the load of the clustered pendent

255 *Right* The cathedral from the north-east, dominated by the late Perpendicular tower with its high turrets and openwork balustrade; the Lady Chapel was kept almost free-standing so as not to obstruct the east window. *Gloucester*

ribs over the transept opening to the crossing piers by flying arches, whose stark, skeletal form is in the functional tradition favoured by the West Country masons at this period (Plate 253). The thrust of the tower itself, reconstructed between 1450 and 1460, in the mature Perpendicular style, was taken by internal flying buttresses which leap across the side aisles with dramatic effect (Plate 254).

At this same later period, a new Lady Chapel was constructed at the east end, repeating in miniature the general form of the choir (25), from which it was separated by a low vestibule. Connection between the Norman tribune galleries over the choir aisles was maintained by a bridge-corridor – the so-called 'whispering gallery' – which opens out into a small chapel over the vestibule, looking down into the Lady Chapel. The whole structure was kept free of the great east window, so that only a reduction in luminosity betrays the presence of the Lady Chapel (Plate 255).

In 1347 a Genoese ship arrived in Messina from the Black Sea, bringing to Europe that most terrible of all diseases, the Black Death: bubonic plague in its most virulent form. This enormous disaster ushered in a new phase of medieval life. Gone forever was the serene confidence of the thirteenth century. In art and literature 'the Dance of Death' became a favoured theme; in sculpture the finest talent was lavished on the tomb. To earlier – and later – ages, such an epitaph as, 'Here lies dust, ashes – nothing!' sufficiently evokes the transience of human existence. After the Black Death this was not enough. Not even the skeleton, scoured clean by time, embodied the contemporary vision of death. Only the putrefying corpse sufficed, preferably rendered all the more ghastly by contrast with the healthy body. The 'cadaver-tombs' gave expression to this morbid philosophy: above, the deceased ruler or ecclesiastic, splendidly attired in his robes of state, lies as if merely asleep; below, as if in a tomb, lies a rigid and emaciated corpse, naked or clad in a winding sheet, with open mouth, hollow eye sockets and decaying flesh crawling with worms (Plate 257).

From the early years of the fourteenth century, the more elaborate tombs in English churches were often associated with chantry chapels (26). These commonly took the form of cage-like constructions of stone enclosing the tomb and an altar where special masses could be chanted in perpetuity for the soul of the founder, the cost being borne by a liberal endowment. At the time of the Reformation, the churches were crowded with chantry chapels of which only a fraction have survived the wrath of the iconoclasts and the zeal of the restorers. An example can be seen on the left of Plate 254.

The Perpendicular style has in the past been attributed directly to the influence of the Black Death. While this is disproved by the fact that the genesis of the style antedates the advent of the plague, there is no doubt that its simplified forms – compared with the preceding Decorated style – the oft-repeated details capable of virtual mass-production, and also the preference for remodelling rather than rebuilding, were peculiarly suited to the straitened circumstances of an age plagued by an acute shortage of skilled labour.

Competing with the choir and its great east window for supreme honours at Gloucester is the cloister with its magnificent fan vaulting. The fan vault is a characteristically English form; hardly surprising, since it represents a logical development of the vaulting evolved in the polygonal chapter houses, themselves uniquely English. The vaulting springing from the

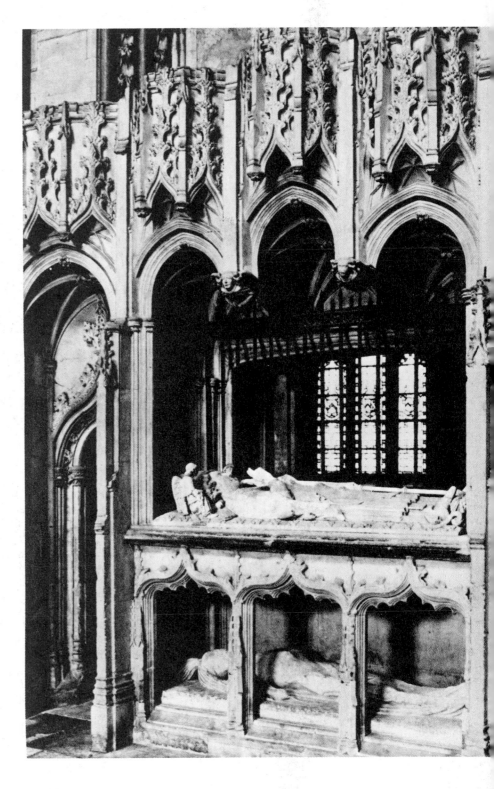

central pier of the Wells chapter house creates a great funnel-shaped conoid of the type associated with fan vaulting (Plate 223). The ribs have virtually the same curvature and would be identical if the ridge rib were circular – a form found in the demolished chapter house of Hereford Cathedral, dating from 1360-1370, which may well have had the first true fan vault. In the Gloucester cloister, commenced about 1370 (27),

256 *Left* South walk of the cloister with its superb fan-vaulting; it served as a *scriptorium*, each of the monks being provided with a study cell. *Gloucester*

257 *Above* A 'cadaver tomb', typical of the obsession with death which followed the Black Death; here, Bishop Fleming's tomb (died 1431). *Lincoln*

the same principle was applied to a continuous walk composed of square bays.

Impeccably proportioned and honey-hued, the Gloucester cloister is not only unrivalled for sheer beauty, but preserves several unique features which vividly evoke the monastic life of the Middle Ages. The southern walk was used as a *scriptorium*. Here each bay of the window wall was further subdivided for half its height into two, forming a total of twenty cubicles, each with its own tiny, two-light window (Plate 256). With the probable addition of wooden wainscoting partitions, individual studies were thus created where senior monks could work in semi-privacy. In the north walk, near the now vanished refectory, the *lavatorium,* where the monks washed their hands, projects into the cloister garth (Plate 258).

A lead cistern originally stood on the continuous wall-shelf, discharging water over the graded stone channel, and on the opposite side of the walk a wall recess for towels completed the singularly beautiful and eminently practical arrangement.

258 Detail of the *lavatorium* where the monks washed their hands before entering the adjoining refectory. *Gloucester*

Germany and Austria

6 Germany and Austria

The middle of the thirteenth century proved a decisive turning point in the history of Germany in both the political and artistic spheres. The end of the Hohenstaufen dynasty in 1254 led to a decline in the political power of the German emperors and an acceleration of the process whereby the country was divided into a series of semi-independent states. At the same time, the Romanesque style, which had survived so long and been so closely associated with the Imperial aspirations of the Hohenstaufen rulers, gave way to Gothic.

In 1235 work was begun on the Church of St Elizabeth at Marburg, the earliest truly Gothic structure in Germany, followed soon after by the equally significant *Liebfrauenkirche* at Trier, and in 1248 by the epoch-making new Cathedral of Cologne. Whereas the Gothic style in England had evolved from the interaction of French influence and native traditions, which had a powerful Gothic potential of their own, in Germany the new style was imported in a fully-developed form from France, and some time elapsed before the national genius asserted itself and a specifically German Gothic came into being.

The most significant German contribution to the evolution of Gothic architecture was the *Hallenkirche*, or 'hall-church', with nave and aisles of equal or near-equal height. An expression of the 'preaching-hall' favoured by the mendicant Orders who played an exceptionally important part in German religious life, it resulted in an interior with an appropriate and very marked sense of spatial unity. The hall-church achieved its ultimate development in the parish and pilgrimage churches of the late-Gothic era. Externally the characteristic feature of the *Hallenkirche* is the monumental roof covering both nave and aisles, and of a pitch steep enough to shed heavy snowfalls. The *Stephansdom* in Vienna is a classic example of this type of building.

German masters showed a marked preference for a single west tower. At Strasbourg this was imposed upon a twin-towered façade in the classic French manner, but at Freiburg-im-Breisgau and Ulm a single central tower was planned from the outset. As on an only child, the designer lavished all the more love on his single tower, which grew to a prodigious height, dominating the entire composition, and often terminated in an openwork spire, a major German contribution to the repertoire of Gothic forms.

The chivalric ideal of measured restraint, expressed to such perfection in the classic Gothic sculpture of France, and so effectively associated with the more 'expressionistic' German manner at Strasbourg, soon succumbed to the national ten-dency towards exaggerated realism and violent emotionalism that achieve great poignancy in the *Pietà* and Crucifixion groups of the late-Gothic period. In architectural ornament the final phase of this so-called *Sondergotik* style is characterized by a riotous profusion of forms, of an almost diabolical intricacy, executed with a technical dexterity that has no equal.

Cologne

The great esteem enjoyed by the Cathedral of Cologne in the Middle Ages was very largely the result of the exceptional collection of relics which the cathedral housed, in particular those of the Three Magi. Purported to have been discovered by Saint Helena, the mother of the Emperor Constantine, they were transferred in the sixth century to Milan and, after the conquest of that city by Frederick Barbarossa, brought to Cologne in 1164. The magnificent shrine built to contain the relics was commenced by Nicholas of Verdun in 1181. Res-

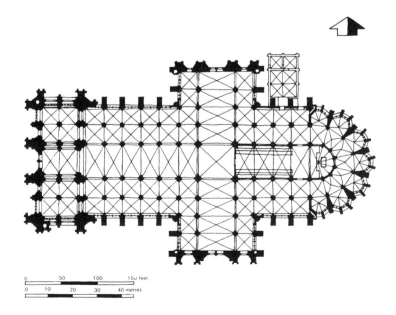

Fig. 18 Ground plan. *Cologne*

plendent with gold and jewels, it is one of the most celebrated examples of the Romanesque goldsmith's art.

The tremendous symbolic significance attached to the adoration of the infant Christ by the Three Magi, and consequently to their relics, can only be fully comprehended in relation to the religious and political background. The act of homage clearly acknowledged the allegiance of the rulers of the four corners of the earth to the supreme King-Emperor, Christ; but, perhaps less obvious, his acceptance of their gifts was in turn interpreted as a mark of his recognition. It was for this reason that the German kings, after their coronation at Aachen, came to offer gifts at the Shrine of the Three Magi at Cologne, thus receiving Divine confirmation, as it were, of their right to rule. This the Church was willing to concede, at the same time stressing the moral of the story: namely, the subservience of temporal power to the Church which, in

259 *Above* The prince archbishop's sword. *Cologne*

260 *Above right* The vertical line is triumphant in the 150ft-high choir. *Cologne*

Cologne itself, in the person of the prince-archbishop, wielded both the temporal and spiritual arm – a fact brought home most vividly by the magnificent gilded sword and scabbard used by the Archbishop in his secular capacity, and still preserved in the Cathedral treasury (Plate 259).

Several Christian shrines had succeeded each other on the site of a Roman Temple of Mercurius Augustus when, in 1247, under the episcopacy of Conrad von Hochstaden, the chapter decided to demolish the Carolingian, five-aisled basilica with its great atrium and build a cathedral in the Gothic style (1). A Master Gerhard is recorded in the archives as the '*iniciator*' of the work. Commenced in 1248 and based on French prototypes, notably Amiens (2), which was then still under construction, Cologne was the first German cathedral to embrace the entire repertoire of high-Gothic elements without reservations, including a fully-developed system of flying buttresses. Progress was initially quite rapid. The choir was formally consecrated in 1322 and closed from the building operations which were continuing in the transepts and nave by a temporary wall. Around the middle of the fourteenth century work commenced on the west front under the direction of Master Michael, a member of the famous Parler family of master-masons. Eighty years later (1473) the southern tower with all its sculptural decoration had been completed up to the level of the belfry. The huge crane for hoisting building material appears as a landmark in every view of the city between the fifteenth and mid-nineteenth centuries (Plate 261). Despite the economic decline of the city, construction continued intermittently for the next hundred years, but when it finally ceased in 1560, the pillars of the nave had been completed only to the height of the capitals and merely the stumps of the piers of the northern tower rose above ground level.

The upheaval occasioned by the French Revolution saw the sack of the cathedral by the Revolutionary Army – though not too drastically one must suppose – and its use as a hay store. In 1803 the transfer of the archbishopric to Aachen reduced the gigantic torso to the status of a parish church. Twenty years later Cologne again became the seat of an archbishopric and with the Gothic Revival came renewed interest and pleas for the completion of the cathedral according to the original plans, which had been discovered under romantic circumstances (3). Goethe's help was enlisted and the German translation of *True Principles of Pointed or Christian Architecture* by Pugin, with its espousal of Gothic architecture for Christian churches on religious as well as stylistic grounds, was also widely read and influential. The interest of the King of Prussia – to whom the territory had been ceded after Napoleon's defeat – was awakened and in 1842 the foundation stone of the new work was laid. In 1863 the 'temporary' partition separating choir and nave was demolished after 541 years and in 1880 the completion of the cathedral at last celebrated.

With a length of 472 feet and covering some 91,000 square feet, Cologne is the largest Gothic cathedral of northern Europe, exceeded in size only by those of Milan and Seville. The most interesting and beautiful part of the building is, needless to say, the original medieval choir, a variation on the theme of Amiens with the ratio of stone to glass still further reduced, the emphasis on verticality still more pronounced, the scale gigantic: the central vessel is 50 feet wide and the vaults of Cologne, 150 feet to the keystone, are, with the single exception of the ill-fated Beauvais, the highest ever built (Plate 260). The view from the East where the sharp fall in the ground gives added dignity to the superb bulk of the chevet with its corona of seven chapels, and effectively isolates it from the unsympathetic twentieth-century setting, makes an

261 *Right* Detail from the view of Cologne by Anton Woersam of Worms showing the complete choir of the cathedral and the crane on top of the unfinished west tower; woodcut dated 1531.

TEMPLV S. PETRI ET
S. TRIVM REGVM.

S. GEREON

AD PREDICATORES

AD MARIE GRADV.

unforgettable impression. Viewed more closely, however, the mechanical precision of the architectural detail falls far short of the superlative standard of Amiens.

The interior, particularly of the chancel, is of exceptional importance since it conserves, to a most remarkable degree, the original furnishings which so impressed Petrarch on his visit in 1333. The clerestory glass, though much restored, is fine in general effect, with the central apsidal window occupied, appropriately enough, with a representation of the Three Magi. Mounted on the console brackets on the piers are twelve elegant, if somewhat mannered, figures of the Apostles and a very fine Christ and Virgin, the vertical line being further emphasized by tall canopies crowned with music-making angels. Behind the High Altar stands the incomparable Shrine of the Three Kings, its refulgent gleam offset to perfection by the original altar frontal with its blind-arcading and sculpture in white marble against a black marble background (Plate 265).

The impressive choir-stalls date from about 1320 and with 104 seats form the largest ensemble to have survived in Germany. Their particular distinction lies not so much in the elaborately-carved stalls themselves, as in the frescoes on the masonry wall which separates the chancel from the choir aisles above the level of the stalls. Within an intricate architectural framework of painted canopies of gold, the scenes unfold against a stylized background, alternately red and blue (Plates 275 and 263). The superbly decorative effect recalls a medieval hanging (4). Thanks to being covered for centuries while the Gothic style was in disfavour, the paintings have come down

262 *Left* The piers of the double-aisled nave seen from the triforium. *Cologne*

263 *Below* Detail of a 14th-century painting from the choir enclosure. *Cologne*

264 *Right* Detail of the gable of the St Peter Portal of the west front, completed in the Middle Ages. *Cologne*

265 *Below right* Detail of the high altar dating from the consecration of the choir in 1322; compare this high-Gothic representation of the *Coronation of the Virgin* with that at Laon (plate 102). *Cologne*

266 *Above* Detail of a silver-gilt monstrance (see plate 267). *Cologne*

267 *Above right* Silver-gilt monstrance dating from about 1400, in the cathedral treasury. *Cologne*

to us in a remarkable state of preservation and despite inept restoration in the nineteenth century and considerable bomb damage during World War II, afford a good example of the elegant linear style of the Cologne School of painting in the fourteenth century.

The choir chapels are rich in treasures, including the Gero Cross, a monumental, thousand-year-old crucifix. Outstanding among the many fine sepulchral monuments in the choir chapels is that of Archbishop Conrad von Hochstaden, the founder of the present cathedral, represented not as an old man, but at the 'perfect age' of thirty-three. The idealized portrait has been likened by Jakob Burkhardt to that of a Greek Apollo (Plate 268).

Significant for the grand sense of scale it imparts to the interior is the over-life-size, polychrome stone statue of Saint Christopher (about 1470) (Plate 269). Mounted high on a pier, he looks towards the old entrance of the unfinished cathedral and, according to contemporary belief, anyone who

entered with true repentance and caught the genial giant's eye was saved. Although the cathedral treasury owes its exceptional fame to its collection of manuscripts and works of art dating from the early Middle Ages, there are several important works in the Gothic style. Outstanding is the monstrance dating from about 1400, one of the earliest surviving examples of its kind (Plates 266 and 267). Of silver-gilt, with the Eucharist enclosed between two laminae of rock-crystal, the monstrance is surmounted by figures of the Madonna and Child and attendant music-making angels in an elaborate architectural setting, complete with flying buttresses, pinnacles and minute, exquisitely-chased gargoyles. Fine, too, is the bishop's crozier, probably of Cologne workmanship, dating from the mid-fourteenth century and inlaid with translucent enamels (Plate 115).

The indifferent architectonic quality of the west front is due not so much to the fact that most of it only dates from the nineteenth century, as to inherent defects in the original design. The space between the two enormous towers, soaring to over 500 feet, is an uninviting, canyon-like slit, while the horizontal subdivision of the lower stages of the tower, though logical as an expression of the double aisles, and attractive enough at the second stage, results in the totally incompatible pairing below of a side portal and a window of such enormous height that the main portal appears depressed. Particularly uninspiring, too, is the manner in which the bulk of the towers is whittled away as they ascend by weak and indeterminate setbacks; the bold horizontal accents of the French gargoyle are also lacking here. Cologne, of all cathedrals, would have benefited had only one of the twin spires been completed as at Strasbourg, but such 'imperfection' would never have been countenanced by the nineteenth-century patriots to whom the completed cathedral was to be a symbol of German unification.

In spite of these drawbacks it must be admitted that the west front, thanks to its size alone, is extremely awe-inspiring and the distant view of the twin towers, suspended disembodied above the morning mist, is particularly dramatic.

268 *Right* Bronze sepulchral effigy of the founder Archbishop Conrad von Hochstaden (died 1261), represented at the perfect age of 33 at which, according to medieval belief, the dead would rise. *Cologne*

Freiburg

The rose-red Minster of Freiburg-im-Breisgau combines the grandeur of the cathedral and the intimacy of the parish church.

Around the year 1200 it was decided to rebuild the old parish church of Freiburg from which St Bernard had so passionately exhorted the faithful to join the Crusades. Progress on the over-ambitious project proceeded slowly and only a simple polygonal apse flanked by chapels (5) surmounted by the lower stages of the choir towers, the crossing and the square transept arms had been completed, when construction was unexpectedly interrupted in 1218 by the death of Berthold V, last of the Dukes of Zähringen, whose succession was much disputed.

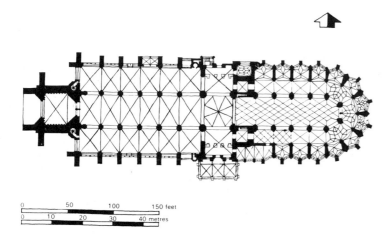

269 *Left* St Christopher, a genial peasant, looks towards the old entrance of the cathedral. *Cologne*

Fig. 19 *Above* Ground plan. *Freiburg*

270 *Right* Interior with votive Madonna dating from about 1500. *Freiburg*

271 *Overleaf* The splendid openwork spire of the Minster. *Freiburg*

The interval before funds were again available (by about 1250) had seen the introduction and acceptance of the Gothic style in the region of the Upper Rhine and when work began at Freiburg once more, the nave was to some extent adapted from that of Strasbourg (6).

Even before the completion of the nave; work started on what was to become the minster's special pride: the west tower. A certain Master Gerhart was responsible for the design to the height of the clock, comprising a deep hall-porch which also served on occasion as a court-room; the Chapel of St Michael above, opening into the upper portion of the nave and expressed externally by a single large window; and the bell-chamber proper, originally left open. Commenced in 1275, this much of the tower had been completed by 1301. Only ten years later was work continued under the direction of another master, an enigmatic figure known as 'Heinrich der Leiter' (7) of whom, as is ironically so often the case with the creators of the greatest masterpieces, almost nothing is known. He enclosed the bell-chamber within the lower half of a great octagon, effecting the visual transition from square to octagon with the greatest subtlety by means of tall buttress pinnacles placed on the diagonal. The upper half of the octagon is an

airy chamber with traceried openings surmounted by gables which effectively mask the base line of the octagonal-pyramid (Plate 271). The effect inside the octagon is even more startling. Emerging from the narrow spiral stair which leads upward from the claustrophobic bell-chamber, with its enormous beams felled in the nearby Black Forest, one finds oneself inside the most magnificent cagework of stone imaginable, while the view upward is of filigree lightness and delicacy (Plate 272).

Nearly all critics have been carried away by their enthusiasm for the tower at Freiburg. The German art historian of the end of the last century, Georg Dehio, called it 'the boldest declaration of independence of an art-form serving a useful purpose' and, indeed, the dematerialized surfaces of the spire, not even providing protection from rain or snow, seem to proclaim that we are dealing with a purely symbolic art form. One of the rare examples of the typically German openwork spire to be completed in the Middle Ages – those at Cologne, Ulm and Regensburg all date from the nineteenth century – the spire of Freiburg is truly one of the unique creations of the Gothic spirit. Whether it really is '*der schönste Turm der Welt*' (the most beautiful tower in the world) as the Germans claim is naturally open to dispute. A similar claim could be made for the south tower of Chartres (to which I, personally, would be inclined to hand the palm) or, equally, for Salisbury.

The entrance porch under the west tower contains a wealth of late-thirteenth-century sculpture forming one of the most comprehensive and detailed iconographic schemes in Germany. Included are personifications of the Seven Liberal Arts (Plate 274) and a variation on the '*Tempter*' theme of

272 *Previous page* Interior of the openwork spire. *Freiburg*

273 *Right* Interior of the choir. *Freiburg*

274 *Below* Personification of the Liberal Arts, left to right: *Grammar, Rhetoric* and *Arithmetic;* from the west porch. *Freiburg*

in 1359 Johann Parler was appointed master-mason for life. Seen across the nave with its relatively meagre clerestory windows and the sombre Romanesque crossing, his soaring, late-Gothic choir, flooded with light, is a fitting goal of the pilgrim's symbolic journey towards the East – and light (Plate 273).

One of the happiest creations of German late-Gothic, the choir was an important milestone in the evolution of the final phase of *Sondergotik*. The manner in which the attenuated vaulting shafts of the piers sweep upward without interruption, metamorphosing into the twisting reed-like ribs that arch diagonally over the vault in a seemingly organic manner only to arrive at a point mid-way between the points of support, certainly expresses to perfection the restless and irrational spirit of the later Middle Ages, with its endless search for novel effects. The diagonal emphasis of the vaulting pattern is echoed in a subtle manner by the disposition of the choir chapels. Instead of the customary odd number of chapels so that the central chapel on the main axis presents a frontal view from the choir, there are at Freiburg an even number of chapels, so that the pier separating the two central chapels is on the axis line and the eye is deflected diagonally into the chapels. The same theme is repeated in the chapels themselves which also have a pier on the centre-line between two windows.

The vaulting of the choir ambulatory and chapels (which was not finished until about 1500) is a masterpiece of the 'Parler School' which had its own concepts of beauty (Plate 278). How far from the logic and clarity of classic French Gothic is this arbitrary interlacing of the ribs as they spread frond-like from the vaulting shafts of the piers, or the random truncation of the intersecting ribs. The *pièce de résistance* has been reserved for

Strasbourg. Here 'The Prince of the World', likewise elegantly clad and with his back being devoured by toads, offers a flower to his neighbour, a comely woman clad only in a goatskin draped casually over her shoulders, and symbolizing 'The Lust of the World'. Both ignore the next figure, an angel with an insufferably smug smile, carrying a scroll bearing the warning words, '*Ne intretis*', 'that ye enter not' (i.e. 'Watch and pray, that ye enter not into Temptation' - *Matthew 26, 41*).

Towards the middle of the fourteenth century additional storeys were added to the Romanesque choir-towers, terminating in openwork spires calculated to harmonize with the recently completed west tower, and crowned by the gilded weather-vanes from which the 'Cock Towers' derive their name. At the same time it was decided to rebuild the choir and

275 *Right* Paintings of the choir enclosure, dating from the consecration in 1322, showing two incidents from the *History of the Emperor Constantine*. *Cologne*

276 *Overleaf* Prisoners scream in anguish, two squinting with distraction, as a soldier sets the building ablaze; detail from a 14th-century window in the main aisle. *Freiburg*

constantin̄ ... ... s̄·Silvest

ī·stantin·

ſar ē m̄ ērabēa conferē īſigniā dara ... ... papā ſaqo bapaſmatē rēr rēnoiētur

Regensburg

Situated at the westernmost navigable point on the Danube, at its confluence with the Regen, Regensburg is one of the oldest and most historic cities of Germany. In turn a Celtic

the 'Imperial Chapels' (8), where the ribs that converge, touch, and diverge again to form an hour-glass shape, are kept quite free of the vault.

Freiburg boasts some exceptionally fine glass. Particularly expressive is a scene from a cycle depicting lives of the saints, in which prisoners scream in anguish, two quite squint-eyed with distraction, as a soldier sets the building ablaze (Plate 276). Very different is the regal Madonna and Child exhibited in the Augustine Museum on loan from the *Münsterfabrik,* one of the most beautiful specimens of South German stained glass of the first half of the fourteenth century (Plate 277).

settlement dating from 500 BC with the name *Rathaspona* (whence the alternative name Ratisbon), a mighty Roman fortress, capital of the Eastern Frankish Empire and flourishing trading centre during the early and high Middle Ages, the city has preserved a wealth of monuments of all periods.

The eleventh-century Romanesque cathedral, a three-aisled basilica with a wooden roof, was several times damaged by fire and restored, and had finally to be entirely rebuilt after the disastrous fire of 1273. The resemblances between the design of the new Cathedral of Regensburg (whose foundation stone was laid in 1275) and the church of Saint Urbain at Troyes (9) can perhaps be explained by the fact that Leo of Tundorf, Bishop of Regensburg attended the Council of Lyons in 1274, where he met, among other important clerics, Cardinal Archer, under whose patronage the Church at Troyes was being built.

Although the new cathedral was far larger than the former

277   *Previous page* Virgin and Child. Stained-glass window dating from the first half of the 14th century. *Freiburg, Augustiner Museum*

278   *Above* Choir ambulatory and chapels. *Freiburg*

279   *Above* South transept with well drawing water from the Danube. *Regensburg*

280   *Right* Apsidal end of the north aisle showing two of the ciborium altars. *Regensburg*

one and existing foundations could not be utilized, the novel French forms rose from a ground plan that retained such typical Bavarian-Romanesque features as the termination of the nave and aisles in parallel, polygonal apses without ambulatories. The choir was completed under the episcopacy of Nicholas of Stachowitz (1313-1340) and is thus contem-

281 *Left* Caryatid corbel figures; that on the left is presumed to be a self-portrait of the sculptor. *Regensburg*

282 *Right* An angel rescues St Peter from prison; tympanum from the west front. *Regensburg*

porary with, but far less revolutionary than that of Cologne. The nave, recalling Strasbourg, was only completed far later. A continuous walkway in the manner of a *galerie champenoise* runs along the aisle walls, stepping up over the transept doors, the effect being most striking in the southern transept, seen in conjunction with the sculptural accent of the elaborate, late-Gothic well-head (Plate 279).

How does one account for the extraordinarily powerful emotional impact of the interior? This cannot be attributed solely, or even primarily, to purely architectonic factors, for the forms used are often not particularly distinguished, though in certain instances the very evidence of groping indecision and change has a charm and interest of its own. The secret is, rather, to be sought in the evocative ambience.

The cathedral has preserved much of its fine glass – including some brought from the previous Romanesque cathedral – while a whole series of rare ciborium altars, which, almost miraculously, survived the wrath of the iconoclasts and the refurbishing zeal of devotees of the '*grand goût*', effectively articulate the architectural space and provide an inimitable note of warmth (Plate 280).

There is besides, much fine sculpture. Two equestrian groups of St George and St Martin and the Beggar, are particularly effective in their setting (Plate 3). Of exceptional interest among the numerous corbel-bracket sculptures is the caryatid figure on the inner face of the west wall, squirming restlessly

under his burden (Plate 281). These acutely characterized features may perhaps be a self-portrait of the sculptor. Belonging to the front rank of early German Gothic sculpture are the figures of the Virgin of the Annunciation and the Messenger Angel – the justly celebrated 'Angel of Regensburg', with his irresistible smile and 'Archaic-Greek' ringlets – who commune with each other across the nave from their high pedestals (Plates 283 and 284). Carved in about 1280 by that wayward, independent genius, the so-called Erminold Master, the figures have an engaging spontaneity and sincerity.

The most interesting feature of the exterior of the cathedral is the west front. Work had already started in 1340 on the south tower with its low doorway of insignificant scale, not unlike English practice. The enchantingly naive contemporary tympanum sculpture represents the 'Rescue of St Peter', with the angel casually tilting up the top of the prison while he lifts out a rather bewildered St Peter. The gaolers, meanwhile, sleep unconcernedly (Plate 282). Work on the north tower could not start simultaneously, as the site was still occupied by the Collegiate Church of St John (the detached baptistry of the previous cathedral). Only in 1380 was agreement reached to demolish the structure and build a new church elsewhere.

Wentzel Roriczer, one of the outstanding masters of the time, assumed charge of building operations in 1411. By then the third stage of the south tower was already under con-

283 *Below The Virgin of the Annunciation. Regensburg*

284 *Right The Angel of Regensburg,* detail of the head; it faces the Virgin across the nave.

285 A view of the west façade of Regensburg from a lithograph by Domenico Quaglio, 1820. *London, Victoria and Albert Museum*

struction. Roriczer's solution shows a rare sensitivity in the manner in which he wedded his new design to the existing portion. On the lower stages and in the great ogee arches he employed the currently fashionable late-Gothic vocabulary of forms, but in the upper stages deliberately reverted to forms similar – though not identical – to those used on the older tower, thus achieving a harmonious overall effect.

To Wentzel Roriczer's son, Conrad, is due the charming, if capricious, triangular porch (completed in 1482, two years after he died)(10), which has excited such praise and scorn. The lavish but delicate ornamentation in no way obscures the diagonal lines which contrast dramatically with the cliff-like façade behind. Less happy is the manner in which the porch seems hemmed in between the strongly projecting buttresses, all the more irritating since the triangular design seems to invite one to view the porch from the side. At Conrad Roriczer's death c. 1480, he was, in turn, succeeded by his son, Matthäus, celebrated, as we have seen, for his revealing treatise, '*On the Ordination of Pinnacles*'.

After 1530 work on the cathedral ceased. Stucco and fresco transformed the interior in the Baroque style in the early eighteenth century, but this decoration was removed a century later at the instigation of Ludwig I of Bavaria, who shared the Romantic passion of his countrymen for both Classical antiquity and the Gothic 'National Style'. A lithograph by Domenico Quaglio, dated 1820, shows the appearance of the west façade before the ill-advised addition of octagons and pierced tracery spires based on the precedent of Freiburg. Attractive enough from a distance, seen purely as townscape, especially in the famous view from across the Danube, the spires with their inflated scale and precise, mechanical forms are completely out of character with the façade below (Plate 285).

Ulm

The history of the building of the Ulm Minster is unusually interesting for the light it throws on the civic pride and independence of the burghers of the late Middle Ages. A missionary church to convert the heathen German tribes was already established at this convenient crossing of the Danube by the Franks in the year 600 and in 813 Charlemagne made the church, together with the palace on the site, dependent on the Monastery of Reichenau. By the fourteenth century Ulm had become a singularly wealthy free-town. Its chief place of worship, 'Our Lady of the Fields', descendant of the missionary church, however, still stood outside the fortified walls, and the disadvantages became apparent during the unsuccessful siege of the city by the Emperor Charles IV in 1376, and the conflict between the Swabian towns and the Dukes of Württemberg. Determined that they should never again be denied access to their church, and also relishing the idea of freedom from dependence on the Monastery of Reichenau, the burghers dismantled the church and re-erected it within the walls – within a space of six weeks, according to one chronicler. This was, however, merely a temporary measure. The town's proud new status as head of the Swabian League demanded a far more imposing church, and the foundation stone of a vast new structure was laid that same year (1377), significantly enough, not by prince or prelate but by the Mayor of Ulm.

The Master Heinrich first mentioned in the archives and assumed to be the original designer, has generally been identified with the Elder Henry of Gmünd (about 1300-1387), founder of the Parler Dynasty, who had worked at Cologne as a '*parlier*' and had designed the *Kreuzkirche* at Schwäbisch-Gmünd (11). He was succeeded by a Master Michael (probably a son) and later by a second Master Heinrich. When this Heinrich the Younger resigned in 1391 to go to Milan to advise on the design of the new cathedral, the aisleless choir had been completed, except for the vaulting which only dates from 1449. Paul Frankl (12) has suggested a possible reason for the delay: since the Minster was built of a mixture of stone and brick, materials which do not settle evenly, a *50-year period* was allowed for settlement – an almost inconceivable thought in our day and age, but perhaps not so in the Middle Ages. One must also bear in mind that construction was, meanwhile, continuing on other parts of the church.

The *tour de force* of Ulm, the unique west tower, owes its inspiration, at least on its present titanic scale, to Ulrich von Ensingen (about 1350-1419), who was also responsible for the design of the octagon of the great north tower of Strasbourg (see above page 167)(13). Here, too, the most interesting feature of the design lies in the penetration of the solid form to achieve complex spatial effects. The veils of masonry suspended, as it were, one behind the other, create an extraordinary impression of transparency and weightlessness, so that the tower belies its huge mass and seems to wing effortlessly skyward (Plate 287). At Ulm the metallic sharpness of the masonry profiles is all the more noticeable by contrast with the broad surfaces of brickwork below.

Playing on the vanity of the citizens and their determination to outdo all rivals – and notably Strasbourg – Master Ulrich modified the plan of the Minster, increasing the number of bays in the nave to ten and making the narrow aisles the same width as the central nave, resulting in an enormous overall width of

286 Interior showing the double aisles with their lightweight stellar vaulting. *Ulm*

287 *Above* The tower belies its huge mass and seems to rise effortlessly skywards. *Ulm*

288 *Left* Interior of the Besserer Chapel. *Ulm*

147 feet (as compared with a mere 107 feet at Strasbourg). The vaulting of the excessively wide aisles was a remarkable structural achievement. Only a hundred years later, under the threat of failure due to other causes, were they subdivided along their length by the addition of a row of slender columns and revaulted with lightweight stellar vaulting, assuming their present striking appearance of a double-aisled hall-church complete in itself (Plate 286).

The tiny Besserer Chapel entered from the choir and also from the hand of Ulrich von Ensingen, shows quite a different facet of his talents. Beautifully proportioned and retaining most of its original glass and furnishing, its endearing intimacy complements the grandeur of the main spaces to perfection (Plate 288).

Construction continued under the direction of three

generations of the Ensingen family until 1474 when Matthäus Böblinger became the master-mason in charge. He completed the third stage of the great tower according to Ulrich von Ensingen's original design and proposed a still more elaborate octagon above and an even higher spire. He had, however, omitted to strengthen the piers of the tower sufficiently, and signs of failure occurred in 1493. Böblinger was dismissed and a conference of twenty-eight master-masons convened to advise on the necessary action to be taken. One of the members, Burkhard Engelberg, gradually assumed control, successfully consolidated the structure of the tower and, between 1502 and 1507, subdivided the wide side aisles as we have already noted.

In 1530, after the Imperial Diet of Augsburg, Ulm espoused the Protestant cause and the Minster remains today simply the

Lutheran Parish Church of the city, the only building in our volume never to have housed the *cathedra* of a bishop. In 1531 the iconoclasts stormed the Minster and destroyed more than sixty altars and numerous works of art, although the choir escaped being so completely wrecked. Its greatest loss was the principal altarpiece (14), which was then replaced by the singularly attractive work by Martin Schaffner dating from 1521 (Plate 291). The painted wings of the polyptych already show marked Renaissance influence, but the carved centre-piece remains faithful to the old traditions. Still covered with their original glowing colours, the actors could have stepped straight from a 'Miracle Play'.

Between 1469 and 1474, Jörg Syrlin the Elder, 'master carpenter and joiner', carved the choir-stalls, the greatest treasure of the Minster, with their unique and incomparable series of busts on the pew ends. Those on the north represent famous men of antiquity, the balancing female figures on the south the sibyls who had foretold the coming of the Messiah. The figures combine an almost visionary grandeur with remarkable individual characterization: Pythagoras, 'the inventor of music', listens with rapt attention to the harmonies he is plucking from his lute (Plate 289), while Ptolemy, celestial globe held to his cheek, ponders with puckered brow on the mysteries of astronomy (Plate 293).

Apart from the choir-stalls, the most remarkable sculpture at Ulm is the poignant *Schmerzenmann* or 'Christ as the Man of Sorrows' carved by Hans Multscher in 1429 on the central pier of the west portal which stands within a lofty, late-Gothic

289 *Above* Two busts from the choir-stalls carved by Jörg Syrlin the Elder: *left, Pythagoras* in his rôle as inventor of music and *right,* the *Cimerian Sibyl. Ulm*

290 *Left The Man of Sorrows* by Hans Multscher, from the west porch. *Ulm*

291 *Right* Central panel of the altar-piece of Martin Schaffner, 1521. *Ulm*

292 *Overleaf* Vignette with detail from the life of St Stephen from the St Etienne window. *Bourges*

porch (Plate 290). Characteristic of *Sondergotik* is the complex rhythm that results from the triple-arched entrance leading to the paired entrance doors.

Only in the mid nineteenth century were the octagon and the great openwork spire erected according to Matthäus Böblinger's original design (15). Towering to a dizzy 528 feet, it remains the highest stone spire ever built. Although the details, particularly the over-emphatic, knobbly excrescences of the spire, lack the perfection of Freiburg, the impression from a distance, and especially from across the Danube when floodlit at night, is of remarkable splendour (Plate 294).

Vienna

In 1304 the Gothic style was introduced to the Romanesque church of St Stephen in Vienna with a spacious new choir, in the form of a hall-church with nave and aisles of equal height and almost equal width, terminating in three polygonal apses in the German manner. In the later nave the central vessel was raised above the height of the aisles, but without clerestory lighting, so that the basic effect of the *Hallenkirche* was maintained (Fig. 20 and Plate 295). The Romanesque west front was retained and merely modified, and to supplement its meagre single portal, transeptal porches were provided, culminating in two towers.

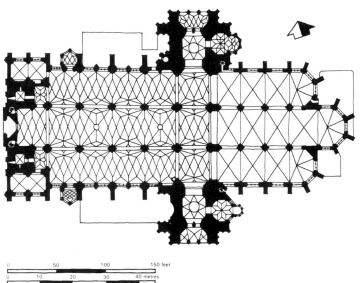

The southern tower, the so-called *Alte-Steffl,* was completed between 1368 and 1433. Only in 1450 was work started on the north tower, but halted in 1511 when only half completed. The Reformation and the Turkish menace, which necessitated extensive additions to the city's defences, were both contributory factors, but there were also serious – and well-founded – doubts as to whether two equally prominent towers would be aesthetically satisfactory. The final decision not to raise the north tower was sealed with the addition of an elegant little cupola in the Italian Renaissance style in the latter half of the sixteenth century. And there the matter rested until the nineteenth century with its obsession to 'perfect' the heritage of the past. The remainder of the elaborate, traceried gables designed by Hans Puchsbaum in the mid fifteenth century were then completed (only the one illustrated in Plate 297 is original) and the cathedral architect prepared elaborate drawings for the erection of the north tower. Mercifully,

293 *Previous page Ptolemy* by Jörg Syrlin the Elder, from the choir-stalls. *Ulm*

294 *Above left* The floodlit old town seen from across the Danube. *Ulm*

295 *Left* The interior of the nave looking west. *Vienna*

Fig. 20 *Above* Ground plan. *Vienna*

296 *Right* Head of St Anne from the statue formerly on the high tower of the *Stephansdom. Vienna, Historisches Museum*

nothing came of this latter project and one of the most audacious and successful examples of architectural massing was saved.

Two perfectly balanced and complementary features dominate the exterior: the great south tower, 448 feet high, looming skyward like an admonishing finger, its elaborate filigree ornament inscribed within a basic obelisk shape, and the enormous roof, that results from covering a hall-type church the width of St Stephen with a pitch steep enough to shed the heavy snowfalls of Central Europe (Plates 300 and 299). With its polychrome tiles arranged in bold chevron and lozenge patterns that could have come from a Khelim rug, the roof resembles the tent of some central Asian nomad and has an irresistibly exotic quality that links it in spirit with the bizarre roofs of Russian architecture.

The treatment of the tower as a semi-independent element of the architectural composition – a favourite device of modern architects – was most unusual in the Gothic period. It is significant in view of Vienna's geographical position at the cross-roads of Europe, that we should find here this interesting compromise between the northern tower, integrated with the structure, and the completely free-standing, Italian *campanile*.

297 *Left* The original gable by Hans Puchsbaum. *Vienna*

298 *Above* The Servants' Madonna. *Vienna*

299 *Above right* General view of the *Stephansdom*. *Vienna*

300 *Right* The roof of the *Stephansdom*. *Vienna*

The position of the tower also effectively distracts attention from the weakest point of the composition, the unhappy junction between the roof of the choir and that of the new and higher nave.

Thanks to commendable restoration, the richly-decorated interior, a mere shell at the end of World War II, has regained its wonderfully evocative atmosphere. Now mounted on one of the nave piers is the 'Servants' Madonna' (Plate 298). According to legend, the statue once stood in a noble household. When a maid-servant accused of theft appealed to the image, her mistress brusquely retorted that the Madonna did not listen to servants. Needless to say, the servant was proved innocent and the penitent countess presented the statue to the cathedral. Certainly one could hardly have appealed to a more gracious intercessor. The elegant stance and tender expression of the Virgin, and the charming attitude of the Child, absent-mindedly fondling her brooch, are typical of the sculpture of the period (1320-1330).

The Habsburgs, who had been intimately connected with the building of the cathedral, figure in its decoration to a very unusual degree. Two windows of the Ducal Chapel dating from about 1390 are given over to large figures of family ancestors, shown not as donors or worshippers but simply as secular rulers, while life-size statues of the Habsburgs and their wives, the epitome of high-fashion and the contemporary chivalric ideal, also decorated the façade and the great tower (Plate 302). Exceptionally interesting for its psychological insight is the head of Duke Albrecht II, the Wise, or the Lame (Plate 303).

Nowhere is the frenzied exuberance of the final phase of *Sondergotik* better exemplified than in the great pulpit (1510-1515), the last example of monumental sculpture in the Gothic style, by the master-mason Anton Pilgram whose likeness adorns the corbel bracket of the organ console (Plate 83). A masterpiece of technical virtuosity, the entire portion illustrated in Plate 301, the pulpit itself, the vivid portraits of Church Fathers and every lacy frond of ornament, is carved from a single piece of stone (16).

The complexity of the ornament evokes Professor Huizinga's brilliant description of late-Gothic architecture as 'the postlude of an organist who cannot conclude . . . decomposing all the formal elements endlessly . . . interlacing all the details . . . with not a line which has not its counterline' (17).

301 *Left* Detail of pulpit carved by Anton Pilgram (1510-15); the part shown is made from a single piece of stone. *Vienna*

302 Two statues of Habsburgs, *left* Catherine of Bohemia and *right* Duke Rudolph IV, done in sandstone about 1365, formerly on the west façade of the *Stephansdom. Vienna, Historisches Museum*

303 *Above* Head of the statue of Duke Albrecht II, 'the Wise', from the high tower of the *Stephansdom. Vienna, Historisches Museum*

304 *Overleaf* Exterior, general view. *Burgos*

Spain

7 Spain

In 711 AD the conquering Moors crossed the straits from Africa, overthrew the Visigothic kingdom of Spain, and within three years had established their rule over virtually the entire peninsula. Only in the mountainous wastes of the North, behind the Cantabrian Mountains and along the Pyrenees, were the Christians – native and refugee – able to maintain a precarious independence and establish pockets of resistance. In time these developed into the principalities of Asturias, Navarre, Aragon and the 'Spanish Marches' or Catalonia, which were to provide a springboard for the reconquest of the South. The Arab civilization of Spain, the most advanced and brilliant of Europe for three centuries, was fatally weakened by internal dissension, and, after the fall of the Umayyad Dynasty in 1031, fragmented into twenty petty states. The *Reconquista* which had already won back considerable areas in the North and West, and assumed the nature of a Crusade against the infidel, now gained momentum, culminating in the great battle of *Las Navas de Tolosa* in 1212. Here the Christian forces, reinforced with contingents from France, Germany and Italy, dealt the death-blow to Muslim power in Spain – although it survived at Granada until 1492, the year of Columbus' discovery of America.

The Gothic centuries in Spain witnessed not only the conquest of the Muslim South, but the assimilation of much of its rich culture. Arab artisans and craftsmen placed their skill at the service of the conquerors, and in architecture the style known as *Mudéjar,* partly Gothic, partly Islamic, was widely used, especially for secular work. In the case of the cathedrals, however, a deliberate effort was made to break with Arab influence which, nevertheless, still often manifested itself, particularly in the design of the *cimborio* or lantern over the crossing, usually octagonal and carried on squinches. We have already discussed the great debt of medieval Europe to Islam in the field of science and in transmitting the heritage of the classical world. Suffice it to note here that in the cosmopolitan Spanish society of the thirteenth and fourteenth centuries, Christian, Arab and Jew coexisted in relative amity and that scholars enjoyed more intellectual freedom there than anywhere else in Europe.

In Spain, as in the Holy Land, European Christendom felt a particular obligation to protect a sacred tomb, that of St James the Greater (Santiago), brother of St John the Evangelist, who, according to tradition, spent seven years in Roman Spain, primarily in Galicia before returning to Jerusalem and martyrdom. By miraculous means his body was borne back to Galicia. Abandoned during the persecutions of the third

305 A French cathedral transplanted to Spain. *León*

century, the tomb was miraculously rediscovered in 812 thanks to a guiding star. The site of the new tomb was given the name *Campus Stella* (Field of the Star), later corrupted to Compostela. The pilgrimage to *Santiago de Compostela* became as famous in the Middle Ages as those to Jerusalem and Rome. Crowded with pilgrims from as far afield as Germany and Ireland, sporting the cockle-shell badge of St James, the 'Road to Santiago' provided the most fruitful single contact between the peoples of Europe. Known in Spain as the *camino francés* or 'French Road' it was also the natural point of entry for French influence. At Santiago de Compostela itself, the great pilgrimage church inspired by the art of France, is probably the finest example of the high-Romanesque style to survive in all Europe. Not surprisingly, some of the earliest buildings in the new *opus francigenum* also arose along its route.

The first Gothic cathedrals of Spain were built by French architects and sculptors following French models, but the powerful *genius loci* soon asserted itself and stamped the adopted forms as inescapably Spanish. The climate rendered great roofs superfluous and the Classical and Islamic heritage both favoured their suppression. At Burgos the low-pitched tile is hidden behind a modest parapet (Plate 304), and at Seville we have the ultimate negation of northern practice with the stone vaults virtually exposed to the elements (Plate 341). In the torrid Spanish summer the glass-walled Gothic church of the North only too easily became a hot-house, and many of the great windows provided as a matter of course by the foreign architects of the early cathedrals were subsequently blocked with masonry. The later cathedrals were provided with smaller windows from the start. It is the spotlight effect of these relatively small, but extremely bright, light sources playing on sumptuously decorated, gilded furnishings that is largely responsible for the drama and mystery of Spanish church interiors. Outstanding among these furnishings are the enormous carved *retablos* or altarpieces and the beautiful *rejas* or grilles of hammered and chiselled iron, often elaborately crested, and decorated with figures in *repoussé* work, placed back to back (1).

If French cathedrals are notable for their height, and English cathedrals for their length, Spanish cathedrals are distinguished by their great width and the sheer area that they cover. This tendency became ever more marked as foreign influence was assimilated and a truly national style evolved. Spanish plans are comparatively short, despite the large space reserved for the clergy, and this gave rise to the feature which, more than any other, gives the Spanish interior its special character: separation of the sanctuary containing the high altar (*Capilla Mayor*) and the choir (*coro*) and the removal of the latter to a position west of the crossing. This became the standard arrangement even in completely new structures where the eastern arm could easily have been lengthened, as in England, to provide adequate space for both activities. The separation must, therefore, have been deliberate and it has been suggested that, to the Spanish temperament, the transcendental nature of the Sacrifice at the Altar made it unfitting that the same space be shared by any lesser function (2).

306 Tympanum of the *Puerta del Sarmental,* with the Evangelists represented not only by their symbols but also as scribes. *Burgos*

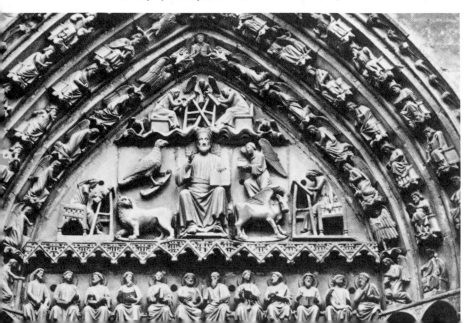

Burgos

It was at Burgos, capital of Old Castile, birthplace of the heroic Cid and seat of the dynasty of León-Castile which took the lead in the reconquest of the South, that the foundation stone of the first great Spanish cathedral in the Gothic style was laid on July 20, 1221, a year after Amiens and Salisbury, in the presence of the youthful King Fernando III – St Ferdinand, cousin of St Louis (3). A few years previously, the founder-bishop, Mauricio, had travelled to Speyer to negotiate the young king's marriage to a daughter of the Emperor Barbarossa. He also visited France, where the great new Gothic cathedrals, symbols of the new supremacy of the city bishops, must have fired his imagination and strengthened his resolve to replace the modest Romanesque cathedral of Burgos with a structure that would eclipse the splendour of the royal monastery of *Las Huelgas,* on the outskirts of the city.

Bishop Mauricio is said to have been 'English', but, if so, probably only in the sense of coming from the provinces of France under English rule. Certainly the new Cathedral of Burgos is in the French tradition and has particular analogies with Bourges and Coutances (4). The first architect of Burgos, responsible for the apse, was probably the same Maestro Ricardo who had worked at *Las Huelgas* from before 1203 until 1226 or later. The second architect of the cathedral was a Maestro Enrique, already in charge in 1235, who constructed the nave between 1243 and 1260.

The cathedral is built into the steep side of the hill which was dominated by the great castle of the Kings of Castile, the change in levels being bridged by ramps and stairs which add to the many and various impressions of space that reward a walk around it. Passing through the crenellated gateway into the main plaza to the south (5), one sees the full length of the cathedral riding majestically on its high podium, the silhouette bristling with spires and pinnacles. The main entrance to the cathedral from the town is by the monumental flight of steps leading up to the mid-thirteenth-century *Puerta del Sarmental* in the south transept. This is in the French Gothic style (Plate 307). The three major architectural elements of portal, rose and crowning 'Royal Gallery' are separated and enhanced by huge blank areas of wall, providing a good example of the abiding national genius for effectively juxtaposing luxuriant decoration and Spartan austerity – here apparent, even when ostensibly dominated by foreign influence. In the tympanum of the portal, the first major work of Gothic sculpture in Spain, an Apocalyptic Christ, regally crowned and robed, is surrounded by the Evangelists, represented not only by their symbolic beasts but also as industrious monastic scribes, seemingly oblivious to the celestial concert provided by the Kings of Israel ranged in the archivolts (Plate 306). The need to support the upper figures of St Matthew and St John obviously posed a problem for the artist. The solution: a billowing carpet of cloud is solicitously held in position by angel attendants.

A constricted opening leads to the *Plaza de Santa Maria* to the West, excavated out of the hillside like an intimate theatre and embraced by a cobbled stair-ramp leading to the vantage point of high ground to the North-West; the view of the cathedral from here must surely be numbered among the most spectacular examples of 'townscape' in Europe (Plate 304). The lower part of the west front dates from the original period

307 *Left* The *Puerta del Sarmental. Burgos*

308 *Below left* The bristling crockets on the openings of the west towers. *Burgos*

Spanish wife, and his grandson, Francisco, were in charge of both the architectural and sculptural work on the cathedral. Juan de Colonia built the west towers and spires between 1442 and 1458; Simón, the magnificent chapels of St Anna and of the Constable of Castile, while Francisco rebuilt his grandfather's central lantern after its collapse in 1539.

The details of Juan de Colonia's openwork spires – completed centuries before those of his native Cologne – admittedly leave something to be desired, but the towers themselves, with their tall lancets opening into the bell-chambers, are most successful. From a distance the bristling crockets establish a fine sense of scale; seen close-to, their extraordinarily vital, almost 'surrealist' forms, anticipate the extravagant plasticity of Antonio Gaudi's church of the *Sagrada Familia* at Barcelona (6) (Plate 308). Linking the base of the towers, Juan also built the elaborate high balustrade, incorporating a statue of the Virgin and the inscription in Gothic lettering, 'PULCHRA ES ET DECORA'.

of French influence, unfortunately marred by disastrous eighteenth-century improvements, but the upper part reflects a very different tradition. In 1442 Bishop Alonso de Cartagena who had visited Germany, Switzerland, and Bohemia, appointed Juan de Colonia (Johann von Köln) master of the works, and for three generations Juan, his son Simón by a

309 *Above* Detail of the heraldic sculpture, *Capilla del Condestable. Burgos*

310 *Overleaf* Gothic and Islamic influences mingle in the stellar vault of the high lantern over the crossing. *Burgos*

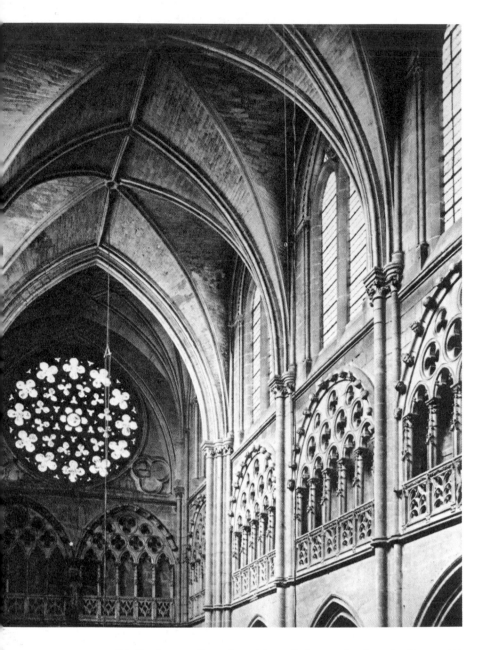

311 *Previous page* Beneath an elaborately decorated arch a pair of furry 'wild women' of medieval legend support the founder's coat of arms; *Capilla del Condestable. Burgos*

312 Interior of the nave looking west. *Burgos*

Continuing our circuit along the North, there is a fine view of Francisco de Colonia's new *cimborio*, its riotous medley of nascent *Plateresque* detail contrasting strangely with the austere grandeur and purity of style of the thirteenth-century Royal Gallery surmounting the north transept; at this point only a narrow lane separates a row of decaying patrician palaces from the magnificent sculpture of the thirteenth century *Puerta Alta* or *Puerta de la Coroneria,* similar in character to that of the *Puerta del Sarmental* to the South. Now closed, the 'High Portal' gave access to the theatrical 'Golden Staircase' in Renaissance Plateresque style in the north transept, which sweeps down to floor level inside the cathedral. East of the transept, the lane opens out and we find ourselves on a terrace looking down on the animated Wheat Market and across to the elegant pinnacles of Simón de Colonia's great eastern chapel, constructed between 1482 and 1495. The *Capilla del Condestable* was erected at the expense of the

High Constable of Castile, Pedro Hernández de Velasco, Count of Haro, to house his tomb and that of his wife, Doña Mencia de Mendoza. The emphasis on rank is pertinent, for both without and within, the magnificent coats of arms constitute probably the most imaginative exploitation of heraldic devices in all architecture (Plates 311 and 309).

Descending a monumental flight of steps, we face a deep, narrow passage at the end of which a richly ornamented Renaissance portal affords access to the north transept at ground level. We, however, skirt the *Capilla del Condestable,* then plunge down a narrow alley with the fortress-like walls of the chapels lining the cloisters towering above (7). At the end of the alley an archway opens into the dark lower walk of the cloister – double-storied thanks to the change of levels – which relieves the congestion in the narrow street and affords tantalizing glimpses into the cloister garden. A moment later we emerge once more into the sunlight, with the *Puerta del Sarmental* looming above us, our walk completed.

The interior of the cathedral may originally have been French in character, but with the centuries has acquired a distinctively Spanish atmosphere with its carved *retablos,* its sculptured stone screens and the great iron grilles connecting the *coro* and sanctuary and closing off the numerous, richly decorated chapels. Most impressive is the interior of the octagonal *Capilla del Condestable,* over 50 feet in diameter, and suffused with light from its clear-glazed, high windows and the partially open stellar vault on even the greyest day. The tomb of the founders stands before the altar with its towering gilded Renaissance altarpiece, flanked by enormous armorial bearings in stone, carved with such *panache* as to be attributed by some authorities to Gil de Siloé, the greatest Spanish sculptor of the day (8). Above each coat of arms an arched recess provides the setting for a pair of free-standing figures of 'wild men' and 'wild women' holding yet another huge coat of arms.

The public area of the nave was almost reduced to a vestibule by the bulky *coro* of 1497, and the western rose can best be appreciated from the organ loft (Plate 312). The most exceptional feature of the nave is the elaborate triforium with its rich variety of heads, beautiful and grotesque, disposed round the circumference of the arch. The effect must have been far finer still before the addition of the late-Gothic balustrade, sprouting finicky pinnacles that grip the columns of the arcade like some parasitic plant.

After the collapse of Juan de Colonia's elaborate *cimborio* – by all accounts the most sensational architectural achievement of the fifteenth century in Spain – the piers of the crossing were strengthened to enormously thick, ungainly cylinders to take the weight of the new lantern constructed between 1540 and 1568 by Francisco de Colonia. After the uncompromising introduction of the piers and the squinches and the interior walls of the lantern, loaded with coarse decoration in a hybrid Renaissance style, the climax of the view upward is all the more stunning. Here, in a superb stellar vault owing nothing to the Renaissance, we have a final summation of Spain's twin Gothic and Islamic heritage (Plate 310).

313 *Right* The Creator as 'Architect of the Universe' imposes order with the compasses of the master mason; detail of the title page of Genesis from *The Bible of St Louis,* a gift to his cousin St Ferdinand, now in the cathedral treasury. *Toledo*

Toledo

On May 25, 1085, Toledo, former capital of the Visigothic kingdom of Spain, was retaken from the Moors by Alphonso VI of Castile.

The old Visigothic cathedral, which had been converted to a mosque, was reconverted to Christian worship and served as the cathedral until demolished at the order of St Ferdinand, who laid the foundation stone of the present cathedral in 1227. A document of that year records that the architect's name was Martín, who was still in charge in 1234. The chevet was completed by 1238 and Master Martín succeeded by a certain 'Petrus Petri' who only died in 1291 after being in charge for

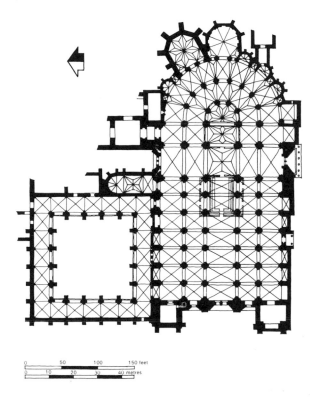

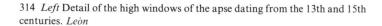

many years. Referred to in Spanish sources as Pedro Perez, it has been suggested (9) he might even have been the same Pierre de Corbie with whom Villard de Honnecourt 'contrived in collaboration' the choir illustrated in the sketchbook, which has a strange alternation of triangular and rectangular vaulting bays similar to that found in the ambulatory at Toledo (Fig. 21 and Plate 315).

The plan with its double aisles and ambulatory, graded in height, is based on Bourges, but with far less vertical drive, coupled with an emphasis on width exceptional even in Spain. Although one of the reasons for the complete rebuilding was a desire to break with the Arab heritage, this manifests itself very clearly in the cusped Moorish arches of the triforium of the ambulatory (Plate 315). In the nave, on which work continued until the end of the fourteenth century, the triforium was completely suppressed, and the classic three-stage interior elevation reduced to two elements only: arcade and clerestory (Plate 318).

Even in a country where the wealth of two continents has

314 *Left* Detail of the high windows of the apse dating from the 13th and 15th centuries. *León*

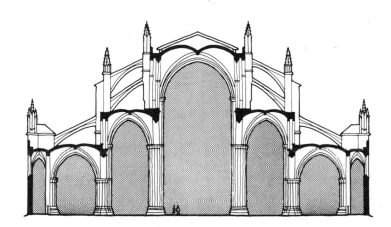

Fig. 21 *Left* Ground plan. *Toledo*

315 *Top* View of the ambulatory looking towards the Santiago Chapel with its delicate stone screen; note the cusped Moorish arches of the triforium. *Toledo*

Fig. 22 *Bottom* Transverse section. *Toledo*

been lavished on the enrichment of the cathedrals and these have seldom been despoiled of their treasures, the Metropolitan Cathedral of the Primate of all Spain is uniquely rich and deserves its epithet of '*Dives Toletana*'. The array of masterpieces is bewildering, ranging from illuminated copies of the Koran and Talmud, and a collection of sacerdotal vestments rivalled only by that in the Hermitage at Leningrad, to splendid paintings by El Greco, including '*The Spoliation*'. Outstanding among the Gothic treasures are the three-volume Bible given by St Louis to St Ferdinand (Plate 313); the enchanting, fourteenth-century French *Virgén Blanca*, preserving its original colouring (Plate 15); the *Reliquary of Sant' Anita*, donated by a Queen of Navarre (Plate 114); and the *custodia* carried in procession through the streets on the Feast of Corpus Christi. Completed by the Flemish goldsmith,

Enrique de Arfe, in 1524, the *custodia* is of gilded silver weighing more than 350 pounds, in the form of an incredibly intricate Gothic steeple nearly 10 feet high, studded with jewels and surmounted by a cross of pure gold made from the first gold brought back from the New World by Columbus.

The immovable furnishings of the cathedral are equally impressive: there is much fine glass, a superb sculptured choir-enclosure, perhaps the finest *reja* in all Spain giving access to the *Capilla Mayor* (10), and a breathtaking altarpiece rising behind the high altar. The carved *retablos* or altarpieces of Spain are unique. Assuming ever more monumental proportions they ceased to be mere furnishings; became attached to the structure and by the end of the Gothic period reached the vaults, while their design took on an appropriately architectonic character (Plates 317 and 339). The work of many specialists—the *trazador* or author of the original sketch, often a painter, a host of wood carvers, *encarnadores* and *estofadores* (tinters of flesh-colouring and painters of ornament) and the *doradores* (gilders)—these *retablos* provide one of the last significant manifestations of that characteristically medieval collaboration of many artists, subordinating their individual personalities to the group endeavour so successfully that it is often impossible to distinguish the contributions of individual artists.

The *retablo mayor* of Toledo (1498-1504) is exceeded in size—though not in beauty—by Seville alone. Surmounted by a huge Calvary group, silhouetted against the vaults, are scenes from the Life and Passion of Christ—the naturalistically coloured figures seeming to enact *tableaux* from a Miracle Play—grouped around a *custodia* carved with exquisite delicacy (Plate 317).

The author of the design was Peti Juan (Petit Jean) who was assisted by the Burgundians Felipe Vigarny and Juan de Borgoñia, the Netherlandish artists Diego Copin and Christiano, the German Rodrigo Aléman, and the Castilian Sebastian de Almonacid. The international cast is typical of the period, with Netherlandish and Burgundian influence even more dominant after the incorporation of these territories within the Spanish Empire through the Habsburg alliance of Juana the Mad.

On three sides the buildings of the old town, still today so oriental in character, jostle the walls of the cathedral, masked to a degree unusual even in Spain by the accretions of centuries. Only on the West do the steep, narrow lanes open out into a plaza of irregular shape defined by the archbishop's palace, the fine town hall and the cathedral (Plate 321). The great portals of the west front date only from the fifteenth century. The slender *trumeau* of the central portal bears a figure of Christ on an exceptionally high pedestal, and on the tympanum is a relief of unusual asymmetrical composition, far earlier in style than its date would lead one to expect. It represents *The Virgin presenting the Chasuble to St Ildefonso*, a miraculous event of the year 666, rewarding the Bishop of Toledo for his

316 *Above left* Silver reliquary of St Eugenio, first Bishop of Toledo, in the cathedral treasury. *Toledo*

317 *Above* Detail of the *Retablo Mayor* carved in larchwood, showing the *Custodia* (bottom right). *Toledo*

318 *Right* View of the nave from the inner aisle. *Toledo*

defence of her impugned virginity. The monumental iron doors with their overall pattern of interlocking emblems of León and Castile and the splendid openwork, double-headed eagles above are not only intrinsically superb, but consort perfectly with their Gothic setting. Not so the elaborate seventeenth-century additions above the portals, particularly the theatrical 'Last Supper', spread across the entire width of the central portal, and set as if on a sloping stage so that the table-top can be seen from below. All that can be said in favour of the curious triangular porch which masks the great Gothic rose, is that it does permit light to penetrate, so that the interior view of the rose, against expectation, remains unspoilt (Plate 318).

Although twin west towers were originally intended, the final design of the north tower leaves no doubt that this concept had by then been abandoned in favour of a single high tower. today balanced surprisingly effectively, despite the disparity of style, by the mass of the classical cupola erected by Jorge Manuel Theotocopuli, the son of El Greco. The great tower rises from a starkly simple lower stage (commenced about 1400) which contained a fortress-like chapel and now, appropriately, houses the fabulously rich treasury. The next stages were built between 1425 and 1440 by Alvar Martínez and are decorated with blind arcading, with the severity of the grey granite relieved by string-courses and a frieze of black and white marble with inserts of blue and white ceramic *azulejos* and with great projecting grilles protecting the openings of the bell chamber (Plate 319). After the conclusive horizontal of the projecting cornice, the crown and spire, erected by Hanquín de Egas (Anequin de Eycken) of Brussels, *maestro de la obra* from 1448, show a renewed vertical impetus. The high, recessed octagon reinforced by pinnacled buttresses, providing a rich play of light and shade, terminates in an octagonal spire ringed with strange but compelling – if unbeautiful – spiky ornaments forming a triple 'Crown of Thorns'.

Master Hanquín de Egas was also responsible for the great

319 *Left* Detail of the grey granite west tower. *Toledo*

portal of the south transept, the *Puerta de los Leones*. The tympanum was subsequently spoilt by an eighteenth-century addition, but the finely moulded jambs contain sculpture by Juan Alemán, 'beautiful in line, noble in design and clear in silhouette' (11) (Plate 322).

320 *Above left* Central portal of the west front. *Toledo*

321 *Above* West front, dominated by the great tower with its spiky triple 'Crown of Thorns'. *Toledo*

322 *Below* Sculptures from the *Puerta de los Leones* by Juan Alemán, after 1465. *Toledo*

León

The little city of León with its remarkably metropolitan air was, during the tenth century, the leading city of Christian Spain and capital of the Kingdom of Asturias, which had early taken the lead in the reconquest of the South. Finally united with her offshoot, Castile, under St Ferdinand, and later rather eclipsed, she could still proudly boast that she had had a line of twenty-four kings before Castile had even had laws!

Work only began on the present cathedral shortly before 1255 and, except for the towers, was completed by 1303, the architect responsible for the design almost certainly being that same Maestro Enrique who built the transepts and nave

of Burgos between 1243 and 1260. The experience and confidence gained at Burgos, and the incentive of starting afresh, seems to have inspired Enrique to attempt something really *avant-garde*. The advance on Burgos is certainly astounding. At León the inspiration derives primarily from Rheims and, as if to compensate for the enforced reduction of scale, Maestro Enrique showed even greater structural daring, further refining and paring down the section of the piers, and introducing a glazed triforium. In so doing, he almost precipitated a disaster similar to that of Beauvais. A couple of centuries later, the structure already showed signs of severe failure and many openings were walled up, including the triforium; by the mid nineteenth century the building was in danger of imminent collapse, necessitating a complete restoration; commenced in 1859, the cathedral was only reconsecrated in 1901. The miracle is that despite these vicissitudes, almost all the original glass has survived.

It is this glass which is the supreme glory of León. Documents in the archives of the chapter record that two glass painters, Adam and Fernán Arnol, were already at work on the windows in 1263, and were joined a year later by Pedro Guillermo, who continued for the following fifteen years.

Unusually interesting is the specific mention, in an entry of 1281, that Juan Pérez, who succeeded Enrique as master-mason, was occupied in painting glass – yet another instance of the multiple skills of the medieval artist. The fourteenth century was a troubled period for León and little progress was made with the windows, but the fifteenth century saw renewed activity and the virtual completion of the work. Seldom, if ever, has thirteenth- and fifteenth-century glass been combined so harmoniously as here, as can be seen from Plate 314, where the large fifteenth-century figures preserve the deep tones of the thirteenth century 'Tree of Jesse' (12). It is this consistent tonality of all the windows – maintained even by the extraordinarily virile nineteenth-century restorations – that enables the glass to be appreciated without the distraction of glare spots. At Chartres and León alone among the great cathedrals of Europe can the magical quality of light, envisaged by the thirteenth-century builders, be fully appreciated.

The most distinctive feature of the west front is the clear expression of the bulk of the nave above the height of the aisles, only the flying buttresses spanning the gap between the nave and the towers placed on either side of the aisles (Plate 328). Combined with this almost aggressive assertion of structural integrity, the very epitome of French *raison* (13), the effect of the great false gables with their rose windows opening to the sky is all the more uncanny – as if the structure were uncompleted or had just been ravaged by fire. At León, with its air of a French cathedral transplanted to Spain, it would seem that a high northern roof was intended to complete the illusion, but never built.

Both the west front and the south transept have triple portals

323 *Left The Entrance to Paradise*, detail from the *Last Judgement* of the west front. *León*

324 *Below* Head of an *Angel of the Annunciation* with the unmistakable 'Rheims smile'. *León*

325 *Right* Sculptured tympanum of about 1300 in the vestibule of the cloister, preserving its original colours. *León*

on the Chartres model with elaborate sculptural decoration. Particularly memorable is the Paradise scene from the 'Last Judgement', for once, more intriguing than the nether regions (Plate 323). On the left, St Peter holds open the gate for a kneeling pope to enter. It is the group on the right, however, that is so interesting in its reflection of the more sophisticated and worldly attitude of the time. Earlier, the eyes of the Elect had been steadfastly fixed on the Gate of Paradise; here the attention of the animated throng, seemingly in no particular hurry to enter, is divided between an elegantly-gowned young king and a boy organist whose assistant pumps merrily at his bellows. Henri Focillon has remarked on the distinctively Spanish colouring of the types and costumes (14). The variegated foliage on the lintel below could, however, come straight from Rheims (Plate 139), the resemblance being even more striking in photographs taken fifty years ago, before the sculptures of León were disfigured by a strange form of stone decay characterized by leprous blistering and scaling. Among the sculptures fortunately spared this fate, is a beautiful 'Angel of the Annunciation', probably from the south portal, displayed in a hall leading off the cloister (Plate 324).

The doorway of the north transept opens into a wide vestibule from which meagre openings connect with the cloister walk. Little light penetrates this double barrier to the richly sculptured portal dating from about 1300 – initially a source of frustration, until one's eyes become accustomed to the penumbra and one realizes how grateful one must be for the poor light, thanks to which the sculpture has preserved its original colours in almost perfect condition. The pensive Virgin on the *trumeau* seems to have a premonition of her son's destiny. Above, on the tympanum, rosy-cheeked angels bear aloft a great *mandorla* from which a triumphant Christ with orb of dominion gives his blessing (Plate 325).

There is much else of great interest in the cathedral (15), but it is the harmonious ensemble of architecture and glass that lingers forever in the memory. If León is not the most original cathedral in Spain, the interior is unsurpassed for sheer beauty, and fully deserves its proverbial medieval title of '*Pulchra Leonina*' (16).

Pamplona

The medieval kingdom of Navarre, which included both the Spanish and French provinces of that name, played a key rôle in the history of Spain. Though ruled by a French dynasty, the soul of Navarre, and the capital, Pamplona, lay in Spain, where its location on the main pilgrim route to Santiago de Compostela, which crossed the Pyrenees at Roncesvalles, gave the kingdom great religious significance and seems to have imbued her people with a missionary fervour which they have retained to this day. There is a solemnity about religious observances in Navarre which is at the opposite pole from the exuberance and almost pagan gaiety with which *Semana Santa* is celebrated in Seville.

The present Cathedral of Pamplona was commenced in 1397, possibly by the French master, Jacques Perut, and much of it completed within the next thirty years (17). The exterior, disfigured by an eighteenth-century west front, is of little interest, but the elegant, if severe, interior is homogeneous and very pure in style, and despite the French derivation of the forms, very Spanish in character with its small clerestory windows punctured in large areas of blank wall – the antithesis of the glass church of the North (Plate 326).

The *pièce de résistance* of Pamplona is the cloister, commenced in 1317 (18), and among the finest in all Europe (Plates 327, 331 and 332). The arcade in the *Rayonnant* style has attenuated, lozenge-shaped, intermediate shafts combining strength with the utmost elegance, and supporting superb

326 *Below left* View up into the vaulting of the crossing; typically Spanish are the small clerestory windows (top right hand corner) punctured in large areas of blank wall. *Pamplona*

327 Detail of the *rayonnant* tracery of the cloister arcades. *Pamplona*

328 *Right* The west front, *León*; portals and elevation of the nave date from the 13th century; the north tower is 14th-century and the south tower 15th-century, the work of Maestro Jusquin from Utrecht in the Netherlands.

tracery framing segments of cypress and palm in the romantic, overgrown garden, and rewarding the solitary visitor at sunrise and sundown with a lace-like pattern, etched on the neutral screen of the cloister wall. A spiral stair leads to the upper cloister walk which affords a splendid overall view. The Spanish genius for balancing light against dark, solid against void, exuberant ornament against ascetic severity, can be seen to perfection in the gable-crowned arcades, the simple upper storey with its lean-to roof and the massive wall of the transept, pierced by a single rose, so framed as to accentuate further its thickness (Plate 331).

On the *trumeau* of the doorway giving access to the cloister from the cathedral, stands the much-venerated *Nuestra Senora del Amparo* at whose feet there are always fresh offerings of flowers. The tympanum above contains an animated and crowded *Death of the Virgin* in high relief, dating from the end of the fourteenth century, and still preserving much of the original polychromy (Plate 330). The child-like figure of the Virgin – traditionally believed to have been untouched by age, but here quite doll-like – contrasts strangely with the lined faces of the Apostles. The Chapter of Pamplona Cathedral lived as a community, and off the cloister opens the former refectory, now a chapel, and the kitchen with its great central fireplace. The well-preserved Gothic murals from the refectory have been transferred to canvas and are now displayed in the *Museo de Navarra*. Most remarkable is the 'Risen Christ' standing triumphant before the open tomb where the Three Marys, bearing jars of unguent, converse with the angel. Below, in a light-hearted, secular vein that accords strangely with the solemn subject, two musicians provide incidental supper music. The work is dated 1330 and signed '*Johannes Oliveri*' (Juan Oliver). Stylistic analogies with contemporary English painting have led some critics to suppose that the artist might have been English (19) (Plate 329).

In the treasury is the silver Reliquary of the Holy Sepulchre, dated 1258, and said to have been a gift to the cathedral from Saint Louis (Plate 333). Within an open shrine whose exquisite detailing recalls that of the Sainte Chapelle, stand the Three Marys and the angel pointing down to the glass-topped sepulchre in which is placed the relic: a fragment of stone from the Holy Sepulchre. Below and of diminutive scale, Pilate's guards sleep. On the mat between them, as in a doll's house, stand a minute jug, mugs and dice.

332 *Overleaf* Detail of cloister. *Pamplona*

333 *Overleaf* Detail of the silver reliquary of the Holy Sepulchre, 1258, said to have been a gift to the cathedral from St Louis of France and now in the cathedral treasury. *Pamplona*

329 *Left The Risen Christ,* detail from a mural by Juan Oliver, 1330, formerly in the refectory of the cathedral. *Pamplona, Museo de Navarra*

330 *Above right* Late 14th-century polychrome relief in the cloister showing the *Death of the Virgin*. *Pamplona*

331 *Right* View of the cloister and south transept. *Pamplona*

Palma

The Balearic Islands, the Greek 'Isles of the Hesperides', fell early to the conquering Moors and were only recaptured in 1229. In that year a great Armada under the youthful Jaime I, King of Aragon and Count of Barcelona, set sail for Mallorca but almost came to grief in a violent storm – the 100 mile voyage from Barcelona taking no less than three days. The city of Palma was taken after a siege of four months and the building of the cathedral on the site of the principal mosque commenced almost immediately, supposedly in fulfilment of a vow made by the conqueror during the peril of the storm at sea.

The *Capilla Mayor* was completed prior to 1264, but progress seems later to have become sporadic, and towards the end of the century the desperate chapter initiated a singularly modern fund-raising campaign, whereby donors were entitled to have their coat of arms emblazoned on vault bosses for a stipulated contribution. Authorities differ as to how much of the conqueror's original building survives in the present structure: probably very little. The authorship of the audaciously original nave, which dates only from the fourteenth century, is much disputed. Master Pere Salvô who commenced the magnificent, and equally unprecedented, Castle of Bellver, built on a circular plan on the hill overlooking the town, for Jaime II in 1309, has been suggested (20); and also the most celebrated of all Catalan masters, Jaime Fabre, a native of Mallorca, responsible for the early work at Barcelona Cathedral and probably also for the great church of *Santa Maria del Mar* in the same city (21). The latter, like Palma,

shows the influence of the wide-naved congregational churches of southern France, hardly surprising since the brilliant independent Kingdom of Mallorca created by Jaime I in 1262 and only united with Aragon in 1344, included Roussillon and the County of Montpellier.

Work continued on the nave throughout the fourteenth and fifteenth centuries – fortunately adhering to the original plan. By the time the west front was reached, the Renaissance style was dominant. Only the central portal, in a rich Plateresque style, was executed and it was not until the mid nineteenth century that work was resumed and the façade completed in a relatively innocuous, if undistinguished, neo-Gothic style.

A more splendid situation than that of the Cathedral of Palma could hardly be imagined, poised high above the great sea-wall, exposed in its entirety on the south, and seeming to embrace the sea. Approached by steamer in the morning mist, the pinnacled silhouette hovers evanescent and seemingly disembodied behind the wheeling gulls; viewed from across the harbour, the taut lines of its serried buttresses are effectively echoed by the rigging of the forest of small craft.

The huge bulk of the nave is assertively Spanish in its 'Cubist' strength and simplicity, and dominated by the recurring *leitmotif* of the buttress wall. Above the level of the monumental, unbroken plinth, the chapels inserted between the main buttresses become polygonal and are strengthened by two intermediate frontal buttresses which, at the same height, step forward slightly and are crowned by matching crocketed pinnacles; these create the effect of a bristling palisade lashed together by the series of horizontal string-courses (Plates 47 and 334). The shade of the deeply recessed and richly sculptured

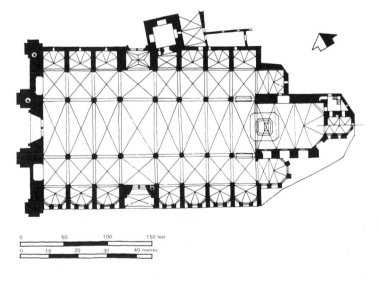

Fig. 23 *Above* Ground plan, *Palma*; the section of the lower half has been taken through the upper portion of the chapels to show the unique arrangement of the intermediate buttressing piers (see plate 334 *right*).

334 *Right* The palisade-like south façade; the chapels inserted between the main buttresses are lit by identical lancet windows, later partially closed with masonry; the two side windows of each chapel are placed diagonally so that the chapels at this level are polygonal. *Palma*

Mirador portal, commenced about 1389 by Pedro Morey, provides the perfect foil to this martial austerity, and invites the worshipper within.

The first view of the interior is overwhelming. The vast nave, 62 feet wide and 141 feet high, is flanked by aisles rising to the level of the springing of the nave vault and, at 98 feet, themselves as high as the nave of any English cathedral. Nave and aisles, together forming an area 364 feet long and 182 feet wide, are separated by fourteen unadorned, octagonal piers only 5 feet 4 inches in diameter and spaced at 29 foot centres – increased to 38 feet for the *Mirador* bay – the whole constituting the lowest ratio of support to enclosed volume in the whole history of Gothic architecture. As might be surmised from these figures, the impression is of one enormous space, articulated rather than subdivided, an effect tracing its ultimate ancestry to Bourges. The climax is provided by the view eastwards towards the sanctuary. Since the earlier choir is only some two-thirds the height of the nave, their junction provides a vast clerestory space into which has been set a great oculus 38 feet in diameter, subdivided by tracery forming a stellar pattern of Islamic inspiration and filled with brilliantly-coloured, non-figurative glass which, in the early morning, bathes the interior in a fiery glow (Plate 5). The great oculus is flanked by two smaller roses at the east ends of the aisles, unfortunately filled with strident modern glass, and the same

motif is repeated yet again at the eastern end of the choir where the rose is flanked by tall lancets. Under this apsidal rose an open arch gives a view of the tiny Chapel of the Holy Trinity, whose special feature is the floor, which is raised nearly 20 feet, so that it can be seen almost in its entirety above the furnishings of the choir.

The *coro* was originally walled and in its normal Spanish location in the nave, but was moved to the choir during the refurbishing of the interior at the beginning of the twentieth century by that exuberant Catalan genius, Antonio Gaudi (22). Eminently successful are his strange but compelling lighting fixtures encircling the great nave piers like spiky chaplets, accentuating rather than interrupting their soaring grace. Nothing daunted by the past, Gaudi relegated the original fourteenth-century *reredos* of the choir to a side wall of the nave, moved the high altar forward, and suspended over it an immense canted chandelier in sculptured metal, a masterpiece of *Art Nouveau,* but hardly sympathetic to its Gothic setting.

335 *Below* Apes carved on the choir-stalls–one dressed as a monk playing the tuba. *Palma*

336 *Right* Detail of sculpture from the *Mirador* portal. *Palma*

Seville

On July 8, 1401, the Chapter of the Cathedral of Seville convened for a historic meeting. The subject was the rebuilding of the great and venerable mosque which had served as cathedral since the reconquest of the city by Saint Ferdinand in 1248, but which was showing signs of age and, besides, seemed an inadequate expression of the religious fervour and civic zeal of the flourishing city. Various grandiose alternatives were considered and a determination voiced 'to build a church so fine that none shall be its equal . . . so great and of such a kind that those who see it completed shall think that we were mad!' The scale of Seville Cathedral – exceeded by St Peter's alone –

covers a rectangle 400 feet long and having an unprecedented, continuous width of some 250 feet.

The unusual rectangular plan (Fig. 24), which occupies the same area as that of the mosque, also shows the ultimate development of that insistent emphasis on area, which, as we have seen, was characteristically Spanish. Despite the great height of the vaults – 132 feet in the nave and transepts, and 85 feet in both of the double aisles – the cumulative impression gained from moving around in the vast, echoing interior is of a dominant, seemingly limitless horizontal extension of space, also, significantly, a salient characteristic of mosque architecture. The two major visual obstructions of the *Capilla Mayor* and the *Coro,* however, make it impossible to find a viewpoint which captures the essence of this spatial sensation,

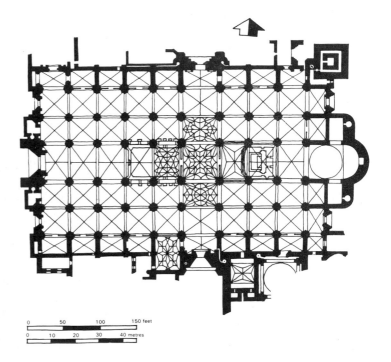

Fig. 24 Ground plan, *Seville* (plan of main structure only, with the *Giralda* tower at the upper right).

338 *Right* View of the vaults rebuilt in 1518 by Juan Gil de Hontañon, with the barnacle-like encrustation of ornament. *Seville*

337 *Above* Interior looking west. *Seville*

certainly does evoke almost incredulous amazement. Apart from the very considerable area of the later additions, the Gothic structure, comprising nave and double aisles of equal height, flanked by chapels inserted between the buttress walls,

and the immensity of the total volume can only be guessed at from the limited view shown in Plate 337. The photograph does, however, convey something of the austere grandeur, saved from bleakness by the extremely fine Renaissance glass.

The details, surprisingly restrained given the late date, nevertheless leave something to be desired. The promise of the interesting pier bases, in the form of an octagon with hollowed sides, is not fulfilled by the piers themselves, with their multiple, indecisive mouldings which obscure rather than reveal the basic form, or the capitals which slice across the vertical shaft piers with a vehemence astonishing for their disproportionately meagre scale. These minor details do little, however, to detract from the general effect of a vast enclosure, which is the particular glory of Seville.

The records of the initial stages of the work were lost in the fire of the Old Alcázar of Madrid, to which they had been transferred on the instruction of Philip II, but the designer was, in all probability, that Alonso Martinez mentioned as being

339 *Left* Detail of the *Retablo Mayor* showing two of the 45 large scenes, each over a yard square; on the left *The Birth of the Virgin,* on the right the *Annunciation. Seville*

340 *Right* The 15th-century *Puerta del Bautismo* of the west front; the flying buttresses over the roof can be seen at the top of the picture. *Seville*

341 *Below* The flying buttresses over the aisles seen from above, and the vaults protected only by a layer of tiles – the negation of the high roofs of the Gothic North. *Seville*

maestro de la obra in 1394, when the initial plans may already have been commissioned. In 1439 a Frenchman, Maestro Carlín, was in charge, at an annual salary of 1500 *maravedis* and two measures of wheat, followed by Juan Norman, under whose direction the first vaults were raised (23). A document of 1496 records the master as one Ximón, who, it has been suggested, might have been Simón de Colonia from Burgos (24).

In 1506 the keystone of the lantern over the central crossing was placed in position, completing the vast project barely a century after work commenced. The lantern, however, collapsed in 1511 and was rebuilt by Juan Gil de Hontañon in

portals, only the side portals of the west front are medieval, the remainder dating from the nineteenth century. Unique and magnificent, though, are the flying buttresses, taking the thrust of the high vaults, particularly seen from above, the elegant 'space-frame' repeating in skeletal form the block-like volumes below (Plate 341).

The parts of the exterior which leave the greatest impression are likely to be of an earlier age: the crenellated walls enclosing the *Patio de los Naranjos,* the former ablution court of the mosque, still fragrant with orange-blossom and cool with the sound of trickling water, and that supreme triumph of Muslim genius, the soaring Giralda Tower, still incomparably lovely despite its incongruous Baroque crown.

342 *Left* Detail of the *Retablo Mayor* showing the east front and the *Giralda* tower as they appeared in about 1510. *Seville*

1518. The triumph of completely different architectural ideals during this brief interval is only too apparent when one compares the sobriety of the general vaulting with the florid exuberance of the rebuilt lantern and adjacent bays (Plate 338). The magnificent *retablo mayor* was designed by the Flemish sculptor, Pieter Dancart, who worked on it from 1482 until his death seven years later. The central part was only completed in 1526 and wings added between 1550 and 1564. 59 feet wide and of virtually the same height, it is the largest *retablo* in Spain and contains forty-five major figure compositions, each over a yard square, within an elaborate architectural framework (Plate 339). Particularly interesting are two subsidiary carvings depicting contemporary views of the city (about 1510), watched over by its patron saints: a general view of the medieval town, crowded within its fortified walls, and a detail of the east end of the cathedral showing the original lantern over the crossing before its collapse, with the small, projecting east chapel (later replaced by the monumental, Renaissance *Capilla Real*) and the Giralda Tower in its original Moorish form (Plate 342).

Subsequent accretions have obscured most of the original Gothic façades, at least for part of their height. Of the elaborate

Italy

8 Italy

Italy constitutes a very special case in the history of Gothic art. The peninsula had never seen so complete a decay of urban life as had the North, and had never been quite reduced to the self-sufficient economy of the *mansus*. Never a completely moneyless society, Italy was the first to witness the revival of commerce and the rise of the banking system which was ultimately to undermine the whole basis of feudal life. Politically, Italy was not a nation, but a series of semi-autonomous principalities and commonwealths, throwing off even their nominal allegiance to the Empire, as that institution crumbled with the fall of the Hohenstaufen Dynasty. Venice, the Papal States, the South and Sicily all cherished independent traditions and were subject to a wide variety of cultural influences. The climate rendered the steep roofs of northern Gothic superfluous and they were quickly discarded, although the high-peaked gable associated with such roofs was often retained for purely aesthetic reasons; the abundance of marble encouraged the use of decorative veneers and inlays of different colours rather than the integral sculptural ornament of the North. Culturally, the ancient classical heritage with its inviolable canons of balance and repose, made it impossible for the Italian artist to accept the dynamism and soaring trans-cendentalism of the Gothic style without reservations.

The northern ideal of a structural framework filled with glass was also modified to retain large areas of wall; the Romanesque tradition of mural painting was continued and elaborated, while the didactic rôle played by stained glass remained supplementary. Italy's unique architectural con-tribution in the Gothic era lay not so much in the religious as in the secular field, in the magnificent buildings housing the seat of government and in the layout of the *piazza* as a focus of civic life. Through the painting of Simone Martini and his school Italy also exercised a major influence on the 'Inter-national Gothic style'.

The modifications which the imported style tended to undergo in Italy are perfectly exemplified by one of the key monuments of Gothic art, the great stained-glass window dating from about 1287, designed as the focal point of the apse of Siena Cathedral (Plate 353). Its design is generally attributed to the great painter, Duccio (1), although it was carried out by two stained-glass specialists. The 'painted glass' technique is uniquely Italian and presages Renaissance methods when compared with the mosaic treatment of thirteenth-century northern stained glass. The discipline imposed by the leading and iron armature has been tolerated rather than exploited, and the decorative possibilities of the rose largely ignored in

343 Upper part of the highly elaborate façade, *Siena*; the oculus appears as a gaping void. In the background is the striped tower.

favour of a rather arbitrary subdivision into nine panels. In fact, one has the impression of a design for painted panels transferred to glass with the minimum modification consistent with technical exigencies, an effect which contrasts strongly with the glass of Chartres which it is almost inconceivable to visualize in any other medium. The dynamic rose-window has become a static oculus (2). Particularly significant is the fact that whereas the tracery of the typical Gothic rose stresses the radius with its implication of rotation and dynamism, here we have a play on verticals and horizontals within a circle, with the perimeter emphasized – an effect that prefigures the Renaissance style in its serenity and balance.

Orvieto

In medieval times the ancient Etruscan town of Orvieto on its almost impregnable plateau dominating the surrounding countryside, achieved considerable importance. Long before its incorporation in the Papal States in 1354 it had very close ties with Rome. A favourite place of residence – and refuge – of the Popes, it witnessed the historic canonization of St Louis.

In 1263, while a sceptical priest from Prague was celebrating Mass at Bolsena, not far away, the Host appeared as living flesh and drops of blood fell from the wafer staining the corporal-cloth, '*uno miracolo stupendissimo*', as the Vulgate chronicles relate. Pope Urban IV, at the time holding court at

Orvieto, ordered the sacred relics to be brought to the city and the following year celebrated this dramatic confirmation of the Doctrine of Transubstantiation by instituting the Feast of Corpus Christi for which Saint Thomas Aquinas composed the Office and the Mass.

A cathedral was already under construction at Orvieto, but

344 *Left* The vertical lines of the Gothic buttresses are accentuated by the horizontal zebra stripes of the Romanesque nave. *Orvieto*

345 *Above* Detail of the *intarsia* decoration from the choir showing St Christopher. *Orvieto, Museo dell' Opera del Duomo*

346 *Right* Interior looking towards the Gothic apse. *Orvieto*

the acquisition of these valuable relics and the income derived from their possession fired the citizens to build a far greater church. It is quite possible that Arnolfo di Cambio (3) himself at the time engaged on other work in Orvieto, submitted a design in the Gothic idiom. The conservative faction among the canons triumphed, however, and, in accordance with their explicit instructions, the design of the new church was to be modelled on that of the Basilica of Santa Maria Maggiore in Rome. The general effect of the nave, with its columns striped in grey and white basalt and travertine, of the round arches, and the exposed timber roof, is strongly reminiscent of the Early Christian basilica, even if the vocabulary of forms is Romanesque with subsidiary Gothic features.

By the time the nave had been completed, the advance of the Gothic style could, however, be resisted no longer and the aspiring character of the eastern portion of the cathedral, where the shafts of the transept piers sweep up to the springing of the vaults with an uninterrupted vertical movement rare, indeed, in Italian Gothic, is proclaimed from afar by the immensely tall, narrow, traceried window of the apse, and its reflection in the polished pink marble paving of the nave (Plate 346). Gleaming like a beacon, it attracts the eye towards the apse where the fine stained glass, the frescoed scenes on walls and vault, the wooden crucifix by Maitani and the Gothic choir-stalls form an unusually harmonious ensemble. Executed between 1330 and 1340 under the direction of Giovanni Ammanati, the stalls and lectern have exceptionally fine *intarsia* decoration (Plates 345 and 352) and were so prized that a special statute of 1357 stipulated that they be dusted only with fox-tail switches.

While the traditional nave had posed no unfamiliar structural problems, the same could not be said for the essay in the new

Three details from *The Creation* by Maitani and his school on the façade. *Orvieto*

347 *Top left* Angels, detail from the *Creation of Eve*.

348 *Bottom* God takes Adam's rib, detail from the *Creation of Eve*.

349 *Top right* The *Creation of the Animals*.

350 *Opposite top* Detail of the 14th-century Reliquary of the Sacred Corporal by Ugolino di Vieri and assistants; two silver and enamel plaques showing a meeting near Orvieto between the bishop sent to fetch the relics and the Pope. *Orvieto, Museo dell'Opera del Duomo*

351 *Opposite below left* Detail of the Reliquary of St Savino by Ugolino di Vieri and Viva di Lando. *Orvieto*

352 *Opposite below right* Detail of *intarsia* (wood inlay) showing St Andrew, from the lectern. *Orvieto, Museo dell' Opera del Duomo*

style, and signs of failure due to insufficient buttressing of the high stone vaults of the transept soon became apparent. Lorenzo Maitani was summoned from Siena in 1305; he reinforced the transepts with flying buttresses and demolished the existing semi-circular apse, constructing in its stead the present rectangular presbytery in the Cistercian manner whose side walls incorporate the necessary buttressing. The lateral flying buttresses of the transepts were originally left free-standing. Only later were they incorporated in additional chapels – but surprisingly enough were expressed on the façade, where their dynamic contours contrast dramatically with the horizontal striping of the walls (4).

The sacred corporal is housed in the north chapel. The marble tabernacle enclosing the reliquary dates from 1358-1364 and the reliquary itself, credited to the Sienese, Ugolino di Vieri (5), and displayed only on rare occasions, is one of the greatest triumphs of the goldsmith's art. Of solid silver and weighing 400 pounds, its finish is either gilt or polychrome enamel whose extreme translucency permits the silver base to shine through, imparting an effect of extraordinary depth and richness. The twin plaques illustrated in Plate 350 depict the meeting of the Pope and the bishop sent to fetch the sacred relics. Particularly noteworthy are the vivacious and highly individualized expressions of the members of the retinue, chiselled with exquisite sensitivity, and the dramatic view of the medieval city with its jostling buildings poised on the edge of a rock and even corbelled out over the beetling crags.

The crowning glory of Orvieto is the west façade (Plate 368), attributed to Lorenzo Maitani who had saved the transepts from collapse, and who was in charge of the works from 1309 until his death in 1330. The Cathedral stands on one of the highest points in the hill-top town and is further elevated on a podium in a piazza which, except for the impressive *Palazzo dei Papi* at a lower level to the south, is surrounded by buildings of inconsiderable scale and height. Consequently, the very last rays of the setting sun still play on the façade. Then arch and gable, rose-window, gallery, buttress and pinnacle – the whole rich repertoire of forms and decoration in marble, bronze and mosaic, combined so successfully – glow with an almost super-natural brilliance against the twilight sky: the whole façade appears to be transformed into a vast glittering reliquary.

Much of the convincing unity of the façade is due to the dominant vertical rhythm established by the powerful butt-resses. Architecturally one could have wished that they had not been interrupted by the marble dado applied almost as a veneer, but had continued down to the base as they do on the sides (Plate 344). However, this would have meant foregoing the reliefs of the dado which are, intrinsically, the most precious part of the whole exterior. Sculpted between 1310 and 1330, their design is attributed to Lorenzo Maitani who may well have executed a considerable number himself. The 'Mirrors' of Nature, Instruction, Morals and History find their allotted place in the reliefs which combine clarity, dignity and vigour with a delicacy worthy of the goldsmith's craft. Particularly fine are the lower registers of the extreme left- and right-hand pilasters devoted to the Creation and the Last Judgement. The vitality and brilliant characterization of the different species of animals who move forward in unison at the Creator's beck are particularly compelling; the poignant tenderness of the gesture with which God slits the side of Adam and creates an Eve lovely as a classical Aphrodite and the grace of the angels whose wings stir the leaves of the primeval

Paradise are also of outstanding quality (Plates 347 and 348). On the pilaster devoted to the End of the World the dead push up the lids of sarcophagi decorated with classical motifs; never have the torments of the damned been portrayed with greater horror – or beauty – than in the anguished figure whose arm is being devoured python-like by a monster and who sinks to his knees fainting with pain and terror (Plate 357).

There is, besides, much other fine sculpture on the façade, especially at the sides of the rose window whose intricate tracery preserves the plane of the façade, evading the unattrac-tive void at Siena (Plates 356 and 343). Truly magnificent are the great bronze symbols of the Evangelists, also dating from Maitani's time, which seem only to await the signal to leap from their precarious perches (Plate 355). The façade which followed Lorenzo Maitani's design so faithfully, took almost three centuries to build, and only in the beginning of the seventeenth century were the high side gables and their mosaic decoration completed, in an illusionistic, Baroque style with three-dimensional perspective effects that are completely out of keeping with the rest (6).

353 *Left* The 13th-century east window, probably designed by Duccio. *Siena*

354 *Above* Detail of the carving on the central portal, consisting of inlaid marble of the *Cosmati* type. *Orvieto*

355 *Overleaf* Bronze eagle, symbol of St John the Evangelist, by Lorenzo Maitani, on the west front. *Orvieto*

356 *Overleaf* The western rose window. *Orvieto*

Siena

Few buildings have successfully survived so many radical changes of concept during construction as Siena Cathedral. The present structure was commenced around 1226 and the Romanesque basilica virtually completed some fifty years later. The central feature was the present great hexagon over the crossing, the width of nave and aisles combined. It was originally far more dominant, particularly externally, since the present nave with its magnificent piers, zebra-striped as at Orvieto but here far more insistent, was then covered – or intended to be covered – at a lower level with an open timber roof. The clerestory wall with its graceful tripartite lancet

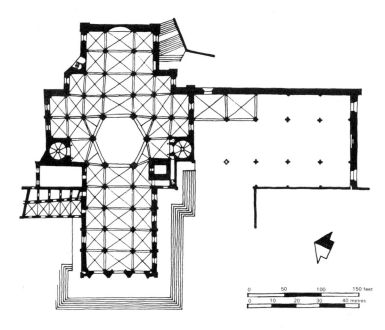

windows and the high stone vaulting were erected later. It was next decided to demolish the existing apse and greatly extend the choir, but this proposal provoked violent opposition on aesthetic grounds, it being argued – with some justification when one surveys the final result – that the disproportionately long choir would throw the hexagon off-balance visually. After much debate the work was, nevertheless, commenced, but while still in progress, the Commune in 1339 resolved on a further and even more radical change.

Siena was then at the height of her prosperity and for a brief period achieved supremacy even over Florence. In a spirit of boundless confidence, and determined not to be outshone by her rival, it was decided to extend the south transept to form a vast new nave at right-angles to the existing one. The choir and the old nave would then form the transepts of an harmonious plan on a vastly increased scale and with a major north-south axis (Fig. 25). The new work was immediately put in hand under the direction of Master Lando di Pietro but, as at Orvieto, problems arose due to an insufficient comprehension of Gothic structural principles. Adequate buttressing of the

357 *Left* Detail from the *Inferno* by Lorenzo Maitani and his school, on the west façade. *Orvieto*

Fig. 25 *Above* Ground plan, *Siena;* on the right the ruins of the nave of the 'new' cathedral.

358 *Top* The cathedral from the ruins of the *Nuovo Duomo;* the high peaked gables associated with the steep roofs of northern Gothic have become a purely decorative screen. *Siena*

359 *Bottom* Interior looking towards the nave; on the extreme right one of the lighter coloured piers of the choir. *Siena*

360 *Left* Detail of *St Simeon* by Giovanni Pisano from the façade. *Siena, Museo dell'Opera Metropolitana*

361 *Above left* Detail of *Miriam* by Giovanni Pisano, from the façade. *Siena, Museo dell' Opera Metropolitana*

362 *Above right* Late 13th-century Reliquary of St Galgano. *Siena, Museo dell' Opera Metropolitana*

high vaults had not been considered as an integral part of the design but signs of failure and distortion were soon apparent in the aisle vaults actually completed. Furthermore, the nature of the site, on built-up ground bounded by precipitous falls, made the inclusion of external buttresses at this late stage all the more difficult.

Meanwhile, the fortunes of Siena had begun to decline, and in 1348 came the Black Death, which killed eighty thousand of her inhabitants. These external factors, as much as technical problems, must have influenced the reluctant decision in 1357 to abandon the *Nuovo Duomo* and concentrate on the completion of the existing structure. The interior walls of the grandiose new nave and the aisle vaults completed were demolished in the interests of safety but the outer walls were left standing. Rebuke to the city though they constituted, it seems that the beauty-loving Sienese did not have the heart to destroy such loveliness, and the walls, partly incorporated in later structures, remain to this day, imparting a Piranesian splendour to the cathedral piazza.

Much of the energy that would have been expanded on the new structure was diverted to the embellishment of the existing cathedral, making it by far the richest of the greater Tuscan churches. Between 1372 and 1562 more than forty artists from the *Maestri Comacini* to Beccafumi—apart from the actual craftsmen—worked on the monumental figure compositions that decorate the marble paving of the entire interior, consisting of inlaid marble designs in a *graffito* technique resembling line engraving.

The extension of the existing choir was completed over a new baptistry at a lower level (made possible by the considerable

363 *Top* Lower part of the façade by Giovanni Pisano; in the background the ruins of the *Nuovo Duomo*. Siena

364 *Bottom* Detail of the pulpit by Nicolà Pisano. *Siena*

365 *Above* Central panel of the *Maestà* by Duccio. *Siena, Museo dell'Opera Metropolitana*

366 *Below The Annunciation* painted by Simone Martini for the Sant' Ansano chapel, Siena. *Florence, Uffizi*

fall in the ground level), and the two elements unified behind a most elegant east front. Internally the form of the new choir followed the precedent of the existing nave with one significant modification symptomatic of the Gothic passion for light: instead of the equal black and white stripes of the nave columns, those of the choir have a far larger proportion of white (Plate 359).

By reverting to the original orientation, the west front resumed its former importance. The lower half of the façade, up to the setback above the great portals, had been executed shortly before 1300 by Giovanni Pisano, in an extremely powerful transitional style, noteworthy for its successful integration of sculpture and architecture. After a hiatus of some seventy years the upper portion was now completed in a

style obviously greatly influenced by Orvieto but lacking its masterly restraint and unity. At Siena it is the detail that entrances, in particular the sculptured decoration by Giovanni Pisano and his school. Giovanni's 'Mary Sister of Moses' (Miriam) and 'Saint Simeon', with their superb quality, dynamism and poignant lyricism, stand in the forefront of Italian Gothic sculpture (Plates 361 and 360) (7).

With the importance attached to the sermon by the influential Mendicant Orders of Franciscans and Dominicans, the pulpit replaced the *ambo* in Italy from the thirteenth century onwards, whereas this change did not generally take place north of the Alps until the fifteenth century; thus some of the finest Italian late-Romanesque and Gothic sculpture is associated with pulpits. Between 1266 and 1268 Nicolà Pisano assisted by his son, Giovanni, and his ablest pupils carved the monumental, octagonal marble pulpit in Siena Cathedral (Plate 364). The pulpit is supported by nine columns: eight around the perimeter, four plain and four resting on the backs of lions devouring their prey, alternating with lionesses suckling their cubs, while the base of the central column has seated female figures of the Seven Liberal Arts and Philosophy, the earliest example of their personification to have survived in Italy. Whereas the epoch-making pulpit in the baptistry at Pisa carved by Nicolà a decade earlier reflects the inspiration of the classical sarcophagi of the Campo Santo, and indeed reveals a most fluent assimilation of Graeco-Roman forms (8), here at Siena we are confronted by the stylistic transition from Romanesque to Gothic sculpture. Gone is the noble simplicity, clarity and balance of Pisa. A restless movement pulsates through the crowded scenes with their complex spatial organization, and the dramatic intensity of mien and gesture anticipates the mature style of Giovanni Pisano (9).

In 1308 Duccio di Buoninsegna, the most renowned artist of the day, had been commissioned to paint a monumental *Maestà* or 'Madonna in Majesty' for the central altar. The contract which is preserved in the cathedral archives, binds Duccio 'to do the best he can, as the Lord shall give him grace to do it.' All materials were to be supplied by the chapter, 'so that the said Duccio shall be bound to put nothing into it but his own self and his labour' (10). The altarpiece was of formidable scale and complexity. The main panel, some 14 feet wide and 7 feet high depicting the Virgin and Child enthroned, surrounded by angels and saints (Plates 365 and 367) was set in an elaborate framework which provided space for numerous subordinate figures and scenes and, since it was free-standing, the back, too, was painted with twenty-six scenes from the Passion.

Despite subsequent dismembering and various vicissitudes, almost the whole survives, constituting Duccio's masterpiece and one of the supreme artistic achievements of all time – and of the Byzantine tradition, but infused with new life and personal vision. The completed altarpiece was acclaimed with the greatest enthusiasm. One chronicler refers to it as 'the most beautiful picture that ever was seen or made, and that cost more than three thousand golden florins' – an enormous sum in the currency of the time, far greater, in fact, than had been spent on Nicolà Pisano's pulpit. On June 9, 1311 the *Maestà* was escorted in triumph from the artist's studio to the cathedral. The expenses are also recorded in the archives:

367 *Right* Detail of The Virgin and Child from the *Maestà* by Duccio (see plate 365).

'Spent on the transportation of the picture painted by Duccio, *Lire* 12, *Soldi* 10, paid to the sounders of trumpets, cymbals and drums for having gone to meet the said picture.' (11) The justified pride of citizenry and artist has been perpetuated in the invocation on the base of the Madonna's throne:

MATER SANCTA DEI–SIS CAUSA SENIS REQUIEI SIS DUCIO VITA–TE QUIA PINXIT ITA

(Holy Mother of God, give peace to Siena and long life to Duccio who has painted thee thus) (12).

Many of the tendencies that had found only tentative expression in Duccio's art were carried to a triumphant conclusion in the work of his successor, Simone Martini. In his masterpiece, the Annunciation painted in 1333 for the Chapel of Sant' Ansano in the cathedral, and now in the Uffizi Gallery in Florence, Gothic lyricism takes flight (Plate 366). The whole pageant of Italian art has produced nothing more poetic than the central figures of this masterpiece: it is the epitome of the Sienese-Gothic style – the rhythmic line, the splendid colour, the aristocratic detachment, the poignant mysticism, all here find their consummate expression. These characteristics were to be disseminated throughout Europe, for the latter years of

Simone Martini's life were spent at the Papal Court at Avignon, from where he was to exercise a profound influence on contemporary French work and on the later 'International Gothic Style'.

Florence

If the Gothic spirit fell on such fruitful soil at Siena and Orvieto, it was quite otherwise at Florence. There the works dating from the period only too often present a real problem of stylistic analysis. Neither Romanesque nor yet early Renaissance, they cannot truly be called Gothic. The Cathedral of Florence is a case in point. Commenced in 1294 on a scale commensurate with the city's growing economic and political importance, to replace the far smaller existing Cathedral of Santa Reparata, the design was entrusted to the celebrated Arnolfo di Cambio, at the time working on the great Franciscan basilica of Santa Croce. Arnolfo's design had as its chief features a nave of four monumental bays and an octagon of unprecedented scale over the crossing. Transepts and chancel conformed to the same shape: five sides of an octagon (Fig. 26).

Progress must initially have been most satisfactory, for by a decree of April 1, 1300, the Commune of Florence granted Master Arnolphus exemption from every tax as long as he should live, in recognition of the 'magnificent and visible

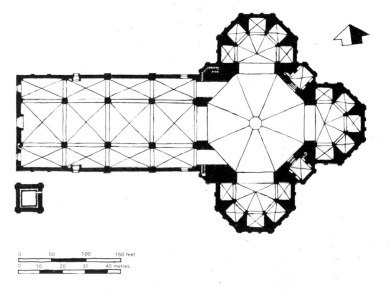

beginning' – a privilege any architect today might envy. At the death of Arnolfo by 1302, however, with only a portion of the west front and the adjoining bays of the side elevations completed, work on the new cathedral came to a virtual standstill.

Florence had entered upon a troubled period in her history with her disastrous campaigns against the great Castruccio Castracani of Lucca who, with far smaller resources, succeeded in defeating her armies and laying waste her territory. Only with Castruccio's death in 1328 did events take a turn for the better, and in 1331 the Commune assigned funds for the continuation of the project and appointed the *Arte della Lana* or Guild of Wool Merchants, renowned for their business acumen, to administer building operations. In 1334 Giotto was appointed master of the works and for the remaining three

368 *Left* The west front, *Orvieto;* the sculptures by Maitani and his school are in the lower half; the mosaics in the upper half are largely 19th-century.

369 *Above left* Entrance doorway of 'Giotto's Tower'. *Florence*

Fig. 26 *Above* Ground plan. *Florence*

years of his life concentrated on the design of the free-standing campanile. Though affectionately known as 'Giotto's Tower', the great painter was, at most, responsible for the design of the lowest of the three main stages. After his death, construction was continued under the direction of his assistant, Andrea Pisano (13), and completed in 1357 by Francesco Talenti; the time lapse is reflected in the stylistic change from a transitional style to the full flowering of Gothic (Plates 369 and 370).

In a land boasting the most superb examples of the detached campanile, Giotto's Tower may with justification claim to be the finest. The way in which the penetration of the solid mass increases as the tower rises, culminating in the great, three-light opening of Talenti's belfry with its intricate tracery and wire-thin spiral columns, is a particularly successful adaptation of the traditional Romanesque practice: with successively more attenuated stages the campanile belies its mass and despite its many Classical features has a soaring Gothic grace, which would have been further accentuated if the originally intended spire had been added. The sheathing of the brick structure with coloured marble veneers and inlays in rectilinear patterns is characteristically Tuscan (14).

With the belfry almost completed, work was resumed in 1357 on the cathedral proper, now envisaged on an even more grandiose scale. Of the opinion that Arnolfo di Cambio's design was somewhat old-fashioned, Francesco Talenti effected several significant changes, the most basic of which was to increase the depth of the nave bays by a third – a very questionable improvement. Three of the new bays, therefore,

370 *Left* General view of the exterior with the tower. *Florence*

371 *Below* The nave of *Santa Maria del Fiore*, looking east. *Florence*

372 *Right* Detail of the fresco of the *Church Militant* by Andrea da Firenze, 1366, in the Spanish Chapel of the *Chiostro Verde* of *Santa Maria Novella*. In the background can be seen the cathedral as designed by the committee appointed in the same year. The tall traceried clerestory windows were superseded by *oculi;* the octagonal dome, although it has no drum, is already the dominant element and in essence remarkably similar to Brunelleschi's solution. *Florence, Church of Santa Maria Novella*

equalled the four of Arnolfo and a fourth was added at the east. The size of the octagon was also enlarged. This design was further modified and a final plan, to which all concerned were formally sworn to adhere, was drawn up by a committee of four architects and four painters in 1366 (15). From then onwards work proceeded smoothly. By 1421 the drum of the cupola was in position and all that remained was the roofing of the central space, of such a scale as to present an apparently impossible task and one to which, rather surprisingly, little attention seems previously to have been given. Brunelleschi's brilliant solution is no longer Gothic, however, but largely Renaissance in character.

The vast and chilly interior of the cathedral inspires awe rather than affection (Plate 371). Anything but ingratiating, it evokes surprisingly different responses, ranging from 'hard', 'bleak' and 'uninteresting' to 'serene', 'stern' and 'noble'. Particularly interesting are individual reactions to the scale. To Ruskin 'the most studious ingenuity could not produce a design for the interior of a building which should more completely hide its extent, and throw away every common advantage of its magnitude' (16), while to the great German scholar, Paul Frankl, on the other hand, it 'possesses a more tangible feeling of bigness than the great French Cathedrals . . .' (17). The proportions of the nave arcades, unpleasant in themselves, do, however, seem to propel one forward irresistibly towards the crossing and the octagon.

Though the vocabulary of forms employed in the nave is predominantly Gothic, they have been combined in such a manner that the end result is a negation of the very spirit of the Gothic. Verticality has been consistently denied. The

373 *Above* Detail of the head of the Virgin by Arnolfo di Cambio, formerly incorporated in the façade. *Florence, Museo dell'Opera del Duomo*

374 *Below* Sixteenth century Florentine drawing showing the unfinished façade of the cathedral shortly before its destruction. *Florence, Museo dell' Opera del Duomo*

375 *Right* View of the south façade; the nearer bay adjoining the *campanile* was built according to the original design but subsequently increased in height. *Florence*

376 *Below right Hope Reaches for the Crown of Immortality,* detail from the bronze south doors of the Baptistry by Andrea Pisano. *Florence*

nave piers, 'Classical' in their insistent frontality, are spaced 63 feet apart as opposed to only 24 feet at Amiens, although the height of the vaults is practically the same. At the same time what little *élan* is generated by the pointed arches is firmly held down by the powerful horizontal gallery-cornice which continues uninterruptedly around nave, octagon and apses,

377 Three hexagonal bas-reliefs by Andrea Pisano from the lowest stage of the *campanile* representing from left to right *Music, Metallurgy, Sculpture. Florence*

378 *Below* Detail from the *Porta della Mandorla* showing the *Assumption of the Virgin* by Nanni di Banco. *Florence*

379 *Overleaf* Detail of bronze bas-relief from the south doors of the Baptistry by Andrea Pisano, showing *St John Baptizing in the Wilderness. Florence*

stepping out above the nave piers and obscuring their connection with the vaulting at precisely the point where the vertical continuity of line would be most effective. Momentarily hiding the cornice from view, the vaults leap skyward and the proportions of the interior are altered to an almost unbelievable extent.

The building of the Duomo was to a remarkable degree a communal undertaking and the concern of every citizen. A sixtieth part of the city treasury was set aside for its construction and also the revenue from a special poll tax of 2 *soldi* levied on every male inhabitant. Public interest was not only tolerated but invited. Thus in 1357, for example, a model indicating the shape of the nave piers was set up in a public place with a notice in large letters advising anyone who found fault with the design to contact the Board of Works within eight days, and assuring him of an attentive hearing. When, later that year, the foundation of the first nave pier was at long last laid, it was to the acclaim of bells, organ and song.

Work on Arnolfo di Cambio's west façade, continued by Francesco Talenti, had ceased in 1420 and was a little more than a third complete when it was demolished in 1588 at the instigation of Bernardo Buontalenti. A Mannerist Florentine drawing gives an idea of its appearance shortly before its destruction (Plate 374) and, together with the quality of the surviving fragments, makes one regret the loss all the more. The present tasteless façade was built to the design of Emilio De Fabris between 1871 and 1887.

Among the sculptures from Arnolfo di Cambio's own hand salvaged from the original façade is his monumental, seated *Madonna and Child* with its compelling synthesis of Classical, Byzantine and Gothic elements (Plate 373). The vitreous inlaid eyes, so disconcerting at first glance, impart a strangely compelling expression, veiled and introspective, to the Madonna's face. Andrea Pisano was responsible for the south doors of the baptistry (1330-1336), the most important work in the neglected medium of bronze during the entire Gothic era (Plates 376 and 379). Truly architectonic in their respect for the integrity of the sculptural plane, they are, in a way, even more appealing to modern sensibilities than the illusionistic marvels of Ghiberti's justly celebrated 'Gate of Paradise' (18). Also to Andrea Pisano are attributed the finest of the hexagonal bas-reliefs from the lowest stage of the campanile (Plate 377).

Outstanding among the architectural sculpture still incorporated in the fabric, is the relief of the *Assumption of the Virgin* by Nanni di Banco (1414-1421) on the northern *Porta della Mandorla*, the last of the cathedral's doorways to be completed (Plate 378). The crockets on the gable are already changing into classical *rinceaux* and the youthful Donatello himself worked on the small statues of prophets, but the agitated movement still conforms to the spirit of *Spätgotik* rather than that of the early Renaissance.

Milan

With the Cathedral of Milan we reach a fitting conclusion, for, together with the Cathedral of Seville, this was the last building enterprise on the truly grand scale and one of the last executed in the spirit of the medieval mason's craft (19). Here, in the bristling forest of statue-crowned pinnacles (some of which, admittedly, are later additions), can be seen the final expression of the spirit that had carved the portals of St Denis and placed the enigmatic oxen on the towers of Laon.

In 1385 Gian Galeazzo Visconti usurped control of Milan from his uncle and set the city on the path to prosperity and power after two centuries of political eclipse. By the very next year construction had started on a vast new cathedral, which the inordinately ambitious Gian Galeazzo had decided should rival, and surpass, the greatest buildings of the North – no mean undertaking considering that no really large structures had been built in Lombardy for centuries. Even at this late stage, certain aspects of the Gothic style seem still to have perplexed Italian masters. Problems soon arose, particularly concerning the abstract geometrical basis to which plan and section should conform, and which would, in turn, decide the height of nave and aisles. Gian Galeazzo therefore consulted the most renowned foreign masters as well, and no fewer than fifty names are cited in the archives in connection with the design and initial constructional phases during the first fifteen years. Unusually well documented, the proceedings provide perhaps our best insight into the medieval mason's philosophy of design.

Initially, a section *ad quadratum,* based on the square and double-square, with accented central nave and both side aisles of the same height seems to have been favoured, but this was soon abandoned in favour of a section based on the equilateral triangle. Since the height of an equilateral triangle is incommensurable with its side the assistance of a mathematician, Gabriele Stornaloco of Piacenza, was sought. He rounded off the incommensurate height of 83.138 to 84 *braccia,* which

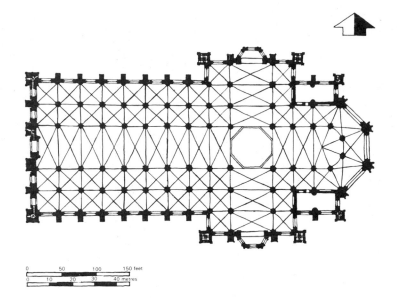

Fig. 27 *Above* Ground plan. *Milan*

380 *Below* Cross-section through Milan cathedral showing the proportional scheme *ad triangulatum.* After Cesare Caesariano's *Vitruvius,* Como, 1521

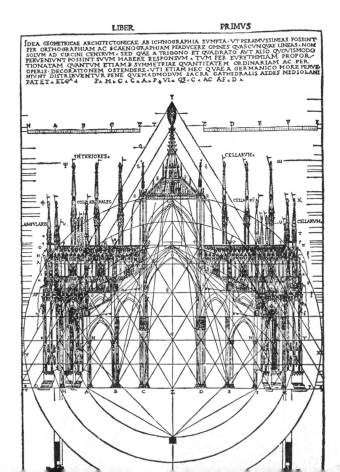

could conveniently be broken down into six 'great units' of 14 *braccia.* The controlling geometrical basis of his scheme is illustrated in the *Comment on Vitruvius* by Cesare Caesariano, published at Como in 1521 (Plate 380). The indication of the hexagon and circle related to the basic equilateral triangle stresses the conformity of the design to universal laws.

Accepted in principle, Stornaloco's scheme was also eventually modified (20), effecting a further reduction in height and conforming more closely still to Classical norms. It was this compromise of 'true measure' which so infuriated the German consultant, Heinrich Parler, and which he felt endangered not only the beauty but also the stability of the structure. Fruitful collaboration between the foreign consultants and the native masters proved impossible since they argued from different premises. In determining the section of the piers, for example, the Lombards resorted to their time-honoured building technique (*ars*) rather than to the theoretical concepts on which the northern masters laid such stress and which they called *scientia.* Working with marble which they knew so well and accustomed to joining the piers with iron binding-rods placed at the level of the capitals, the Lombard masons could pare down the structural sections required – a fact which the foreign consultants were loath to accept. Heinrich Parler was dismissed in 1392, and Ulrich von Ensingen, finally persuaded to come to Milan from Ulm in 1394, stayed only six months; the Italian masters struggled on alone until a number of unresolved problems forced them to call in another group of consultants in 1399, this time French.

At a tempestuous meeting at the beginning of the year 1400, called to discuss the numerous criticisms by the French master, Jean Mignot (Giovanni Mignot), a complete ignorance of Gothic principles of construction was shown by the Lombard masters, who went so far as to deny that pointed arches exerted a thrust. Flabbergasted, Master Jean flung at the Lombard masters a contemptuous '*ars sine scientia nihil est*', to which they promptly retorted '*scientia sine arte nihil est*'.

The following year Mignot returned to Paris, his criticisms largely unheeded, and the Italians went ahead with their own

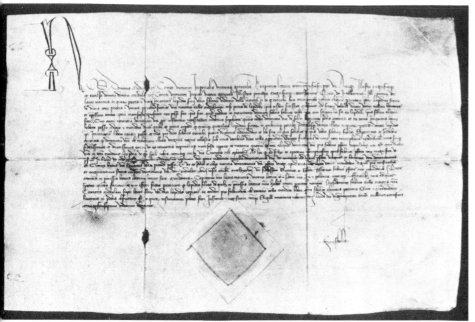

design and vindicated themselves in practice rather than in theory, for despite the critical defects found by the erudite northerners – the poor foundations, weak piers, and inadequate buttresses – the cathedral has survived to this day (21). The choir and transepts were completed in about 1450 but the construction of the great lantern and the nave dragged on for centuries and the west façade was only finally completed at the order of Napoleon in 1809. Covering an area of some 126,000 square feet, Milan comes second in size to Seville alone among Gothic cathedrals and is unique in its marble finish.

In a deed dated October 19, 1387, still preserved in the cathedral archives, Gian Galeazzo Visconti granted the right to work the marble quarries of Candoglia for the construction of the cathedral (Plate 381). Quarried in the vicinity of Lake

Maggiore, the stone could conveniently be transported by *barconi* across the lake and by river and canal to a dock in the very heart of the city, a mere stone's throw from the building site (22). With a few insignificant exceptions, the entire cathedral is faced – and still today repaired – with Candoglia marble, whose characteristic rosy tint, still glowing through the accumulation of industrial grime, faithfully reflects the slightest change in the quality of light and takes on a wide variety of hues through orange, pink, mauve and violet, at the hour of sunset (Plate 382).

The nave vaults are 148 feet high (almost as high as those at Cologne) but appear far less lofty. This is due primarily to their strange capitals in the form of enormous drums, 20 feet high with canopied niches containing over-life-size sculptures. Though the detail is Gothic, this deliberate interruption of the vertical line shows quite a different spirit. The abiding memory of the interior is, nevertheless, of a dark, brooding, mysterious, northern forest, an impression strengthened by the elaborate tracery pattern of the vaults – the only part of the structure not finished in marble – painted in an astoundingly convincing, if regrettable, *trompe l'œil* style (Plate 383) (23).

The wide-flung nave and double aisles of gradated height are based on Bourges, but with the emphasis on width rather than height. The clerestory windows are very meagre and filled with deep-toned stained glass, so that the nave is plunged in semi-gloom. This makes the blaze of light admitted by the three great windows of the polygonal apse all the more

381 *Above left* Deed of Gian Galeazzo Visconti, of 19 October 1387, ceding the marble quarries of Candoglia in perpetuity to the Cathedral Chapter. *Milan, Archives of the Veneranda Fabbrica*

382 *Left* Exterior, general view. *Milan*

383 *Above* View of the vaults with their *trompe l'œil* tracery. *Milan*

384 *Right* Detail of the central apsidal window with the giant *razza* in its centre, the heraldic device of the Visconti family. *Milan*

compelling, and draws one irresistibly towards the choir, the oldest and finest part of the building. These apsidal windows are truly monumental, each measuring 68 feet by 28 feet. The *Razza,* that curious heraldic device of the Visconti, resembling a halo of gyrating flame, occupies a focal position in the central window and sets the whole vast composition in motion as effectively as the whirling *Flamboyant* tracery of the flanking windows (Plate 384).

It is on the easternmost façades that one finds the oldest and most interesting of the vast number of statues that adorn the cathedral – 2,245 to be precise – executed by an international cast of sculptors, French, German and native Italian, from the fourteenth to the twentieth centuries, in a bewildering variety of styles: Gothic, Renaissance, Baroque, neo-Classic, neo-Gothic, and 'Monumental Mason's Modern' (Plates 386 and 387).

Characteristically Italian is the roofing surface of great marble slabs laid to such a slight fall as to permit promenading. On a sunny day it is difficult to be hypercritical as one strolls on marble terraces dappled with intricate filigree patterns cast by pierced and crested balustrades, as one surveys the great lantern and *flèche* with its colossal gilded bronze statue of the Virgin, 350 feet above the bustling pavements, or glances out through a palisade of statue-crowned pinnacles to the distant Alps (Plates 385 and 388): beyond them lies the 'barbarian' world of the North which found its finest artistic expression in that *opus modernum* of the thirteenth century, the Gothic cathedral.

385 *Left* View on to the shadow-dappled, marble roof terraces. *Milan*

386 *Above right* The buttresses, pinnacles and statues, from the roof. *Milan*

387 *Right* The populated pinnacles. *Milan*

388 *Overleaf* View of the apse and octagonal lantern over the crossing, crowned by the 350ft-high gilded statue of the *Madonnina. Milan*

Glossary

Ambulatory
The aisle enclosing the apse. Usually semi-circular or polygonal, it could also, particularly in the case of English churches with their characteristic square east end, be rectangular.

Apse
The semi-circular or polygonal termination of the east end of the chancel or a chapel.

Archivolt
The reveal or inner surface of an arch, often decorated with concentric rows of sculpture or mouldings.

Barrel vault
A semi-circular tunnel or waggon vault (Fig. 1).

Boss
A projecting block at the intersection of vaulting ribs, often elaborately carved (Plate 251).

Capilla mayor
The sanctuary housing the high altar in a Spanish church.

Centering
Temporary wood support used in the construction of a masonry vault or arch.

Chantry chapel
A small chapel endowed with land or other source of regular income for the maintenance of a priest to say masses for the soul of the donor.

Chevet
The French term for the east end (head or *chef*) of a Gothic church, comprising an apse, ambulatory and radiating chapels.

Ciborium
A decorative canopy or *baldachino* over an altar or tomb (Plate 280).

Cimborio
The name given to the lantern over the crossing admitting light to the interior in a Spanish church (Plate 310).

Clerestory
(Most probably from the French *clair*: light.) The upper stage of a wall, rising above the adjoining roofs and pierced with clerestory windows (Fig. 7).

Corbel
A projecting bracket bonded into the wall and supporting a weight (Plate 214).

Coro
The choir of a Spanish church, usually located in the eastern bays of the nave.

Crocket
(From the French *croquet*: a hook.) A projecting spur with foliate ornament spaced at regular intervals along the edges of a gable, pinnacle, etc.

Crocket capital
A capital with crocket-like foliate forms, characteristic of classic French Gothic (Plate 158).

Cusp
The projecting point formed by the intersection of two segmental arcs or foils.

Fig. 28

Decorated style
The name given to the lavishly ornamented second phase of English Gothic, extending from the late thirteenth century to the mid-fourteenth. It is sometimes further subdivided into an earlier Geometric Period and a later Curvilinear Period, the names referring primarily to the pattern of the window tracery.

Diaper
A small-scale, overall surface-pattern comprising such forms as lozenges or squares (Plate 197).

Dog-tooth
An early English ornamental motif consisting of raised pyramids with a stylized foliate pattern (Plate 202).

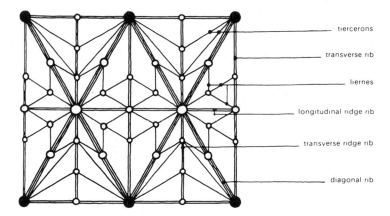

Fig. 29 Plan of two bays of stellar vaulting clarifying the nomenclature of Gothic vaulting ribs.

Early English
The name given to the first and classic phase of English Gothic, spanning most of the thirteenth century. Particularly characteristic are the tall, narrow, pointed windows (hence the alternate name 'Lancet Style').

Fan vault
A regularized highly decorative form of vaulting developed in England in which the ribs all have the same curvature (Plate 256).

Finial
(From the Latin *finis*: end.) A carved terminal ornament at the apex of a gable, etc.

Flamboyant
Used to describe tracery with sinuous flame-like forms. The late phase of French Gothic is known as *Style Flamboyant*.

Flèche
(Arrow.) A slender wooden spirelet over the crossing; particularly characteristic of French Gothic.

Foil
Name given to each of the small arcs separated by cusps. The number of foils are designated by the terms trefoil, quatrefoil, etc. See diagram under *Cusp*.

Formeret
A vaulting rib abutting the external window wall; known in England as a wall rib. See Fig. 29.

Groined vault
A vault formed by the intersection of two barrel or tunnel vaults, the line of intersection of the vaulting surfaces being known as a groin (Fig. 2).

Hall-church
A church with nave and aisles of equal or near equal height. A form particularly characteristic of German Gothic (Plate 295).

Jamb
The upright surface (frequently splayed) forming the side of an archway or window.

Jubé
The French term for a screen separating the choir from the nave (Plate 179).

Lancet
A slender pointed arch resembling a lancet; strictly speaking, more sharply pointed than an equilateral arch. Lancet openings are particularly characteristic of the early English style (Plate 242).

Lantern
A tower, usually over the crossing, glazed to admit light to the interior.

Lierne
(From the French *lier*: to bind, tie.) A short, purely decorative, intermediate vaulting rib which does not rise from the main springer and is not a ridge-rib. See Fig. 29.

Mandorla
An almond-shaped aureole enclosing the figure of Christ or the Virgin Mary (Plate 378).

Misericord
(Pity.) A projection under the hinged, tip-up seat of a choir stall, frequently elaborately carved, which, together with the arm-rests, affords a measure of support for members of the clergy required to stand during the offices.

Mouchette

A curvilinear, dagger-shaped tracery motif characteristic of the English Decorated and French Flamboyant styles.

Fig. 30

Mudéjar

Spanish style of markedly Moorish character produced by Moorish craftsmen under Christian rule.

Oculus

A circular opening or window without stone tracery (Plate 343).

Ogee

A continuous, S-shaped, reverse-curve. An ogee arch: a pointed arch with a head so shaped, inscribed by means of four centres.

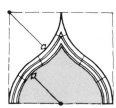

Fig. 31

Perpendicular style

The last of the three great styles of English Gothic, so named from its emphasis on the vertical line and generally considered to extend from the early fourteenth to the early sixteenth century.

Pier

The preferred term for a support other than a column in Gothic architecture. Particularly characteristic of the mature Gothic style is the 'Compound Pier', composed of a cluster of colonnettes which continue the line of the vaulting shafts to ground level (Plate 107).

Plateresque

Literally, resembling the art of the *platero*, or silversmith. The name given to a Spanish style of the late Gothic and early Renaissance periods, characterized by lavish, delicately chiselled ornament.

Presbytery

The portion of the church east of the choir reserved for the priests and housing the high altar.

Pulpitum

The screen closing off the west end of the choir. The English equivalent of the French *jubé*.

Quadripartite vault

The classic Gothic solution, with each vaulting bay divided by diagonal ribs into four triangular cells (Plate 142).

Rayonnant

The name given to the French style of the period 1250-1350, characterized by the ultimate paring down of supports to create veritable window-walls, a certain linearism in the detail, and a particular fondness for rose windows with 'radiating' tracery – hence the name (Plate 108).

Reredos or retablo (Spanish)

An altarpiece of carved and painted wood, stone or precious metal rising above the rear edge of an altar.

Retablo mayor

The principal altarpiece or *reredos* of a Spanish church.

Retrochoir

An area behind the high altar, particularly applicable to English Gothic, where the retrochoir between the presbytery to the west and the Lady Chapel to the east often functions as a rectangular ambulatory (Plate 219).

Ridge-rib

A decorative rib following the ridge of a vault, either longitudinally or transversely.

Rood loft

A gallery surmounted by a monumental Crucifixion or Rood (from the Anglo-Saxon for a rod).

Sedilia

Seats for the priests, generally of masonry, on the south side of the presbytery.

Severy

A compartment or section of the vaulting web enclosed between vaulting ribs.

Sexpartite vaulting

A compromise system evolved in the search for the perfect solution to the problem of vaulting oblong bays. A square composed of two nave bays constitutes the vaulting unit, sub-divided by an intermediate transverse rib on the line of the intermediate pier, thus creating a six-part compartment with the diagonal ribs (Fig. 4 and Plate 64).

Sondergotik

The bizarre final phase of German Gothic, with vaults characterized by interlacing blade-like ribs, often arbitrarily truncated (Plate 278).

Soufflet

An elongated quatrefoil with one pair of opposite ends pointed, popular as a tracery motif in the Flamboyant style (Fig. 32).

Fig. 32

Spandrel

The triangular space enclosed between an arch, a vertical line rising from the springer and a horizontal line at the level of the apex.

Springing

The point at which an arch begins to curve upwards from the impost block.

Squinch

An arch bridging the angle between two walls. Placed diagonally in the internal angles, squinches may, for example, conveniently be used to convert a square to an octagon.

Stiff-leaf

The name given to the crisp, conventionalized, multi-lobed, decorative treatment of foliage in the Early English style; usually anything but 'stiff' in effect.

Strainer arch (or beam)

An arch or beam inserted across an opening to resist an end thrust tending to cause distortion of, for example, a pier (Plate 217).

String-course

A projecting horizontal course or moulding.

Tierceron

An intermediate vaulting rib, rising from the main springer and terminating at the ridge-rib. (See Fig. 29).

Tracery

The stone framework of a Gothic window. Tracery is conveniently divided into two types: *plate tracery*, the earlier form, in which the effect is of a solid surface pierced with openings (Plate 95); and mature Gothic bar tracery, in which a filigree of thin stone members subdivides the glass area into manageable sizes and provides the necessary degree of stiffening (Plate 108).

Tribune gallery

A vaulted gallery above the aisles which helped to take the thrust of the high nave vaults before the evolution of the flying buttress; characteristic of the earliest Gothic cathedrals (Plate 103).

Triforium

An arcaded wall passage opening towards the nave, at the height of the sloping roof over the aisle vaulting and below the clerestory (Fig. 7).

Trumeau

A central pillar supporting the tympanum and dividing a wide doorway in two; in French Gothic frequently carved with figure sculpture of major iconographic importance (Plate 156).

Tympanum

The triangular space between the lintel and an arch over a doorway (Plate 163).

Vault

A ceiling or roof of masonry constructed on the principle of the arch.

Vaulting shaft

A vertical member supporting a vaulting rib and extending for a part or the entire height from the springing of the vault to the ground (Plate 235).

Voussoirs

The wedge-shaped blocks of masonry used in the construction of an arch.

Notes

Introduction – The Cathedral in Medieval Society
The relations between patron and builder, and the social background to medieval cathedrals and architecture in general is most fully worked out (for France) in Joan Evans, *Art in Mediaeval France* (Oxford, 1948); G. Duby, *Europe of the Cathedrals, 1140-1280* (Geneva, 1966). For the relation of design and religious sentiment, see C.N.L. Brooke in *Bulletin of the John Rylands Library* Vol. L (1967, pp. 13-33). For general, but penetrating sketches of medieval society and its religious setting, see S. Painter, *Mediaeval Society* (Ithaca, 1951); C. Dawson, *Mediaeval Religion* (London, 1934); R. W. Southern, *The Making of the Middle Ages* (London, 1953). A study of the economic setting of medieval towns, and a full bibliography are to be found in the *Cambridge Economic History of Europe*, vol. III (Cambridge, 1963).

On cathedral clergy and chapters, see K. Edwards, *The English Secular Cathedrals in the Middle Ages* (2nd edn., Manchester, 1967); C. N. L. Brooke in *A History of St Paul's Cathedral*, ed. W. R. Matthews and W. M. Atkins (London, 1957); on chantries, K. Wood-Legh, *Perpetual Chantries in Britain* (Cambridge, 1965); and for ecclesiastical institutions in general, G. Le Bras, *Histoire des Institutions Ecclésiastiques*, I (Paris, 1959).

The building of Milan Cathedral is vividly described by E. Bishop in *Liturgica Historica* (Oxford, 1918), pp. 411-21: see also p. 311.

On the Dance of Death, see H. Holbein, *Dance of Death*, ed. J. M. Clark (London, 1947), and T. S. R. Boase in *The Flowering of the Middle Ages*, ed. J. Evans (London, 1966).

On Eadmer and Canterbury Cathedral, see R. W. Southern, *St Anselm and his Biographer* (Cambridge, 1963); his *Historia Novorum* was edited by M. Rule, London, Rolls Series, 1884, and translated by G. Bosanquet (London, 1964).

For the Merchant of Prato, see I. Origo, *The Merchant of Prato* (2nd edn., London, 1963).

Chapter 1 – The World of the Cathedral Builders
1   Raoul Glaber or Rudolf the Bald (*c*. 985-*c*. 1046). The importance of the so-called 'Millenary Psychosis' and its aftermath has been grossly overestimated by one school of historians, provoking an equally violent reaction minimizing its rôle. That it was significant is obvious. The thing to bear in mind is that this was but one of the factors contributing to the extraordinary revival of Europe in the eleventh century.
2   Cluny was founded in 910 and its first abbot was St Berno. Cluny began to reform other houses in the time of St Odo, the third abbot. The congregation of Cluny eventually assumed enormous importance – especially for the arts. The third Abbey Church at Cluny commenced in 1088, and wantonly destroyed during the French Revolution, was, in its day, one of the greatest churches in Christendom.
3   After the wholesale slaughter and destruction of the great tenth-century invasions of Norsemen, Magyars and Muslims, this was a relatively peaceful period. The idea of a 'Truce of God' between the feudal lords was first proclaimed by the Church at Le Puy in 990 and bore its first fruit in Aquitaine – one of the factors accounting for the great prosperity of the dukedom. Later, rulers in northern France, Italy and Germany joined the movement.
4   Henri Pirenne: *A History of Europe from the Invasions to the XVI Century*, London, 1939 (quoted by permission of Messrs George Allen and Unwin Ltd). Pirenne's view is now no longer accepted without qualification. It is generally thought that the local lords also played an important part in the early stages of the revival of urban life.
5   *idem*
6   Such episcopal sees, 'cities' by mere virtue of the presence of the bishop, were, however, simply ecclesiastical administrative centres for a purely agrarian society until revitalized by the merchant community.
7   The bourgeois himself was, from the start, a free man.
8   The exceptionally important rôle played by English scholars in this transmission may be partly explained by the rule of a Norman dynasty in Sicily, where Englishmen held high office: 'Walter of the Mill' was archbishop of Palermo, and Robert of Selby the chancellor of King Roger II; English students were particularly welcome at the University of Salerno.
9   The classic formula as exemplified by the *Summa* of St Thomas Aquinas, was to divide each topic into four sections. First the arguments against the conclusion were stated (*videtur quod* . . .); the arguments in favour followed (*sed contra* . . .); the teacher then stated his opinion (*respondeo dicendum* . . .); and finally attempted to explain away the apparent objections noted, one by one (*ad primum, ad secundum* . . .).
10   Erwin Panofsky: *Gothic Architecture and Scholasticism*, Latrobe, 1951 (quoted by permission of the Archabbey Press). For a complete exposition of the relationship of architecture and philosophical thought in this period, the reader is referred to this book.
11   Brunetto Latini gave as his reasons for writing his *Le Trésor* in Romance (French), the inimitable sound of the language and the fact that it was universal.
12   A sustained number symbolism based on the sacred number of the Trinity and its square, nine – perfection raised to a higher power as it were – permeates both formal structure and narrative. Not only are the *Inferno*, *Purgatorio* and *Paradiso* each subdivided into nine sections, but Dante first meets Beatrice when each is nine years old, and they first speak nine years later; this kind of number symbolism was of the utmost significance to the medieval mind.
13   Confirmed in a description of the ceremony by Pierre de Corbeil, Archbishop of Sens.
14   Extract from a letter to the King of France from the authorities of the University of Paris, asking for the suppression of the feast. Quoted by Sir Edmund K. Chambers, *The Mediaeval Stage*, Oxford, 1903. (By permission of the Clarendon Press, Oxford.)
15   This view is from a high vantage point in the tribune gallery; from ground level the organ obscures even more of the great western rose.
16   Quoted by G. G. Coulton, *Art and the Reformation*, London, 1928 (quoted here by permission of the Cambridge University Press).
17   *Works of François Villon*, translated by Geoffrey Atkinson, London, 1930.
18   Repeated by William Durandus (*c*. 1220-1296) in his influential work on the symbolism of church architecture and ornament, the *Rationale Divinorum Officiorum*.
19   Emile Mâle: *L'Art religieux du XIIe siècle en France*, Paris, 1922; *L'Art religieux du XIIIe siècle en France*, Paris, 1902; *L'Art religieux de la fin du moyen age en France*, Paris, 1908. The author acknowledges his profound debt to these inspired volumes. The product of a lifetime's work in the field, they are the starting point of all modern studies of medieval iconography. The volume on the XIIIth century is available in an English translation under the title *The Gothic Image*, London, 1961.
20   All four creatures are winged, a fact which has often led the human figure to be mistaken for an angel, but the medieval commentators are specific on this point.
21   Emile Mâle, *The Gothic Image*, Collins, London, 1961, quoted by permission of the publishers.
22   Honorius of Autun (active 1090-1120), *Speculum Ecclesia*.
23   Arnold Hauser, *The Social History of Art*, London, 1951. (By permission of Alfred A. Knopf, Inc., New York.)
24   Vincent of Beauvais uses the word, '*doctrinale*', to include work of every kind, manual and intellectual.
25   Concordances were found in the smallest details of the story: 'The Ass which bears the implements for the sacrifice, not knowing what it does, is the blind and undiscerning Synagogue. The wood that Isaac bears on his shoulders is the very Cross. The thorn-bush in which the horns of the ram are entangled is an allusion to the Crown of Thorns.' Emile Mâle: *The Gothic Image*, London, 1961. (Quoted by permission of Messrs Collins.).

Chapter 2 – The Gothic Style
1   Abbreviated, paraphrased and edited rendering of the translation by Erwin Panofsky: *Abbot Suger on the Abbey Church of St Denis and its Art Treasures*, Princeton University Press, 1946.
2   The floor of the *camera* was raised above that of the chapels over the side aisles, the difference probably being bridged by a wooden stair which could be removed, making the treasure-house a defensible refuge.
3   The translation is that of Otto von Simson, *The Gothic Cathedral*, copyright 1956 by Bollingen Foundation, New York. The expression 'sacred windows' occurs elsewhere in the text. The literal translation of Erwin Panofsky reads: 'an elegant and praiseworthy extension . . . by virtue of which the whole (church) would shine with the wonderful and uninterrupted light of most luminous windows, pervading the interior beauty.'
4   The phrase is Suger's.
5   Viollet-le-Duc, *Dictionnaire raisonné de l'architecture française du XIe au XVIe siècle*, Paris, 1854-1868, 10 vols.
6   Pondering on the mystery of Christ's sacrifice for man's twofold death of body and soul (through the Fall), St Augustine in his treatise, *De Trinitate*, considers that the octave (1 : 2), most easily recognized of all consonances, will best convey to the listener the meaning of the mystery of the Redemption.
7   The analysis is according to E. de Bruyne, *Etudes d'esthétique médiévale*, Bruges, 1946, quoted by Otto von Simson, *The Gothic Cathedral*, New York, 1956. Subtitled *Origins of Gothic Architecture and the Medieval Concept of Order*, von Simson's book provides a brilliant exposition of the rôle of light, and 'measure, number and weight', in Gothic architecture.

8 Abbreviated rendering of the translation by George Coulton, *Art and the Reformation*, London, 1928, of the 'Apologia' of St Bernard to William, Abbot of St Thierry (quoted by permission of the Cambridge University Press).

9 Excerpt from the translation by Erwin Panofsky, *Abbot Suger on the Abbey Church of St Denis and its Art Treasures*, Princeton University Press, 1946.

10 *ibid*

11 *ibid*

12 Louise Lefrançois-Pillion, *Les sculpteurs français du XII et XIII siècles*, Paris, 1931.

13 Paul Frankl, *Gothic Architecture*, Harmondsworth, 1962. (Quoted by permission of Penguin Books Ltd.)

14 Examples of the pointed arch occurred in ancient Assyrian architecture chiefly in utilitarian structures such as aqueducts and drains. From there it travelled to Persia where the conquering Arabs learnt its use.

15 Henri Focillon, *The Art of the West in the Middle Ages*, Vol. II: *Gothic Art*, London, 1963; a translation of the French original: *Art d'occident*, Paris, 1938. (Quoted by permission of Phaidon Press Ltd.)

16 Pol Abraham, *Viollet-le-Duc et le rationalisme médiéval*, Paris, 1934.

17 The arched openings customarily provided for circulation in the roof may have suggested the idea.

18 Arnold Hauser, *The Social History of Art*, London, 1951. (Quoted by permission of Alfred A. Knopf Inc., New York.)

19 Before this date the glass had been supported in position by a framework of stone or a trellis of woodwork.

20 During the thirteenth century the bars formed a simple vertical and horizontal grid; in the fourteenth century they were bent to follow the outlines of the medallions.

21 James Rosser Johnson made a microscopic examination of a fragment of twelfth-century Chartrain ruby glass and reported: 'To the naked eye the pigmented half appears to be a solid colour, but under the microscope it presents an extraordinary sight, a highly complex structure composed of many thin laminations of red alternating with striae of colourless glass, totalling as many as fifty-six laminae in certain sections of this fragment . . . possibly resulting from successive gatherings made from alternate pots . . . after which the metal was spun out by centrifugal force.' James Rosser Johnson, *The Radiance of Chartres*, London, 1964. (Quoted by permission of Phaidon Press Ltd.)

Chapter 3 – How the Cathedrals Were Built

1 The translation is by Henry Adams, *Mont Saint-Michel and Chartres*, Boston, 1904. (Quoted by permission of the New English Library Ltd.)

2 The Archbishop of Rouen in a letter to Bishop Thierry of Amiens, also dated 1145, cites the example of Chartres as inspiring the faithful of his own and neighbouring dioceses to form similar associations for the transport of materials to build churches.

3 In the case of monastic establishments, the sacrist normally performed this function.

4 The author acknowledges his debt to the researches into medieval building methods by Professors Douglas Knoop and G. P. Jones, published in *The Mediaeval Mason*, Manchester, 1949.

5 Analysed in great detail by Professors Douglas Knoop and G. P. Jones: *The First Three Years of the Building of Vale Royal Abbey*, in the masonic periodical, *Ars Quatuor Coronatorum* XLIV.

6 Lionel Vibert, *Freemasonry before the Existence of Grand Lodges*, London, 1932, comments: 'Exactly what *free* meant has been much discussed. That the original meaning was a mason who worked in freestone is one explanation, but it is not without philological difficulty. Another interpretation is that the *free* mason was the workman out of his indentures, and so free of his guild or his borough. Another is that he was independent of his guild; free from it and its restrictions; free, for instance, to travel and work where he liked; or he may even have been free from certain restrictions of the borough, by reason of his having to work outside of the city as well as in it.'

G. G. Coulton, *Art and the Reformation*, London, 1928, states: 'It is probable that *freemason* means *worker in freestone*, for freestone is mentioned in much earlier documents than *freemason*.' (Quoted by permission of the Cambridge University Press.)

7 French documents contain several such references, also to women plasterers, and at Cærnarvon there is mention of '*Juliana filia fabri, Emmota filia fabri, Elena de Engelond and Juliana uxor Ade.*' D. Knoop and G. P. Jones, *The Mediaeval Mason*, Manchester, 1949.

8 This, and the figure for the earlier period are taken from John Harvey, *The Gothic World*, London, 1950. The author, who has made an important contribution to our knowledge of medieval building practice, and is, perhaps, the foremost authority on the lives of the medieval master-builders, suggests

a multiplier of 100 to obtain a rough modern equivalent for medieval money values for the period up to 1348, and a multiplier of 80 for the following century and a half (to account for the sharp rise in prices after the Black Death).

9 The estimate is that of G. H. Cook, *Portrait of Salisbury Cathedral*, London, 1949.

10 John Plantagenet, Duke of Bedford, brother of Henry V of England and Regent of France.

11 The Communes of Italy provide a notable exception, but many features of medieval life in Italy were unusual from the point of view of the northern Europeans.

12 For example, to the Archbishop of Canterbury in 1396.

13 Quoted in George Edmund Street, *Some Account of Gothic Architecture in Spain*, London, 1865.

14 *ibid*

15 The *Relatio Translationis corporis Sancti Geminiani* (Modena ms Cod. OII ii).

16 Abbreviated to the letters in heavy type; the missing portions are familiar from old engravings and records. The inscription was removed when the small chapel constructed by Master Erwin and the ancient *jubé* were destroyed during the refurbishing of the cathedral in the *grand goût* following its return to the Catholic cult in 1681.

17 The quotations are from the translation of the Rev. Robert Willis, *Facsimile of the Sketch-book of Wilars de Honecort*, London, 1859.

18 Particularly interesting in this regard are two rather grotesque male nudes sharing the Recto of the leaf with a superbly drawn foliage-head. If copied from the antique, as one would naturally suppose, why is the one man wearing typical medieval footwear fastened on the inner side, the other a worker's cap of the period? The explanation must surely be that they were drawn from life. The treatment of the drapery is outstandingly competent, as in all Villard de Honnecourt's work, but the same can hardly be said for the drawing of the nudes; obviously a field in which the Gothic artist had little experience or interest.

19 The Cathedral of Kassa (Kaschau) is considered by some authorities as having stylistic affinities and a possible link with Villard de Honnecourt.

20 Quoted in translation by Professor Paul Frankl, *The Secret of the Medieval Masons*, The Art Bulletin, XXVII, 1945.

21 Matthäus Roriczer: *Das Büchlein von der Fialen Gerechtigkeit*, Regensburg, 1486.

22 Abbreviated excerpt from the translation of the dedication by John W. Papworth *Roriczer on Pinnacles* published by Architectural Publications Society, London, between 1848-1853.

23 See Paul Frankl, *The Secret of the Medieval Masons*, The Art Bulletin, XXVII, New York, 1945.

24 See B. Kossmann: *Einstens massgebende Gesetze bei der Grundrissgestaltung von Kirchengebäuden* (*Studien zur deutschen Kunstgeschichte no: 231*), Strasbourg, 1925.

25 Translation by Geoffrey Grigson, Architectural Review, Vol. 98.

Chapter 4 – France

1 During the fourteenth century, chapels were inserted between the buttresses and a large traceried window placed in the south transept, replacing the early rose. In the sixteenth century the chapels were closed off from the church with rather charming, Renaissance-style stone screens.

2 From quarries, some ten miles distant, ceded to the Cathedral by Jean de Chermizy in a charter dated 1205.

3 The upper medallions of the lancet from which Plate 77 is taken, illustrating the life of the Virgin, tell the ingenuous tale from the Apocrypha of the midwives summoned by St Joseph and of their reaction to the virgin birth. In the Gospel of the Pseudo-Matthew it is related that Joseph had gone to seek a midwife and when he returned to the cave with two midwives the Child had already been born. One of the midwives asked to touch Mary and was amazed to find that she was still a virgin in spite of the birth. The other, unable to believe this, insisted on touching her also and immediately her hand withered as punishment for her incredulity. After a vision in which she was told to touch the Child – which she does – the second midwife's hand is then healed.

The story is quoted in full by Emile Mâle in *The Gothic Image*, London, 1961.

4 The two west towers, two over each transept and a central tower over the lantern.

5 Aggravated by the high and narrow proportion of the nave. The round openings which originally opened into the roof space over the tribunes were suppressed about 1230 and the sills of the clerestory windows lowered, increasing their height considerably. The original arrangement has been restored by Viollet-le-Duc in the bays adjoining the crossing.

6 Introduced for the first time in the interests of unity.

7 In 1638 Louis XIII had consecrated his kingdom to the Virgin and promised to furnish Notre-Dame with a new High Altar surmounted by a Pietà. The vow was fulfilled by Louis XIV. The Virgin of the Pietà by Nicolas Coustou (1723) has been compared rather unkindly, but with some justice, to a swooning actress from the Comédie Française.

8 Particularly those dating from the early Gothic period where the colouring is stylized. The naturalistic flesh tints characteristic of some late-Gothic sculpture can come dangerously close to the ghastly effects of waxworks.

9 The so-called *Caveau de Saint Lubin.*

10 Otto von Simson, *The Gothic Cathedral,* copyright by the Bollingen Foundation, New York, 1956.

11 The third range of nave buttresses was added later.

12 This plausible hypothesis was advanced by Emile Mâle.

13 Louise Lefrançois-Pillion, *Les Sculpteurs français du XII et XIII siècles,* Paris, 1931.

14 The intermediate stage in the evolution of Gothic sculpture can be seen at Laon.

15 A small sacristy in the late thirteenth century; a chapter house surmounted by the Chapel of St Piat to the east of the cathedral in the fourteenth century, and, fortunately, only one addition to the nave: the fifteenth-century Vendôme Chapel.

16 Seven years later, Jean de Beauce was already working in the Renaissance style, when he built the charming little Clock Pavilion at the foot of the tower.

17 It is a contested point whether Aubry de Humbert, the founder-archbishop, or Robert de Coucy occupied the central plaque.

18 The cathedral endured four years of attack from German artillery fire. Incendiaries set fire to scaffolding erected around the north tower for restoration work, and the fire spread to the great roof which was entirely destroyed. Although the walls and vaults held, much of the stonework was calcined and many sculptures also destroyed by shelling. The restored cathedral was only reopened in its entirety in 1938.

19 The central shaft of the triforium was made only slightly thicker than the others (Plate 133). The lower arcade was abandoned altogether, but the wall surface kept far forward, forming a walk-way at sill level – a feature characteristic of the region, and known as a *galérie champenoise.*

20 The dating of the sculpture of Rheims has given rise to bitter controversy among scholars and has been further complicated by the fact that many of the figures were moved from one location to another – a veritable game of 'musical chairs' as one critic has described it – so that adjoining figures are often quite unrelated, chronologically and stylistically.

21 This final 'Gothicization' of the Romanesque wheel-window by the artists of the north should be contrasted with the tendency of Italian masters to reduce the dynamic rose window to a static oculus (Plate 343).

22 The same drapery *motif* also occurs in the porches outside. A magnificent series of real tapestries, the oldest dating from the fifteenth century, formerly only displayed for coronations, now covers the walls of the nave aisles, imparting an inimitable touch of warmth to the interior.

23 Forming part of the Royal Treasury of France, the reliquary is supposed to have originally been given by Henry II to Renée of Lorraine, abbess of Saint-Pierre-les-Dames at Rheims.

24 The second is of Geoffroy d'Eu (died 1236), his successor.

25 Those medieval 'adders' that, as we have seen, were so susceptible to the lure of song.

26 From the *trumeau* of the south portal. Even more regal is the Virgin from the tympanum of the St Anne Portal at Paris, about 1170 (Plate 20).

27 John Ruskin, *The Bible of Amiens.*

28 The evil deeds are here symbolized by a bloated head with huge ears and a toad-like creature clinging underneath the scale.

29 The Archbishop of Bourges, Henri de Sully (1183-1199) and the Bishop of Paris, Eudes de Sully, the successor to Maurice de Sully, but no relative.

30 Chiefly in the interiors of the towers and in the roof spaces over the nave aisles.

31 His body rests at the Abbey of Fontevrault.

32 A symbolic or even a seriously satiric intent is discounted by such authorities as Emile Mâle.

33 Their 'floating' appearance contrasts forcibly with the successful integration of the sculpture of the central portal in the late *Flamboyant* style of the beginning of the sixteenth century.

34 See Glossary.

35 Erwin Panofsky: *Gothic Architecture and Scholasticism,* Latrobe, 1951 (quoted by permission of the Archabbey Press).

36 Eventually Pope Clement V could no longer ignore the complaints, and despatched a group of prelates to Albi, who found the charges only too well substantiated, and freed prisoners confined in pitch darkness in the dungeons of the episcopal prison, still awaiting trial after five years or more.

37 Since destroyed.

38 During the Hundred Years' War and again in 1562, when a Protestant army besieged Albi, the fortress-like character of her churches proved a major deterrent, commemorated in a contemporary verse:

. . . Les églises furent bien asseurées
De Sainct Salvi et de Saincte Cécile.
Les portes sont, forsque l'une, murées,
Entrer dedans n'eut pas été facile . . .

39 A symmetrical door on the north, reserved for the clergy, afforded access to the complex of the episcopal *Palais de la Berbie* but was subsequently walled-up. The present north doorway, leading to the narrow lane opened up in the nineteenth century, was formerly connected to the fifteenth-century sacristy.

40 Basil Spence has acknowledged his debt to Albi in the design of the new Coventry Cathedral.

41 Although the *Baldaquin* was only erected between 1519-1535, it was paid for with money specially left for the purpose by Louis I.

42 Now replaced by replicas; the originals may be seen in the Musée de l'Œuvre Notre-Dame.

43 The secular authority charged with the allocation of funds and the general administration of the cathedral building operations; first mentioned in Letters of Indulgence dating from the period 1190 to 1202.

44 Master Rudolf I, author of the earlier drawing 'A', about 1275.

45 As if the Tempter were already a corpse; the symbolism is of the death of the soul through sin.

46 This sculpture, dating from about 1280, reflects the mannerism of the contemporary School of Paris in the elegant and slightly affected gestures.

47 The façade without the towers forms a square; the length of the diagonal of this square determines the height of the towers and an isosceles triangle inscribed within the overall rectangle determines the angle of inclination of the gables. An analysis by H. Reinhardt and E. Fels, *La façade de la Cathédrale de Strasbourg,* appears in the *Bulletin de la Société des Amis de la Cathédrale de Strasbourg,* Strasbourg, 1935.

48 Such was the amazement inspired by the great tower of Strasbourg, that when the corporations of master-builders and master-masons of the Empire assembled at Regensburg (Ratisbon) in 1459 to form a common association, they conferred the title of Grand-Master on the master of the Strasbourg Lodge, while the city became the Grand-Chapter of the Order – supreme honours granted in perpetuity and, in fact, retained until the dissolution of the guilds by Louis XIV in 1707 for political reasons.

49 The eventful history of the city has left its mark on the cathedral. From 1525 to 1681 it was a Lutheran church, a change which resulted in no more serious loss than the destruction of the subsidiary altarpieces. The union of Alsace with France under Louis XIV and the return to Catholicism saw a major refurbishing of the choir in the *grand goût,* involving the destruction of the ancient *jubé,* Master Erwin's Lady Chapel and, later, of the original high altar. After serving as '*The Temple of Reason*', during the Revolution, the cathedral was reconsecrated in 1801 and the damage repaired as far as possible. Between 1848 and 1850 the decoration in the *grand goût* was in turn removed and an attempt made to return the choir to its original appearance, as conceived in terms of nineteenth-century Romanticism. The cathedral suffered serious damage in the German bombardment of Strasbourg during the Franco-Prussian War. The city became part of Germany in 1871, and remained so until 1918 so that the major work of restoration, like that of the actual construction, was done by Germans. The cathedral was damaged by bombing in World War II, fortunately not too seriously.

Chapter 5 – England

1 For a most diverting account of the effects of national preferences and idiosyncrasies on English art through the centuries, see Nikolaus Pevsner, *The Englishness of English Art,* London, 1956.

2 In a Vatican entry of 1295 the term *opus anglicanum* occurs no fewer than 113 times, far more often than embroideries of any other specified origin.

3 Gervase of Canterbury (1141-1210), *Chronica.* The excerpts are from the translation of the Rev. R. Willis, *The Architectural History of Canterbury Cathedral,* London, 1845.

4 Geoffrey Webb, *Architecture in Britain in the Middle Ages,* Harmondsworth, 1956.

5 An interesting and scholarly account of his career is given by John Harvey, *Henry Yevele: the Life of an English Architect,* London, 1944.

6 Paul Frankl, *The Crazy Vaults of Lincoln Cathedral,* Art Bulletin XXXV, New York, 1953.

7 Earlier scholars found a twelfth century date for the Lincoln vaults

unthinkable in view of the precocity of the design, and assigned them to 1239, when the fall of the crossing tower necessitated a certain amount of reconstruction; the consensus of expert opinion today favours 1192.

8   The spatial possibilities of the Lincoln arcading were brought to complete realization in the thirteenth-century arcading of the cloister of the Abbey of Mont St Michel in Normandy, where the similarly staggered arcades are separated by an extremely narrow vaulted mock walkway.

9   John Harvey, *English Cathedrals,* London, 1950.

10   The member of the chapter entrusted with education in the diocese and the keeping of the chapter seal and library.

11   John Ruskin, *The Seven Lamps of Architecture,* London, 1849.

12   Certain details, notably the fenestration, were remodelled in about 1440 in the Perpendicular style.

13   Geoffrey Webb, *The Sources of the Design of the West Front of Peterborough Cathedral,* Archaeological Journal (London), LVI (supplement for 1952).

14   The earliest surviving example of fan vaulting, and the most beautiful, is to be found in the cloister of Gloucester Cathedral (Plate 256).

15   Commonly so-called. Actually a misnomer since the cathedral is dedicated to the Virgin.

16   A more precise, if less evocative comparison would be with steel lally columns. Even in steel, they could hardly be thinner.

17   Wyatt, who removed most of the old glass on the usual pretext that it darkened the interior, also demolished the fine – if somewhat dilapidated – campanile standing to the north of the nave and removed the chancel screen, a fragment of which, however, survives in the north choir transept (the Morning Chapel).

18   Although the period of true chivalry, epitomized by St Louis, passed with the thirteenth century, it was in the fourteenth century that the symbols and trappings of chivalry were displayed most ostentatiously.

19   So-called after Christ's words to his Apostles, 'Behold I go before you into Galilee', chanted by the cantor as he led the procession through the porch and back into the church before High Mass on Sundays.

20   In the section on Rouen.

21   Paradoxically, considerable French influence can be traced in the formation of the eminently English Perpendicular style. The most important source of inspiration for the Royal Chapel of St Stephen was the Sainte Chapelle and various Perpendicular motifs can be traced back to Clermont-Ferrand, Limoges and Narbonne.

22   Nineteenth-century historians generally credited the origin of the Perpendicular style to 'West Country' masons. The consensus of modern opinion favours a London origin, although it is acknowledged that some of the transitional Perpendicular style work in the south transept of Gloucester can be only a few years later than the very earliest examples in the capital.

23   Joan Evans, *English Art 1307-1461,* Oxford, 1949.

24   Henri Focillon, *The Art of the West in the Middle Ages,* London, 1963; a translation of the French original, *Art d'occident,* Paris, 1938.

25   The minor stylistic changes between the choir and the Lady Chapel, completed a century and a half later, underline the inherently conservative character of much late-Gothic work.

26   Derived from the French *chanter:* to sing or chant. See G. H. Cook, *Mediaeval Chantries and Chantry Chapels,* London, 1947, for a detailed discussion of the subject.

27   Although only completed *c.* 1412, it is known that several bays had already been vaulted during the period of Abbot Horton. The design had, therefore, been completed prior to his death in 1377.

Chapter 6 – Germany and Austria

1   Possibly the choice of the new style was influenced by the political opposition of the Archbishop to the Hohenstaufen with whom the currently fashionable, late-Romanesque style was so closely associated.

2   With elements also from Beauvais.

3   Sulpiz Boisserée had found a thrifty *hausfrau* in Darmstadt using the great drawing of the west front stretched in a frame for drying beans.

4   This is, perhaps, no coincidence for both figures and decoration show the influence of the East Anglian style at the end of the thirteenth century which so captivated Europe and found one of its two major expressions in the embroideries known as *opus anglicanum.*

5   Later converted to passageways leading to the ambulatory of the present choir.

6   At Freiburg, too, the controlling figure for the proportions of the new work was the equilateral triangle.

7   Perhaps to be identified with Master Heinrich Müller.

8   The two chapels at the head of the choir, disposed on either side of the central axis. They were built from Imperial Austrian benefices and revenues in

honour of members of the Habsburg family.

9   And to the architecture of Champagne generally.

10   Recalling that at Erfurt, the so-called 'Triangle', built some two generations earlier.

11   If not the Elder Heinrich himself, it is reasonably certain that he was a member of the family and certainly well acquainted with the design of the church at Gmünd.

12   Paul Frankl, *Gothic Architecture,* Harmondsworth, 1962. (Quoted by permission of Penguin Books Ltd.)

13   It is quite probable that the original design of Ulm Minster, based on that of the *Kreuzkirche* at Schwäbisch-Gmünd, envisaged no western tower whatever.

14   By Jörg Syrlin the Elder, responsible for the unique choir-stalls.

15   As at Cologne, the original drawing had been preserved.

16   The equally elaborate 'stem' supporting the pulpit is carved from a second piece. The vertical joint where the pulpit joins the stair leading up to it, can be seen on the right.

17   J. Huizinga: *The Waning of the Middle Ages,* London, 1924.

Chapter 7 – Spain

1   Only widely used towards the very end of the medieval period to close off chapels and areas for the exclusive use of the clergy, most *rejas* are in the Renaissance style.

2   John Harvey, in the excellent introduction to his *Cathedrals of Spain,* London, 1957.

3   Berenguera, Queen of Castile in her own right, and mother of St Ferdinand, and Blanche de Castile, wife of Louis VIII of France, were sisters.

4   Whether Burgos reflects the influence of Coutances or *vice versa* is a disputed point; both choirs were possibly influenced by a common source: the Cistercian monastery church of Pontigny.

5   The difficult, steeply sloping terrain no doubt dictated the unusual orientation of the cathedral, with the main axis running not from East to West, but North-East to South-West. For the sake of easy comprehension we have ignored this irregularity in our circuit of the cathedral, preferring to speak of a 'west front' rather than a 'south-west front', for example.

6   Commenced in 1884 and still under construction.

7   The cloisters were built by Juan Pérez, successor of Maestro Enrique, between about 1290 and 1324. The arcades have unfortunately been glazed, robbing them of much of their charm.

8   Author of the magnificent tomb of Juan II of Castile and his queen, Isabella of Portugal, the parents of Isabella la Católica, and of her brother, the Infante Alonso, in the church of the *Cartuja de Miraflores* on the outskirts of Burgos, rebuilt by Juan and Simón de Colonia.

9   Notably by Camille Enlart, in *Manuel d'Archéologie Française,* Paris, 1902-4. This would mean that the ambulatory vault post-dated 1234, when Master Martín was still in charge, and also that Pierre de Corbie was something of a prodigy when he collaborated with Villard de Honnecourt. Most authorities today, however, believe 'Petrus Petri' to have been a Spaniard.

10   The *reja* in Renaissance style by Francisco de Villalpando (1548).

11   Theodor Müller, *Sculpture in the Netherlands, Germany, France and Spain: 1400-1500,* Harmondsworth, 1966.

12   Late-Gothic, Spanish stained glass, which in design shows strong Netherlandish influence, is generally exceptionally deep-toned for the period. Here again, the desire to keep interiors cool and dim was probably a contributory factor.

13   The arrangement recalls the expression of the flying buttresses – though not the placing of the towers – in the influential west front of *St Nicaise* at Rheims by Hugues Libergier. A variation occurs on the towerless south transeptal front at León and is there particularly reminiscent of the elevation of a great church in the *Rheims Palimpsest.*

14   Henri Focillon, *Art d'Occident,* Paris, 1938, available in translation as *The Art of the West in the Middle Ages,* London, 1963.

15   A magnificent late-Gothic, painted altarpiece in the style of Rogier van der Weyden, reconstituted from fragments of the original which had been replaced during the Baroque era and distributed among various provincial churches; good late-Gothic choir-stalls enclosed within an effective Renaissance screen; many fine tombs, particularly in the cloister, which, however, was revaulted in the sixteenth century in a singularly unsuccessful Renaissance style; and in the interesting cathedral museum, outstanding tenth-century Mozarabic manuscripts.

16   The saying defining the salient characteristics of four great cathedrals, ran: *Sancta Ovetensis, Dives Toletana, Pulchra Leonina, Fortis Salamanca.* 'Oviedo the holy, Toledo the rich, León the beautiful, Salamanca the strong.'

17   Under his successor, most probably the Fleming, Jannin Lhomme, who started work in 1416 on the monumental alabaster tomb of Charles the Noble

and his wife in the nave.

18 The north and east walks were completed in the first campaign, the south and west walks only much later, between 1492 and 1507.

19 John Harvey, *The Cathedrals of Spain,* London, 1957.

20 *idem*

21 Ralph Adams Cram, *The Cathedral of Palma de Mallorca – an Architectural Study,* Cambridge, Mass., 1932.

22 And completed by his disciple, Juan Rubio.

23 The name betrays his origin, as the continuous ridge-rib of the high vaults betrays English influence.

24 See John Harvey, *The Cathedrals of Spain,* London, 1957.

Chapter 8 – Italy

1 John White, *Art and Architecture in Italy: 1250-1400,* Harmondsworth, 1966, favours an attribution to Cimabue.

2 The complete absence of stone tracery has the great disadvantage that however effective such a window may be from within, externally it only too easily appears as a gaping hole, disrupting the architectonic unity of the façade, a defect which is clearly evident in the corresponding oculus of the west front (Plate 343).

3 The famous Florentine architect; author of the design for the Cathedral and the Basilica of Santa Croce.

4 See Renato Bonelli: *Il Duomo di Orvieto e l'Architettura Italiana del Duecento Trecento,* Citta di Castello, 1952, for an analysis with diagrams of the various stages of construction.

5 Although Ugolino di Vieri is acknowledged as the chief author, responsible at the very least for the basic features of the design, his collaborators and their precise share of the whole are the subject of considerable controversy. See Enzo Carli: *Il Reliquiario del Corporale ad Orvieto,* Milan, 1964, and Paolo Dal Poggetto: *Ugolino di Vieri: Gli Smalti di Orvieto,* Florence, 1965.

6 The one jarring note is, in fact, provided by the mosaics, not *per se,* for they have constituted an integral – if strongly un-Gothic – part of the composition from its inception, but because even the early designs have been repaired and reworked. The excellent quality of the original mosaics may be gauged from the 'Birth of the Virgin', dating from 1365 and executed to a design by Ugolino di Prete Ilario, formerly over the right-hand doorway and now in the Victoria and Albert Museum in London.

7 See also Enzo Carli, *Sculture del Duomo di Siena,* Turin, 1941.

8 Nicolà Pisano who may be considered the first of the long line of 'Italian' sculptors, received his early training in Apulia, where the Emperor Frederick II with his nostalgia for the grandeur of Rome had crowned the entrance to *Castel del Monte* with a proto-Renaissance, Classical pediment, and had revived an interest in classical sculpture.

9 Seen to perfection in the pulpit of Sant' Andrea at Pistoia.

10 Quoted by Charles Eliot Norton in *Historical Studies of Church Building in the Middle Ages,* New York, 1880.

11 *ibid*

12 After reigning on the high altar for almost two centuries, the *Maestà,* in turn considered 'old-fashioned' by the men of the Renaissance, was taken down and broken up. Most of it has been preserved, however; it has recently been brilliantly restored and is spectacularly displayed in the *Museo dell'Opera Metropolitana.*

13 Often referred to in Italian sources as Andrea da Pontedera.

14 Already a feature of the Baptistry, which established the decorative 'key' of the cathedral ensemble, the style persisted right down to the Renaissance.

15 A fresco by Andrea da Firenze, dating from the same year, in the Spanish Chapel of the *Chiostro Verde* of Santa Maria Novella, depicting the 'Church Militant' has, in the background, a view of the cathedral with its nave of four bays. This must be the modified design of the committee. Compared with the final, executed version, it is far more Gothic in flavour, with its tall, traceried, clerestory windows, later superseded by oculi. The octagonal dome, although it has no drum, is however, already the all-dominant element and, in essence, remarkably similar to Brunelleschi's solution.

16 John Ruskin: *Mornings in Florence,* Orpington, 1875.

17 Paul Frankl: *Gothic Architecture,* Harmondsworth, 1962. (Quoted by permission of Penguin Books Ltd.)

18 The Baptistry has three pairs of doors: those on the South by Andrea Pisano (1330-1336); on the North (1403-1424) by Lorenzo Ghiberti, inspired by Pisano's earlier work and with the scenes within identical Gothic quatrefoils; and Ghiberti's eastern doors (1425-1452) completely Renaissance in style and pronounced by Michelangelo to be fit for the 'Gate of Paradise'.

19 If one excepts the Cathedral of Salamanca as being too hybrid a growth.

20 The 14 *braccia* unit was retained for four divisions, while the upper two were reduced to 12 *braccia* each.

21 See James S. Ackerman, *Ars Sine Scientia Nihil Est,* The Art Bulletin XXXI 1949, for an excellent account and analysis of this historic confrontation of Italian and Northern Gothic masters.

22 The very name of the street now on the site of the dock, the *Via Larghetto,* recalls its former state.

23 By the nineteenth-century illusionistic-perspective school of Sanquirico and Gobetta.

389 The 13th-century gold coronation 'Chalice of St Remi', used at the coronation ceremony of the French kings and still in the cathedral treasury. *Rheims*

Bibliography

The Medieval Scene

CHAMBERS, SIR EDMUND K.
The Mediaeval Stage, Oxford, 1903.

COULTON, GEORGE G.
Life in the Middle Ages, 4 vols, Cambridge, 1930.

COULTON, GEORGE G.
Art and the Reformation, Cambridge, 1953.

GILSON, ÉTIENNE
La Philosophie au Moyen Age, Paris, 12th edition, 1952.

HASKINS, CHARLES H.
The Renaissance of the Twelfth Century, Cambridge, U.S.A., 1927.

HAUSER, ARNOLD
The Social History of Art, London, 1951.

HOLT, ELIZABETH
A Documentary History of Art, Vol 1, New York, 1957.

HUIZINGA, JOHAN
The Waning of the Middle Ages, London, 1924.

JOINVILLE, JEAN DE
Histoire de Saint Louis (contemporary chronicle).

MARITAIN, JACQUES
Art et Scholastique, Paris, 1927.

PERNOUD, RÉGINE
Lumière du Moyen Age, Paris, 1944.

PIRENNE, HENRI
Mediaeval Cities, Princeton, 1925.

PIRENNE, HENRI
Economic and Social History of Mediaeval Europe, London, 1936.

PIRENNE, HENRI
A History of Europe from the Invasions to the XVI Century, London, 1939.

The Gothic Style

ABRAHAM, POL
Viollet-le-Duc et le Rationalisme Médiéval, Paris, 1934.

ADAMS, HENRY
Mont Saint-Michel and Chartres, Boston, 1904.

BRANNER, ROBERT
Gothic Architecture, London, 1961.

BRANNER, ROBERT
St Louis and the Court Style in Gothic Architecture, London, 1965.

CALI, FRANÇOIS
L'Ordre Ogival: Essai sur l'Architecture Gothique, Paris, 1963.

DEHIO, GEORG and BEZOLD, GEORG VON
Die Kirchliche Baukunst des Abendlandes, Vol II, Stuttgart, 1901.

FOCILLON, HENRI
The Art of the West in the Middle Ages, Vol II, *Gothic Art*, London, 1963—a translation of the French original: *Art d'Occident*, Paris 1938.

FRANKL, PAUL
The Gothic, Literary Sources and Interpretations During Eight Centuries, Princeton, 1960.

FRANKL, PAUL
Gothic Architecture, Harmondsworth, 1962.

GALL, ERNST
Die Gotische Baukunst in Frankreich und Deutschland, Leipzig, 1925.

HARVEY, JOHN
The Gothic World, London, 1950.

HOPPER, VINCENT F.
Mediaeval Number Symbolism, New York, 1938.

KARLINGER, HANS
Die Kunst der Gotik, Berlin, 1926.

LETHABY, WILLIAM R.
Mediaeval Art, London, 1904.

MÂLE, EMILE
L'Art Réligieux du XIIIe siècle en France, Paris, 1902.
Also available in translation as: *The Gothic Image*, London, 1961.

MÂLE, EMILE
L'Art Réligieux de la Fin du Moyen Age en France, Paris, 1908.

PANOFSKY, ERWIN
Abbot Suger on the Abbey-Church of St Denis and its Art Treasure, Princeton, 1946.

PANOFSKY, ERWIN
Gothic Architecture and Scholasticism, Latrobe, 1951.

PEVSNER, NIKOLAUS
An Outline of European Architecture, London, 1948.

SIMSON, OTTO VON
The Gothic Cathedral, New York, 1962.

VIOLLET-LE-DUC, EUGÈNE E.
Lectures on Architecture, translated from the French, 2 vols, London, 1877-81.

WORRINGER, WILHELM
Form in Gothic, London, 1927.

Building Methods and Techniques

ACKERMAN, JAMES S.
Ars sine scientia nihil est, Gothic Theory of Architecture at the Cathedral of Milan, Art Bulletin, XXXI, New York, 1949.

BOOZ, PAUL
Der Baumeister der Gotik, Munich, 1956.

COLOMBIER, PIERRE DU
Les Chantiers des Cathédrales, Paris, 1953.

FITCHEN, JOHN
The Construction of Gothic Cathedrals, Oxford, 1961.

FRANKL, PAUL
The Secret of the Mediaeval Masons, The Art Bulletin XXVII, New York, 1945.

GIMPEL, JEAN
Les Bâtisseurs des Cathédrales, available in translation as *The Cathedral Builders*, New York, 1961.

HAHNLOSER, HANS
Villard de Honnecourt, Vienna, 1935.

KNOOP, DOUGLAS and JONES, G. P.
The Mediaeval Mason, Manchester, 1949.

KNOOP, DOUGLAS and JONES, G. P.
The First Three Years of the Building of Vale Royal Abbey, in the Masonic periodical *Ars Quatuor Coronatorum XLIV*.

KOSSMANN, B.
Einstens massgebende Gesetze bei der Grundrissgestaltung von Kirchengebäuden (Studien zur deutschen Kunstgeschichte no: 231), Strasbourg, 1925.

LEFRANÇOIS-PILLION, LOUISE
Maîtres d'Œuvre et tailleurs de pierre des Cathédrales, Paris, 1949.

MORTET, VICTOR
Recueil de textes relatifs à l'histoire de l'architecture et à la condition des architectes en France au Moyen Age, Paris 1911-1929.

PAPWORTH, JOHN W.
Roriczer on Pinnacles, London, 1848-1853.

SALZMAN, LOUIS F.
Building in England down to 1540, Oxford, 1952.

VIBERT, LIONEL
Freemasonry before the Existence of Grand Lodges, London, 1932.

WILLIS, REV. ROBERT
Facsimile of the Sketchbook of Wilars de Honecourt (Villard de Honnecourt), London, 1859.

France

AUBERT, MARCEL
French Sculpture at the beginning of the Gothic Period, 1140-1225, Paris, 1929.

AUBERT, MARCEL; CHASTEL, ANDRÉ; GRODECKI, etc.
Le Vitrail Français, Paris, 1958.

AUBERT, MARCEL
Gothic Cathedrals of France and their Treasures, London, 1959.

*BOINET, AMÉDÉE
La Cathédrale de Bourges, Paris, 1911.

*BOINET, AMÉDÉE
La Cathédrale d'Amiens, Paris, 1922.

*BROCHE, LUCIEN
La Cathédrale de Laon, Paris, 1926.

*COLMET-DAAGE, PATRICE
La Cathédrale de Coutances, Paris, 1933.

*DEMAISON, LOUIS
La Cathédrale de Rheims, Paris, 1910.

EVANS, JOAN
Art in Mediaeval France, Oxford, 1948.

GRODECKI, LOUIS
Le Vitrail et l'Architecture au XIIe et au XIIIe Siècles, Gazette des Beaux-Arts, Paris, 1949.

GRODECKI, LOUIS
The Transept Portals of Chartres Cathedral; the Date of their Construction according to Archaeological Data, The Art Bulletin, XXXIII, New York, 1951.

GRODECKI, LOUIS
Chartres, Paris, 1963.

*JALABERT, DENISE
Notre-Dame de Paris, Paris, 1963.

JANTZEN, HANS
High Gothic, London, 1962.

JOHNSON, JAMES ROSSER
The Radiance of Chartres, London, 1964.

KATZENELLENBOGEN, ADOLF
The Sculptural Programs of Chartres Cathedral, Baltimore, 1959.

*LARAN, JEAN
La Cathédrale d'Albi, Paris, 1911.

LEFRANÇOIS-PILLION, LOUISE
Les Sculpteurs Français du XIIe et XIII Siècles, Paris, 1931.

*LOISEL, ABBÉ ARMAND
La Cathédrale de Rouen, Paris, 1913.

MÂLE, ÉMILE
L'Art Réligieux du XIIIe Siècle, Paris, 1902.

*MERLET, RENÉ
La Cathédrale de Chartres, Paris, 1909.

RODIN, AUGUSTE
Les Cathédrales de France, Paris, 1921.

TEMKO, ALLEN
Notre-Dame of Paris, London, 1956.

VERRIER, JEAN
La Cathédrale de Bourges et ses Vitraux, Paris, 1942.

VIOLLET-LE-DUC, EUGÈNE E.
Dictionnaire Raisonné de l'Architecture Française du XIe au XVe Siècle, 10 vols, Paris, 1854-1869.

*WALTER, JOSEPH
La Cathédrale de Strasbourg, Paris, 1933.

* Monographs on French Cathedrals in the series *Petites Monographies des Grands Édifices de la France*, edited by Marcel Aubert.

England

ATKINSON, THOMAS D.
Architectural History of the Benedictine Monastery of Saint Ethelred at Ely, Cambridge, 1933.

BOND, FRANCIS
Gothic Architecture in England, London, 1906.

BOND, FRANCIS
Introduction to English Church Architecture, 2 vols, London, 1913.

BONY, JEAN
French Influences on the Origins of English Gothic Architecture, Journal of the Warburg and Courtauld Institutes, XII, London, 1949.

BRIEGER, PETER H.
English Art 1216-1307, Oxford, 1957.

CHAPMAN, F. R.
Sacrist Rolls of Ely, Cambridge, 1908.

COOK, G. H.
Mediaeval Chantries and Chantry Chapels, London, 1947.

COOK, G. H.
Portrait of Canterbury Cathedral, London, 1949.

COOK, G. H.
Portrait of Salisbury Cathedral, London, 1949.

COOK, G. H.
Portrait of Lincoln Cathedral, London, 1950.

COOK, G. H.
The Story of Gloucester Cathedral, London, 1952.

COOK, G. H.
The English Cathedral, London, 1957.

EVANS, JOAN
English Art 1307-1461, Oxford, 1949.

FRANKL, PAUL
The Crazy Vaults of Lincoln Cathedral, The Art Bulletin, XXXV, New York, 1953.

HARVEY, JOHN
Gothic England 1300-1550, 2nd edition, London, 1948.

HARVEY, JOHN
English Cathedrals, London, 1950.

HARVEY, JOHN
English Medieval Architects: A Biographical Dictionary, down to 1550, London, 1954.

KNOWLES, JOHN A.
The York School of Glass Painting, London, 1936.

PEVSNER, NIKOLAUS (editor)
The Buildings of England, Harmondsworth, 1951.

PEVSNER, NIKOLAUS
The Englishness of English Art, London, 1956.

PRIOR, EDWARD S.
A History of Gothic Art in England, London, 1900.

PRIOR, EDWARD S. and GARDNER, ARTHUR
An Account of Mediaeval Figure Sculpture in England, Cambridge, 1912.

RACKHAM, BERNARD
The Ancient Glass of Canterbury Cathedral, London, 1949.

RAINE, JAMES
Fabric Rolls of York Minster, Surtees Society, XXXV, Durham, 1859.

READ, HERBERT
English Stained Glass, London, 1926.

STONE, LAWRENCE
Sculpture in Britain: The Middle Ages, Harmondsworth, 1955.

WEBB, GEOFFREY
The Sources of the Design of the West Front of Peterborough Cathedral, Archaeological Journal (London) LVI (Suppl. 1952).

WEBB, GEOFFREY
Architecture in Britain: The Middle Ages, Harmondsworth, 1956.

WILLIS, REV. ROBERT
Architectural History of Canterbury Cathedral, London, 1845.

Germany

BAUM, JULIUS
German Cathedrals, London, 1956.

CLASEN, KARL HEINZ
Deutsche Gewölbe der Spätgotik, Berlin, 1958.

CLEMEN, PAUL
Der Dom zu Köln, Düsseldorf, 1937.

DEHIO, GEORG
Geschichte der deutschen Kunst, Berlin, 1921.

DEHIO, GEORG
Handbuch der deutschen Kunstdenkmäler, 5 vols, Berlin, 1927.

GERSTENBERG, KURT
Deutsche Sondergotik, Munich, 1913.

GERSTENBERG, KURT
Das Ulmer Münster, Burg, 1926.

HORN, ADAM
Der Dom zu Regensburg, Bayreuth, 1939.

HOSTER, JOSEPH
Der Dom zu Köln, Cologne, 1965.

JANTZEN, HANS
Das Münster zu Freiburg-im-Breisgau, Burg, 1929.

MÜLLER, THEODOR
Sculpture in the Netherlands, Germany, France and Spain, 1400-1500, Harmondsworth, 1966.

PANOFKY, ERWIN
Die deutsche Plastik des elften bis dreizehnten Jahrhundert, Munich, 1924.

SCHMITT, OTTO
Gotische Sculpturen des Freiburger Münsters, 2 vols, Frankfurt-am-Main, 1926.

SEIFERT, HANS
Das Chorgestühl im Ulmer Münster, Konigstein-im-Taunas, 1958.

STANGE, ALFRED
Deutsche Malerei der Gotik, Berlin, 1934.

Spain

AINAUD DE LASARTE, J.
Ars Hispaniae Vol X: Cerámica y Vidrio, Madrid, 1952.

*BERRUETA, DOMÍNGUEZ
León. Madrid. 1953.

BEVAN, BERNARD
History of Spanish Architecture, London, 1938.

CALLAHAN, GALE GUTHRIE
Revaluation of the Refectory Retable from the Cathedral at Pamplona, Art Bulletin, XXXV, New York, 1953.

CRAM, RALPH ADAMS
The Cathedral of Palma de Mallorca–an Architectural Study, Cambridge, Mass., 1932.

DURÁN, SAMPERE A. and AINAUD DE LASARTE, J.
Ars Hispaniae Vol VIII, Gótica Escultura, Madrid, 1955.

*GAYA NUÑO, J. A.
Burgos, Madrid, 1949.

*GUDÍOL RICART, JOSEF
Toledo, Madrid, 1947.

GUDÍOL RICART, JOSEF
Ars Hispaniae Vol IX, Pintura Gótica, Madrid, 1955.

*GUERRERO LOVILLO, L.
Sevilla, Madrid, 1952.

HARVEY, JOHN
The Cathedrals of Spain, London, 1957.

LAMBERT, ÉLIE
L'Art Gothiqué en Espagne aux XIIe et XIIIe Siècles, Paris, 1931.

LAMPÉREZ Y ROMEA, V.
Historia de la Arquitectura Cristiana en la Edad Media, Barcelona, 1904-9.

LOZOYA, JUAN DE CONTRERAS, MARQUES DE
Historia del Arte Hispánico, Barcelona, 1934.

MÜLLER, THEODOR
Sculpture in the Netherlands, Germany, France and Spain: 1400-1500, Harmondsworth, 1966.

STREET, GEORGE EDMUND
Some Account of Gothic Architecture in Spain, London, 1865.

TORRES BALBÁS, L.
Ars Hispaniae Vol VII Architectura Gótica, Madrid, 1952.

*VERRIÉ, FEDERICO
Mallorca, Madrid, 1948.

* Monographs on Spanish Cathedrals in the series *Guias Artisticas de España,* edited by Josef Gudiol Ricart.

Italy

BASCAPE, GIACOMO
Il Duomo di Milano, Milan, 1965.

BONELLI, RENATO
Il Duomo di Orvieto e l'Architettura Italiana del Duecento Trecento, Città di Castello, 1952.

CARLI, ENZO
Sculture del Duomo di Siena, Turin, 1941.

CARLI, ENZO
Il Pulpito di Siena, Bergamo, 1943.

CARLI, ENZO
Vetrata Duccesca, Florence, 1946.

CARLI, ENZO
Le Sculture del Duomo di Orvieto, Bergamo, 1947.

CARLI, ENZO
Il Reliquiario del Corporale ad Orvieto, Milan, 1964.

CARLI, ENZO
Il Duomo di Orvieto, Rome, 1965.

CRISPOLTI, VIRGILIO
Santa Maria del Fiore, Florence, 1937.

DAL POGGETTO, PAOLO
Ugolino di Vieri: gli smalti di Orvieto, Florence, 1965.

DECKER, HEINRICH
L'Italie Gothique, Paris, 1964.

EDGELL, GEORGE H.
A History of Sienese Painting, New York, 1932.

LUSINI, ALDO
The Cathedral of Siena, Siena, c. 1955.

MARCHINI, GIUSEPPE
Italian Stained Glass Windows, Siena, 1957.

NORTON, CHARLES ELIOT
Historical Studies of Church Building in the Middle Ages, New York, 1880.

POPE-HENNESSY, JOHN
Italian Gothic Sculpture, London, London, 1955.

RUSCONI, ARTURO J.
Il Campanile di Giotto, Bergamo, 1943.

SIEBENHUENER, HERBERT
Deutsche Künstler am Mailänder Dom, Munich, 1944.

TOESCA, ILARIA
Andrea e Nino Pisano, Florence, 1950.

TOESCA, PIETRO
Il Trecento, Turin, 1951.

WHITE, JOHN
Art and Architecture in Italy, 1250-1400, Harmondsworth, 1966.

Index

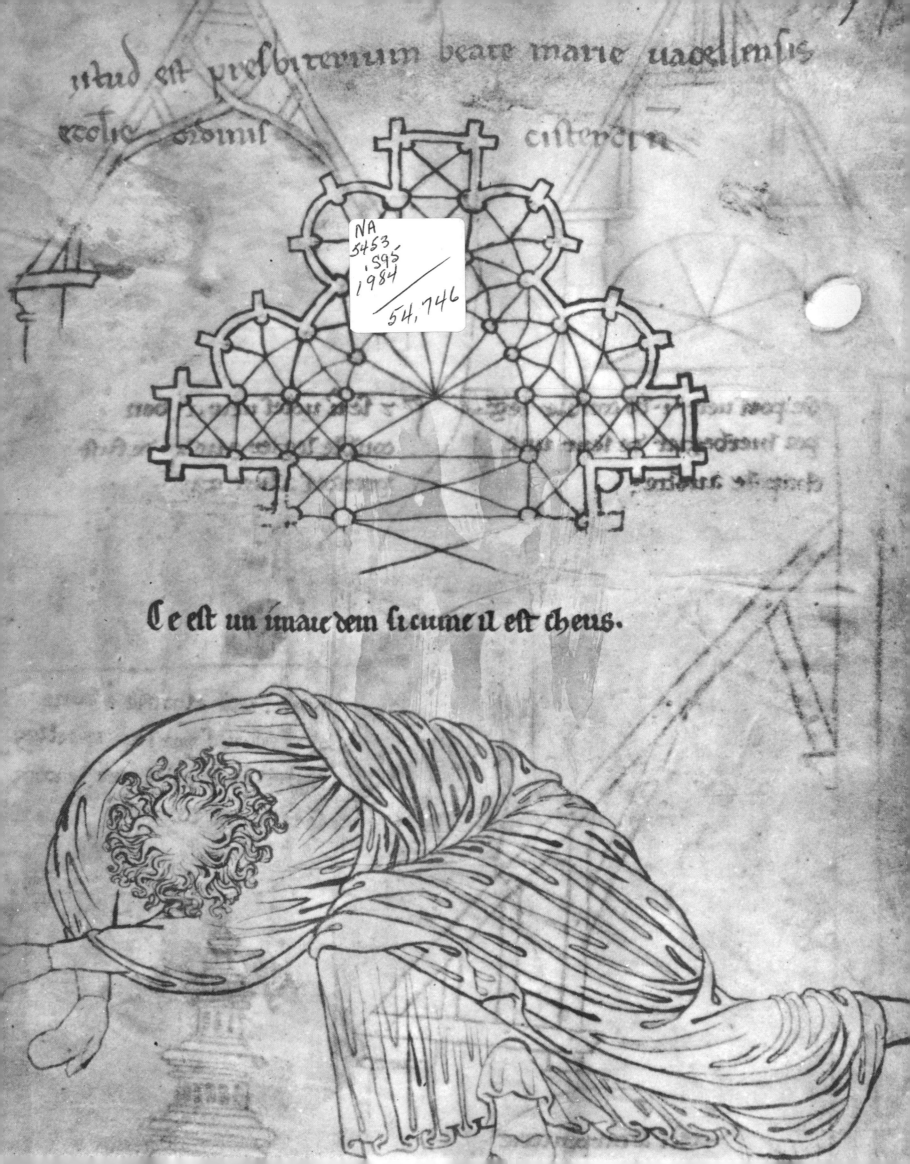

istud est presbiterium beate marie uacellensis

ecclie ordinis   cistercin

Ce est un imaie deu si cume il est cheus.